THE
CHICANO
HERITAGE

CABALLEROS

Ruth Laughlin Barker

ARNO PRESS

A New York Times Company

New York — 1976

Editorial Supervision: LESLIE PARR

———◆———

Reprint Edition 1976 by Arno Press Inc.

Reprinted from a copy in
   The Princeton University Library

THE CHICANO HERITAGE
ISBN for complete set: 0-405-09480-9
See last pages of this volume for titles.

Manufactured in the United States of America

———◆———

Library of Congress Cataloging in Publication Data

Laughlin, Ruth, 1889-
   Caballeros.

   (The Chicano heritage)
   Reprint of the ed. published by D. Appleton, New
York.
   1. Santa Fe, N.M.--History. 2. Santa Fe, N.M.
--Description. 3. New Mexico--Description and
travel. 4. New Mexico--Social life and customs.
I. Title. II. Series.
F804.S2L3 1976   978.9'56   76-1237
ISBN 0-405-09484-1

CABALLEROS

Old Castles in New Spain

CABALLEROS

BY
Ruth Laughlin Barker

Illustrations by
Norma van Sweringen

D. APPLETON & COMPANY
NEW YORK   1932   LONDON

To the memory of my father
N. B. LAUGHLIN
who loved the old town

CONTENTS

I

Gentlemen-on-Horseback

SANTA FE'S main street is the calle de San Francisco. At the western end there are houses of an older day with small native shops opening on the street and sunny patios beyond the open doorways. Yesterday I was walking there as two Caballeros passed each other. Both had reached an age where a cane is a comforting assurance. Don Pedro's face, as he came toward me on his way to the Plaza, had a full, somber dignity. His gray mustache and hair set off the brown skin of heavy jowls and large, arrogant nose. Eyebrows bushed over dark eyes, watchful and yet aloof to passing motors and the paved street. His clothes were as gray as his hair, and an old-fashioned gold watch chain dangled across his vest. I followed Don Miguel's tall spare figure in the black suit with the coat settled into old wrinkles from the stooped shoulders. As they passed, each raised his hand to his broad-brimmed black hat with a single word of greeting:

"Caballero!"

"Caballero!"

In that single Spanish word—Gentleman!—there was all the history of their people. It implied pride of race, aristocratic recognition, innate courtesy, and punctilious formality. As the oldest European title in the Americas it merited respect. More than four hundred years ago Cortés brought it to North America when he unloaded the first horses at Vera Cruz. Caballeros were horsemen, those who rode caballos. But because the luxury of a horse was the outward and visible sign of a gentleman of means, Caballero took on the meaning of Gentleman-on-Horseback.

Now Don Pedro and Don Miguel ride only their canes, yet the old title springs to their lips. Horsemanship has faded in this day of motors, but the significance of Gentleman remains.

New Mexico is characteristically the country of the Caballeros, particularly northern New Mexico, the old division of the upper Rio Grande and Chama valleys that was known as the Rio Arriba. Here is the last stand of Spain in North America. It is a mark left upon the land as indelible as the one-fifth quinta mark on old Spanish silver.

This life naturally focuses in Santa Fe, flowing into it from a wide radius. For more than two centuries the City of the Holy Faith was the northernmost seat of royal rule in the Kingdom of New Spain, the headquarters of a province whose vast boundaries extended from the Mississippi river to the Pacific and from the Mexican city of Parral to the unknown north. It is the oldest capital in what is now the United States, with a Spanish heritage that is as important in the American scene as the English tradition is on the Atlantic coast. Its prestige was due not only to vested Spanish authority but to its importance as a hub of western trails. The Chihuahua Trail, the Spanish trail to California, the fur trappers' trail from north of Taos, and the Santa Fe Trail ended here, bringing cargoes to be redistributed to the western half of a continent.

Yet the trails of those early days were too hazardous for any but the most necessary trade and rare official notices. A fifteen-hundred-mile trek over blazing deserts and grim mountains left the northern province to an isolation that must be self-contained if it continued to exist. Oñate's entrada in 1598 brought four hundred colonists to settle in the Rio Grande Valley. They formed the nucleus of a purely Spanish culture whose traditions were so intensified in their isolation that the Andalusian folk ways of 1900 were not so different from those of 1600. They flavored life with the sal andaluz—the salt of Andalusian wit and character retained in their speech to-day with pithy proverbs and the grandiloquence of Don Quixote.

It is a curious fact that this province has remained more Spanish than the rest of New Spain, as Mexico was called. Spaniards conquered the Aztecs, who had attained a high state of civilization and a simplified government under Montezuma. An abundance of gold and silver, emeralds and pearls gave the conquered people a certain material authority in treasure-seeking Spanish eyes. Caballeros married chieftains' daughters, starting the mestizo class who would later rule Mexico. There the Indian strain is a proud heritage, but in New Mexico it is ignored for a valiant upholding of Spanish purity.

The northern Indians were less advanced. Navajos, Apaches and Comanches were living in the aboriginal, hunting stage. The Pueblos, as the Spaniards called the town-dwelling Indians, had progressed to agriculture and architecture. None of the tribes had ever heard of gold. Since they had no material wealth, Spaniards discounted them as ignorant, lowly vassals, taking their women only as slaves and disqualifying the men's voice in government.

These Indians had no conception of a centralized government, united against a common foe. The first and only time they joined in the Pueblo rebellion of 1680 they ousted the Conquistadores in three days. For, a century before that, a few Spaniards had subdued unnumbered red men, scattered and defenseless in their own country. The nomadic tribes fought each other and preyed upon the Pueblos. Each pueblo defended itself as a small, independent city republic. Though the villages were separated by only a few miles up and down the rivers, they were entirely separated from thought communication by four different language groups—the Tano, Piro, Tewa and Keres. Distrust, bred by fear and ignorance of each other, brought ceaseless intertribal wars.

For three centuries the Spaniards ruled the land by quelling one tribe after another. Perhaps they lacked the grace of ruling a subject people wisely, for theirs was a day when might made right. Even in peace, Indian subjects gave only a negative submission and were never a coöperative factor in government.

In our present warless days we appreciate the Indian's right of self-defense in his own country and forget the bitter struggle of life and death that surrounded the Spaniards. Even fifty years ago men remember that they dared not take their families as far as Española without an armed escort. Scalping raids were seared into their memory so vividly that they marvel to-day at our careless picnic parties. Now the Indians are our friends. They have shrunk into their picturesque pueblos like strange, anachronous islands in our overflowing civilization. Clinging to their ancient self-respecting standards, they survive to teach us lessons interpreted in art and spiritual poise and even in government, for the Pueblos are the most successful of all communists.

Since written history began on this continent, this has been Spanish domain. Those first Spaniards were heroic men of a heroic time. The stock was so virile that it still characterizes half the population of the state as vital, living element, not yet diluted to romantic memories and bygone glories. The quick changes taking place before our eyes now are not as remarkable as the fact that Indians and Spaniards have remained intact through so many centuries.

In the long judgment of time the Caballero is more important to this country than the Conquistador. The Conquerors cleared the land with fierceness and force, but the Gentlemen-on-horseback planted it with the seeds of faith, art and tradition. The cruelties of the Conquistadores have vanished, but the harvest of the Caballeros' culture flourishes to-day.

The Caballeros carried three symbols into this Kingdom of New Spain—gold, the cross, and the horse. The search for gold, that lure that drew Spaniards across oceans and deserts, is a part of the mystery of the mountains and the legends of the land. Every placita has its chapel with the cross set above it to show the march of Christ in a pagan land. More than either, the horse is the symbol of the Caballeros. Where the horse has vanished before the inroads of a mechanical age, Spanish backgrounds have vanished. But where the horse still brings men home in the sunset to warm, adobe placitas, the old folk ways continue and the horse's trot echoes in the rhythm of love songs and the click of high heels in the Varsoviana.

Columbus started the gossip of gold in the Indies and made it a reality when he returned to Sevilla in a triumphal procession with Indians gleaming in golden ornaments and forty sailors carrying forty gorgeous parrots. Every Spanish port swarmed with men whose eyes sparkled with the get-rich-quick dream of finding gold, eager to cross the seas as fast as slow sails would carry them. Spain was Queen of the Seas and the most powerful nation in their world. With a typical far-flung gesture the distant rich lands were included as Spanish possessions. Conquering them and gaining their gold was part of the high adventure and daring that stirred men in a day when little Spanish ships had accomplished the tremendous feat of crossing an ocean and finding a new world. To these primitive adventurers gold was a tangible reality to be exchanged for the luxuries of the Orient—cloth of gold, taffetas, gauze and brocades, heavy perfumes, numberless slaves, and spices to flavor rich foods. Of these spices pepper was the most precious and rare; pepper that was forever after to color the food of Mexico and New Mexico with hot, red chile.

Contrasted with the greed for material wealth was the devout faith of Christians who had succeeded after eight centuries in conquering the infidel Moors. The cross of Christ and the banners of Castilla had led the victorious army against the crescent. Now they would go forward in a pagan land and redeem it for the Saviour. With faith to absolve them as proselyting overlords and national pride, greed and adventure to spur them on, a small band of Caballeros overcame Montezuma and the fertile land of the Aztecs.

Horses were the unexpected factor of greatest consequence in the conquest after Hernán Cortés landed at Vera Cruz in 1519. Before he burned his ships to impress upon his handful of men that the march to Mexico City meant conquest or death, he unloaded sixteen Spanish horses. The Indians, seeing horses for the first time, believed that man and horse were "all in one part." Even more than arquebuses and "sticks that shot thunder and lightning," horses terrified them into fleeing before this new supernatural monster. Medicine men hid in the jungle thickets to dispel the evil magic. By the time they discovered that horses were unsaddled at night and that man and horse could not be one animal, since a captain had pitched over his horse's head on a coast trail, it was too late to stop them. In two years the strange, pale-skinned, bearded conquerors had taken the white temples of Mexico City.

Cortés riding his rose-garlanded stallion there was a magnificent Gentleman-on-Horseback. The first Spanish word the Aztecs learned was caballo, the name for the awe-inspiring animal the Conquerors rode. Soon the Spaniards found that the distinction of being Caballeros brought more homage from Indian chiefs than the proud Castilian title of Hidalgos. Hidalgo had been shortened from Hijo de Algo, Son of a Somebody. These Somebodies might be powerful princes in far-away Spain but in Mexico the Caballero had his horse under him to prove his leadership.

Of the sixteen horses there were eleven snorting stallions and five high-stepping mares. They were Arabian barbs whose colors of chestnut, sorrel and silver gray were to be repeated indefinitely in the mustang breed of western horses. Each boatload of restless younger sons of the Castilian court brought more horses to Mexico. They were richly caparisoned with tooled leather saddles and bridles ornamented with silver, yet this extravagant equipment was not worth one-tenth the price of a five-thousand-dollar horse. Horses were not for sale, even for money worth three times its value to-day. One cavalier refused a ten-thousand-dollar offer for his horse and slave.

But within a century, the increase of horses lowered their price to ten dollars a head. Turned out to forage for themselves, they strayed away and formed the bands of horses who would overrun the western plains. Stallions, leading their mares, were as wild as though their sires had never known a Spanish bridle. Surviving in spite of short mountain grasses and winter blizzards, they became stunted and sturdy, like all semi-arid growth. Piebalds and pinto ponies had the curious marks of inbreeding. Acclimated to a dry country, the small, tough successors of the Arabian barbs were to carry the Caballeros up and down the farthermost trails.

From that day to this the Spanish domain of the wide Southwest has been known as the horse country.

Sentiment and necessity made horses preëminent figures in its story, first as the symbol of Spanish conquest, then as means to "run meat" by buffalo hunters, later pulling covered wagons and carrying cowboys over unfenced ranges and now reverting to the luxury class as swift-turning polo ponies. Navajos riding across red deserts and Spanish-Americans intent on a local horse race owe their mounts to the original Spanish horses. They belong to a day of romance and individualism that is lost before a standardized, twelve-cylinder motor.

The first explorers to penetrate the Southwest failed, perhaps because they were not mounted. Alvar Núñez Cabeza de Vaca had lost his horse in Florida. With two companions and the black slave Estevan he made the first difficult trip across the continent on foot. After nine hard years of wandering, captured by Indians and escaping to push their way to the Pacific as medicine men and jugglers, they reached Mexico in 1536. Cortés and the Viceroy Don Antonio de Mendoza received them to hear from Cabeza de Vaca's own lips an account of the country to the north. They had heard reports of fabulous gold there which would rival Alvarado's explorations in Central America. Cabeza de Vaca told of the country of the Seven Cities of Cíbola—seven terraced cities, larger than the City of Mexico, and so rich that doorways were encrusted with gold and precious stones. The cíbola, or buffalo, blackened the plains in vast herds, providing an unlimited meat supply.

Within the next year the shrewd Mendoza sent a small scouting party north to verify these extravagant reports. If he had equipped them with horses, these first two men to discover New Mexico might have had a happier fate. But the chief scout was friar Marcos de Niza, and frailes were accustomed to go afoot into their wilderness field, armed only with their breviary and cross. His guide was the black slave Estevan of Cabeza de Vaca's party. It was not fitting to mount a slave on a master's horse. So the two, accompanied by six Indian interpreters, set out on foot for the trackless northern wilderness.

Black Steven, used to nine years of foot travel, went ahead. He was to send back a small cross if the land was poor, a larger one if it was good. Indians staggered under the man-sized cross they brought back to Friar Marcos. The cross was typical of the grandiose visions the slave threw around himself, once he was free from his masters. He traveled ahead in state, decked in gaudy feathers and followed by credulous Indians and their prettiest women. His vanity was his undoing. When he reached Hawikuh, the first of the Seven Cities near modern Zuñi, the caciques killed him as an evil man and a spy. Friar Marcos, hurrying to overtake his guide, was warned not to approach the pueblo. Like Moses he looked at the Promised Land from the height of a mesa, planted a cross in this new "Kingdom of St. Francis" and made his lonely, discouraged way home.

He wrote a faithful report of the Cíbola country for

11

the Viceroy, but the gente did not read it. They heard and repeated, and each telling grew more golden, the tale of the barber who shaved the fraile after his return. Not even a Franciscan missionary should have been held too responsible for anything he might have told a barber mowing off a three-months' beard, and the barber lost no glory in talking of the illustrious patron who had visited his little shop. "There," the barber cried, "the people are shrewd and marry only one wife at a time. The cities are populous and surrounded by walls. The women wear golden beads and the men girdles of gold, and white woolen dresses."

Perhaps the barber's gossip had more to do with the expedition that was to claim one-half of the Western continent than the truthful but uninteresting report of the Friar. Mendoza himself was taken with the gold fever and ordered a tremendous royal subsidy to outfit an expedition to the Seven Cities. Within a few days three hundred men had signed up for the gold rush.

There was no question of this expedition going on foot. They were mounted on the best Spanish horses. Many of the captains were young Castilian nobles whose restless energy had stirred up intrigues and fights in Mendoza's capital. Don Antonio blessed them fervently and gratefully as they rode off to the north, scarlet and gold banners flying, the cross upraised. At their head rode their leader, Francisco Vásquez Coronado, the sun glinting on his golden helmet and the polished flanks of his horse. Their valor would repay the huge royal subsidy by finding mountains of gold; and the Church, the King and his Viceroy, Don Antonio, would profit with a vast new kingdom. After months of riding they came to the land of the Seven Cities to find primitive mud and stone huts instead of rich palaces. Yet Hawikuh was not conquered before arrows had pierced Coronado's golden helmet and killed many of his horses. They camped for the winter in a broad valley of the Rio Grande y Bravo at Tiguex, near Bernalillo. From there they rode as far west as the Grand Canyon and east to the Gran Quivira in Kansas. But they failed to search the mountains within twenty miles of their camp, where future generations were to pick up gold nuggets as thick as piñones after the first frost. Nor did they find the hill of Chalchihuites near Los Cerrillos where Indians burrowed for their sacred turquoise. Adventure blinded them to nearby opportunities and romance led them to chase the rainbow.

After two years of disappointments, the bedraggled Caballeros mutinied and Coronado was forced to lead them back to Mexico, riding now with drooping head. He cursed Friar Marcos as a faithless liar, yet Coronado had found just what the friar had officially reported—terraced towns beside each river, people whose jewels were turquoise, and many buffalo. But he had not found that which lent magic to the barber's tale —gold.

What traces did the Caballeros leave on this first entrada? The country reverted to the Indians as

13

worthless, yet they left a geographical imprint upon it, setting boundaries for Spain far beyond their imaginations. It was worth indeed a thousand times the royal subsidy, but Coronado died in humiliated poverty because he had not found mountains of gold.

The cross was left with its dawning influence, for three friars refused to return with Coronado. Padre Juan de la Cruz and the lay brother Luis Descalona were martyred before Coronado reached Mexico. Padre Juan de Padilla went back to the Gran Quivira and lived long enough for a legend to form around him. It is said that his body is buried at Isleta, the sunny pueblo below Albuquerque. How he came to rest there, so far from Kansas, no one knows. But according to the legend, Padre Padilla rises in his coffin, hollowed out of a cottonwood log, every twenty years. Some say that his emaciated body is as dry as a mummy and his brown gown crumbling, as well it might after four centuries, but when his coffin bursts the mud floor before the altar, it is the blessed omen of a good year.

The two years' stay left the Indians with corroding memories which would influence them for the next three hundred years. To them the bearded strangers were not Cabelleros, but buccaneers attacking peaceful villages, burning alive two hundred Indians at Pecos, turning the Tewas out of their warm, winter homes so that the soldiers might be comfortable at Tiguex. They looked with pitying wonder at the babies born to their women that year, babies with pale eyes and reddish glints in their hair. These were not their ruddy

Children of the Sun but the bleached Children of the Moon. The ancient prophesy that a strange white people would conquer them had been fulfilled.

Horses and perhaps a few sheep were left behind by the Caballeros. Being miraculous and unknown creatures, horses were soon woven into the Indian's rich mythology. Johano-ai was the god who carried the golden disk of the sun from east to west. Now, on this daily journey, he rode one of five great horses—a horse of turquoise, a horse of white shell, a horse of pearl shell, a horse of red shell and a horse of coal black. The Children of the Sun knew which horse he had chosen, for at dawn, if the sky was blue and clear, he had mounted the turquoise horse or the one of white or pearl shell. But if there was the sweep of the dust-red wind or black clouds piled up, he was riding the fiery red horse or the one of coal black.

Other legends told of a white stallion with flowing mane and tail ridden swiftly by a mysterious unknown god and never overtaken. He was seen only in the twilight, fleeing toward the horizon and followed by his band of black mares.

Horses were to change the entire life of the American Indians. Before the coming of the Caballeros, Indians had carried heavy burdens by dog teams and depended upon their own swift feet in the hunt. By lassoing the wild Spanish horses, and riding them bareback with a noose for a bridle, the roving tribes of Apache, Navajo, the dreaded Comanche and the Plains Indians could ride to distant hunting grounds.

These encroachments were always a cause for war and brought further strife to keep the Indians from uniting.

Coronado's failure to find gold pricked the balloon of northern hopes. The King and his viceroys refused to grant further large subsidies for explorations. If other men were foolhardy enough to seek this golden will-o'-the-wisp, they must do so at their own expense. This phrase was so impressed upon the colonial mind that all further chronicles included it. "This, I accomplished at my own expense" became the customary appendage to all documents, whether they related to outfitting an army, exploring new territory, or building and repairing churches.

Three years after Coronado returned, the first great silver mine was discovered by the Spaniards in Bolivia and another at Cerro de Pasco in Perú. In northern Mexico, Zacatecas was the silver bonanza of 1548. Here was silver in such quantities that wine goblets, forks and spoons, wash basins and pitchers, mirror frames and chandeliers were pounded out of the gleaming, white metal. Por supuesto, the luxurious horses, were outfitted with it! There were solid silver horns and stirrups, bits and spurs, silver buttons to ornament the leather of saddles and bridles, silver shoes for the captains' horses.

If there was so much silver, surely there must be some of the precious gold north of Zacatecas, so pure that little energy would be lost in refining it. With the Spaniards the dream of gold could not die. These

16

pioneer prospectors had the same malady that is chronic with all men who seek riches from the earth—the faith that on the next trip they will discover pay dirt. They refused to be stopped by the hardships and disappointments of Coronado.

For the next sixty years miners, explorers and missionaries rode to the north—always at their own expense. Some expeditions, failing to find gold, made up for their expenses as slave-catching raids. In 1561 Francisco Ibarra came back to tell the homefolk of a new land he had seen, "as marvelous as a new Mexico." New Mexico was advertised under her own name for the first time. Fourteen years later Chamuscado and two friars marked the north trail with their bleached bones. In 1583 Antonio de Espejo and his fourteen men were the first tourists to see New Mexico and return in ten months. Espejo was a practical promoter and made his trip pay by trading with the Indians. He returned with a promoter's enthusiasm for the mineral wealth and colonization possibilities of New Mexico.

Mañana is a word that is characteristic of Spaniards anywhere. In spite of Espejo's rosy propaganda, the colonizing scheme was put off until mañana. The viceroy was too busy keeping his own seat to start a northern colony. He was beset with plots and intrigues, for the highly individualistic Spaniard chafed at being under any one man's authority. Finally Don Juan de Oñate volunteered to lead a colonizing expedition to New Mexico "at his own expense."

The unstinted magnificence of spending a million pesos on this project came from silver mines in Zacatecas—a magnificence to be trebled from the gold mines he hoped to find on the thousands of acres of land the King would grant him in the new province, where he would rule as governor and captain-general. His wife, Doña Isabel, helped him to the royal reward, for she was the granddaughter of the great Cortés. The Gentlemen-on-Horseback in his company were the rich and distinguished nobility of Spain, a different type of men from the impoverished religious refugees who were to land on Plymouth Rock twenty-two years later.

The poetic glamour and adventure of a quest worthy of the dramatic Golden Age attracted friars, with names as old as Spanish history, and illustrious men of letters. One of his captains was Don Marcos Farfán, the first dramatist who produced a play in what is now the United States, a comedy given by soldier-actors on the banks of the Rio Grande at El Paso del Norte. Another captain, Don Gaspar de Villagrá, wrote the log of the expedition as an epic poem. Its thirty-two cantos give New Mexico the unique honor of having a poem as the original and accurate authority for its dawning history.

They left Mexico in 1598, a gay and brilliant company, dressed as befitted Caballeros in satin and slashings of scarlet taffeta in their puffed sleeves. Long curling plumes waved from their velvet hats. Lacey ruffles fell from their throats and wrists and garters.

In a final bold gesture of leavetaking they buckled on their shining armor and helmets. Their horses were snorting and eager to be off, the best high-spirited steeds that silver could buy.

Don Juan placed his twelve-year-old son Cristóbal on the charger the child was to ride at the head of the troop, saluted the proud Doña Isabel and leaped on his stallion. There were music and songs, trumpets calling, the quick trot of horses' feet, roses and carnations thrown in their path by excited women, and tearful cries of "Adios! Vaya con Dios." The historic migration had started north.

Behind Don Juan there were resplendent captains and soldiers, somber friars fingering their rosaries, four hundred colonists driving seven thousand cattle and sheep in the clouds of dust. Eighty-three teams of oxen pulled the heavy solid-wheeled carretas, loaded with the luxuries of the day to pleasure Don Juan and his gentlemen. Perched on top of the high-piled wagons were children too small to walk. Beside them trudged their mothers and older children, for one hundred and thirty colonists had brought their families whose pioneer courage would make homes in the wilderness.

Oñate's entrada was a long six months' journey, testing high spirits with hardships and dangers. Forbidding mountain crags and burning deserts offered them no easy welcome, for it is characteristic of this land to hold itself impenetrable to strangers. Sheep, cattle and horses foraged for themselves. The colonists depended upon the never-plentiful provisions in the Indian villages they passed. There was always the dreaded fear of failing to find water—a fear that materialized in the parched wastes called in desperation the Jornada del Muerto—the Journey of the Dead. With swollen tongues and blistered feet they found at the other side of this death valley a pueblo where the Indians succored them, and gratefully named the place for Nuestra Señora de Socorro.

Day by day the sun blazed on the heavy armor, creaking wagons and footsore colonists. They followed the Rio Grande y Bravo del Norte, for the river was an active source of life in this semi-arid land. A wall of purple lava overflow at La Bajada divided the big and fierce river of the north into the warm lowlands of the Rio Abajo and the high, timbered mesas of the Rio Arriba. It was a natural division destined to be important always in New Mexican history.

From the crest of each mesa they searched the clear, blue distance for gold, silver and precious stones glinting in the doorways. In spite of the reports of the earlier travelers, they hoped to reach the fabled Seven Cities where there would be luxurious ease for their tired bodies and gold pouring into their eager hands. Instead they too found clumps of primitive mud houses where Indians wore homespun cotton mantas. Their only wealth was shelled corn and crudely cut sky stones.

Don Juan rode north of Coronado's camp at Tiguex

until the river widened into a fertile, green valley, a welcome sight to hungry men and beasts. As had been the custom with earlier trail blazers, the padres set up a great cross in the nearby village of Kay-pa and blessed it with the new name of a helpful saint. Who was more appropriate for this final stopping place than San Juan de Los Caballeros, Don Juan's patron Saint John, who had aided the Gentlemen-on-Horseback?

The camp remained here three years and was then moved across the river to San Gabriel. Though Oñate had found no gold mines, he realized the importance of governing and colonizing so large a province. It was not an easy job, for the colonists were discouraged and the Indians unruly. The Pueblo Indians submitted outwardly to Spanish rule and Christianity, but inwardly they were festering spots of hostility. The roving tribes were openly rebellious, pillaging the settlements as much as they dared for horses and provisions.

With typical Spanish courage, small bands of Caballeros left the headquarters for explorations east and west. At Acoma, Oñate stormed the high rocky citadel of this city in the sky, seventy soldiers against fifteen hundred angry Indians. The Acomans guarded their pueblo on the high mesa of solid rock with bows and arrows, timbers, stones and boiling water, ready to destroy any invader brave enough to climb the steep trail. Their horses were of no use, but by a ruse the Spaniards gained the mesa up the back trail. The battle wavered on the dizzy edge of the cliff. The Indians barricaded themselves inside their houses, but the

21

Spaniards drove them from room to room, setting fire to the houses behind them. There were only six hundred inhabitants of haughty Acoma left to submit to the Spanish crown. The strongest fortress in the Indian country had met defeat.

Following the road to the sun, west of Acoma, Oñate's horses were stopped by the waves of the "South Sea," as he called the Pacific. On his return he rested at the towering red sandstone pinnacle, thrust up through the plains between Zuñi and Acoma. There he carved his record into the enduring rock— "Pasó por aquí el Adelantado Don Juan de Oñate, del descubrimiento de la mar del sur, a 16 de abril, 1605." It is the earliest historical record to be found in the United States. Oñate's memoir was followed by other famous conquerors for the next two hundred and fifty years, making "El Morro" the huge stone autograph album of western history.

Oñate returned to find his headquarters at San Gabriel confused by disheartened colonists and rebellious Indians. The petty jealousies that beset every leader raised the young Don Cristóbal in his father's place as governor. About 1609 Don Pedro de Peralta was appointed as the third governor of the province with orders to found a "new villa," the future Santa Fe.

Early Spanish explorers were required to keep a minute journal of their expeditions. Many of these journals may be studied to-day in the Federal Building archives, yellowed paper showing the quaint lettering in unfaded black ink. Every expense was itemized from the three pairs of sandals allowed each padre to the elaborate wardrobe of Oñate, the salaries, rations and ammunition for the army. Each Indian village was recorded with its new Christian name.

Yet in no record up to 1614 is there a mention of Santa Fe. Historians who have delved through the archives of "the Indies" believe that the journals between 1609 and 1614 might have been lost in their long-ago travels between New Mexico and Spain or may be hidden among the old manuscripts in Mexico City. Peralta's order to establish a "new villa" was without doubt the cause of the founding of Santa Fe. The records of such an important undertaking as building a permanent capital to be the center of authority in the limitless northern province must have been sent to the king and viceroy. Probably some day this historic file will be found to give the oldest capital an authentic birthday. Until then we must be content with such reliable facts that Oñate's camp was moved from San Gabriel after he came back from the "South Sea" and that Peralta's "new villa," Santa Fe, was established between 1609 and 1614.

There is a tradition that Santa Fe was built upon the site of the pre-Columbian pueblo of Kwa-po-ge. The old men of San Ildefonso tell that in the "long since" this was the place where the Virgin Mother of the Sun and Moon was tossed about in the angry waters of the deluge. Resting upon the high loma, she gave birth here to the twin gods of war.

23

Whether the fighting twins eventually destroyed their mother's home or whether pestilence wiped it out, as it did the pueblo of Pecos, is all a surmise into that dim past. The skeletons dug up each year in the construction of city foundations tell no tales except that their skulls are narrow like those of the Pajarito peoples.

The tradition of Kwa-po-ge is all that remains to give an inkling of the life of people living here half a thousand years ago. Kwa-po-ge, meaning the Place of the Shell-Bead People, suggests that even then this little valley at the foot of the mountains must have been a center of trails coming up from the sea-washed countries, where shells were traded and polished into beads to give their name to a tribe.

The terraced walls of Kwa-po-ge had crumbled to the earth probably two hundred years before Oñate's entrada, leaving no trace of a living pueblo to be listed in the explorer's journals. Yet the location which had attracted the wise Indians later appealed to the Caballeros. Oñate may have noted it as he rode the trail between Pecos and Tesuque and suggested it for the permanent capital.

It had many advantages to recommend it. It was nine miles away from the strife of the nearest pueblo at Tesuque. It was higher than the Rio Grande Valley, giving it a strategic military position and cooler summers. It was surrounded by a high forest, good farm lands and a river to irrigate them. This rio, which mercifully never ran dry, was of importance in a land where the gift of water was mentioned in every one's prayers. To the north and east the valley was protected by snowy peaks, at first called by the Spaniards the "Sierra Nevada." But the seventeenth century was a time when lifeblood was offered and spilled in the name of Christ. Later when devout Caballeros watched the crimson radiance of the afterglow of sunset suffuse the mountains, they likened it to the mystical stain of the blood of Christ, and called the mountains the Sangre de Cristo. Clouds with rain-filled sails floated up from the golden plains to the south and broke on these peaks with life-giving moisture for the new villa. From the watchtower of Atalaya Hill sentinels could give warning of any approach from the plains.

To any one who is familiar with long, euphonious Spanish names "Santa Fe" is too short and impersonal for the title of a royal city. Spanish towns needed the protection of some patron saint who would look after his namesake place in time of trouble. Old records show that Santa Fe was named in accordance with this tradition, but the hurry of the last American century has clipped it to one-fourth its original dignity. The Caballeros had time to roll sonorously over their tongues and print upon their fine manuscripts the full name—"La Villa Real de la Santa Fe de San Francisco de Assisi"—the Royal City of the Holy Faith of St. Francis of Assisi. From the beginning the town had to live up to such a name as that.

There was no haphazard chance about building this

royal city. The rules of city planning of three hundred years ago were ordered in detail in Spain and followed as strictly in this far-away frontier as though King Phillip might ride in any day to inspect the villa real. In this way Spanish towns attained the permanent design of dignified architectural units, instead of becoming an ungainly ramble of shacks on either side of a wide place in the road.

Town plans followed the home feeling of houses built around a patio and centered around a plaza. The Plaza Mayor in Santa Fe was laid out and blessed with a cross and the pomp of royal investiture. It was a rectangle half again as long as it was wide "making it better for horses used upon fiestas and other occasions." At the east end, the church and monastery of San Francisco was begun by Friar Benavides, "raised and set apart from other buildings, so that it might be seen and venerated." Shops and houses filled the southern and western sides of the hollow square, with the "Capilla Militar," or soldiers' chapel, on the south side.

The entire northern side was occupied by the Royal Palace, a long, low adobe building with towers at either end. The west tower guarded the arsenal and the east tower the officers' chapel, "La Hermita de Nuestra Señora." High adobe walls formed a compound of several blocks behind the palace, enclosing the Plaza de las Armas and the officers' homes in the Casas Reales. A zaguán was the one wide entrance into the compound where Caballeros might ride inside and ox-teams could be unloaded. With adobe walls thick enough to be arrowproof and only the few necessary doors and windows, the Palacio Real looked like an Arabian desert fortress. It had a simple, massive dignity essentially different from the ornate colonial palaces of the south. Its stark exterior expressed the necessities of a frontier outpost, a huge, solid protectress in a hostile land. But the inner sales and patios had the grace and beauty of this nucleus of Spanish life, doubly precious to the exiled settlement. Like the Indian pueblos the buildings were projections of the brown earth, moulded from mud by conscripted Indian laborers and Spanish artisans. It basked in the sun as the one European official building in all the oceans-bounded continent north of Mexico.

Across the river a smaller settlement was built for the Tlascaltecan slaves brought along with the colonists. It was called the Barrio Analco, from the Aztec words meaning a Little Suburb across the Water. Its chapel was dedicated to the dragon-slaying San Miguel as the slaves' church.

By 1621 the Mission Supply Service established the first time-tables for freight trains between Mexico and the distant missions at Santa Fe. Financed by the Crown it carried north padres and supplies, including oysters, conserves, copper bells, oil paintings of the saints, nails and axes for the lifetime exile in a pagan field. These freight trains of mules were far from being a daily service. As Friar Benavides wrote in 1631, "Though it is true this dispatch is assigned to be made punctually every three years, five and six years are wont to pass without the royal officials bethinking themselves about us. And God knows what it costs to remind them!" Three years were allowed for the round trip, a year and half for actual travel and the same time for loading and unloading at either end.

Like smaller cousins, the Spanish ass or burro followed the mules up the trail. Leaving Mexico they were loaded with kegs of golden pesetas and bullion. Returning from Santa Fe the kegs were filled with salt, as scarce and precious as gold and found only in the dried salt lakes of the Estancia Valley. A trickle of colonists came up the Camino Real, hauling the few necessities to start homes in the wilderness in crude carretas. The first wagons had been brought into the province in 1590 with the unlicensed expedition of Castaño de Sosa. The creaking of these first wheels to turn in the future United States was the prelude to the death knell of the Spaniard's horse. Later he was not necessary for iron wheels propelled by steam, for gas-driven motors nor for airplanes darting through the sky like dragon flies. But for two and a half centuries horses, ox-drawn carts, packtrains of mules and burros were to be the only transportation between the civilized world and the isolated province.

There in the blue and silver of the far mountain valley the city of Oñate's Caballeros put down its roots. The colonists grappled with the problems of the frontier, fighting for life not only against the Indians but against the forces of nature in a semi-arid country. The Spanish settlement counted only a few armed men against the uncounted hordes of Indians. They held Spanish rule supreme during that dangerous day because the Indians were constantly at war among themselves. In the great rebellion of 1680 they united as a red race for the first and last time. Even their complete victory could not teach them the lesson of a united Indian nation.

A spirit of antichrist quickened the rebellion. The Indians had added the new Christian God to their galaxy of nature gods but He had not brought them happiness or peace. Added to the enforced Christian practices was the age old incentive for war—taxation without representation. The head of each family was required to bring to the royal treasury one vara of cotton cloth and one fanega of corn—the Indian's chief wealth and means of barter. Yet for more than two generations they had had no voice in governing the land that belonged to them.

Witchcraft played its part in the rebellion, made dramatic by the medicine man, Po-pé of Taos. In 1675 he had been put in prison with three other medicine men and was only released upon the insistent demand of the Indians. They had suffered already from years of drought and famine. Now they were terrified for fear some new evil would befall them if their priests of nature magic were executed.

Po-pé proclaimed that he was under the guidance of three dark underworld spirits who commanded him to free the Indians from the tyranny of the Christians. For the next five years he went from tribe to tribe using the one universal language for his propaganda. By signs and war shields painted with symbols as old as pictographs on the rocks, he incited them to reclaim their own land and their own gods.

By 1680 they were ready for the rebellion. It was to be the last great battle between men with horses and men without horses. In their final plans the Indians scorned the symbol of the Caballeros and used their fastest runners who ran the long distance from Taos in the north to western Zuñi and the southern Rio Grande villages. These runners, Omtua and Cantua, carried cords whose knots signified how many days would elapse before the general uprising.

But Omtua and Cantua were betrayed and brought to Governor Otermín in Santa Fe. Not to be balked in their break for freedom, other runners were hastily sent forth from Tesuque. One knot in each cord was untied, hastening the rebellion by one day.

On that day, August 11, 1680, every Indian in the province rose to attack the Spaniards. After murdering the padres and colonists in the outlying missions, they hurried over all the trails to Santa Fe. The Spaniards from the ranches and slaves from the Barrio Analco gathered within the protection of the Palace compound. Cannons were set up in the zaguán doorway, men with arquebuses took their precarious positions in the towers.

Governor Otermín asked for a parley. The war cacique met him, barbaric in bright paint and feathers, with a scarlet taffeta sash tied around him that he had snatched from a dying Caballero in the monastery at Galisteo. The cacique offered Otermín two crosses— a white cross signifying that the Spaniards would be allowed to depart peacefully from the Indian country; the red cross symbolizing the blood that would flow if they stayed. Otermín chose the red cross and prepared for battle, realizing for the first time that the entire province echoed with the murderous war cry.

In the battles the Indians lost more warriors than the Spaniards. But the Indian force was growing hourly as new tribes joined them. The trick that quickly decided the victory came when the Indians cut off the water supply for the Palace, an acequia running from the river through the Casas Reales. Horses and cattle began to die from thirst; men, women and children went mad with swollen tongues. The Indians had blocked any help that might have come from Mexico. To-morrow the savage Apaches would come, for once joining the Pueblos in battle.

Governor Otermín took the only alternative between life and death from thirst and butchery and abandoned Santa Fe. The altar of La Hermita was stripped of its chalices and saints, colonists grabbed their few belongings and the Governor divided the provisions among them. The great doors of the zaguán swung open as the dejected Caballeros rode out on their horses, followed by frightened colonists and the remaining cattle and sheep. The Indians watched them go without assault. Not a living Spaniard could be found on the long march south to El Paso where the refugees made their home for the next twelve years.

As the Caballeros rode away, the Indians danced the drama of victory in the plaza and cried "God, the Father of the Spaniards and Mary, their Mother, are dead. But our own gods, whom we obey, have never died." They plunged into the river, scrubbing off the taint of Holy Water with amole lather. They tore down the buildings around the Palace and built in their place terraced communal houses. Two large underground kivas near the plaza were dedicated to the return of the old gods. A high adobe wall with only one doorway surrounded the town. Horses, crosses and the greed for gold were gone. A pueblo flourished once more on the ruins of Kwa-po-ge.

The Indians were not used to a capital. The Tano tribe lived in the Palace and communal buildings in

Santa Fe, and other tribes began to quarrel over the spoils of the Spaniards. Return to the old freedom meant also a return to more tribal jealousies and raids. But they held the province against invasion for more than a decade.

It was not easy for Spanish pride to relinquish its stronghold. The ex-Santa Feans, huddled beside the Rio Grande at El Paso, were humiliated and restless in their defeat. Several expeditions started bravely north but were forced to turn back. Finally in 1692 Don Diego de Vargas y Luján Ponce de Leon gathered together an army for the reconquest of Santa Fe "at his own expense."

Horses and Gentlemen-on-Horseback again rode up the Camino Real. The success of this third entrada was due more to Caballero kindness than to the fire-arms of the Conquistadores. Diplomat as well as general, de Vargas ordered his soldiers not to harm any Indian on the march. They arrived before the high adobe walls surrounding the Santa Fe pueblo in the dawn of September 13, 1692. Sunrise was a happy portent for the colors of Castilla seemed to have permanently stained the land—crimson cliffs rose above the southern plain, a spreading cloth of gold of flowering chamisa and yellow sand.

But war-painted Indians crowded the terraced roofs of the three- and four-story houses. From the inner plaza came the sounds of war whoops and the deep beat of drums. Trenches had been dug before the walls, and four round towers were armed with cap-

33

tured Spanish cannon. The Spaniards' massive Palacio Real had been turned against them as an impregnable fortress.

De Vargas cautiously camped to the west of the town and began a parley with the Indians. They jeered at him until his soldiers repaid the Indians' trick by cutting off the acequia bringing water into the pueblo. By dawn of the next day the Indians were ready to talk with de Vargas if he would come inside the walls. His captains pleaded with him not to go alone through the one narrow doorway into a death trap of a thousand treacherous Indians.

"That is nothing," exclaimed de Vargas. "Who will not risk himself in order to secure perpetual glory and an illustrious name?" With the Padre Custodio and six soldiers he went through the door.

Individual bravery was the quality Indians most admired. The war cacique met the general with equal dignity. De Vargas explained they had not come to punish the Indians but to forgive and rebaptize them and to offer them the protection of Spain. "Spain" was the most formidable word in all the world at that time. Even in this wilderness frontier it brought submission. De Vargas took possession of the province again in the name of Carlos Segundo, and the Padre Custodio blessed the great cross soon erected in the plaza.

The walled pueblo was left to the Indians while the Spaniards tactfully camped beside the river to the west. A week later the leader Tu-pa-tú, who had succeeded

Po-pé, came to pay his respects to de Vargas. Tu-pa-tú was as grand as any Caballero, with a mother-of-pearl crown upon his head and a splendid horse under him, for the Indians now exulted in their fine Spanish mounts.

For more than a year de Vargas used the camp as headquarters. In the last cold days of December 1693 Father Farfán came up from Mexico with many colonists. De Vargas could not care for them in camp and the Indians refused to quarter them in the warm adobe houses around the plaza. The general decided that the generosity of the Caballeros had been wasted, and it was time for the Conquistadores to retake their Royal City.

The seige of Santa Fe began the next day. For two days the Indians succeeded in holding their strong walled pueblo. Before dawn of the third day the Spaniards attended mass in the camp chapel, and de Vargas raised aloft the image of his patron saint "La Conquistadora," vowing a yearly celebration in Her honor if She would aid them in a victorious assault. With the zeal of crusaders and the cry of "Santiago" on their lips the soldiers rushed the walls in the dawning light and drove the pagans out of the City of the Holy Faith. By New Year's day of 1694, "La Conquistadora" was established in the hastily refurnished tower chapel of La Hermita, and the Spaniards attended a solemn mass of thanksgiving for having regained for Catholic Spain the capital of the northern province.

De Vargas had little time to rebuild the Royal City,

for the last ten years of his life were spent in constant effort to subdue the Indians. He died in the Sandía mountains in 1704, asking that his body be buried under the altar of the church in Santa Fe. In his will he acknowledged his illegitimate son and two daughters, dividing four thousand pesos between them. To his friend Don Antonio Maldonado Zapata he left "one pair of yellow silk stockings embroidered in silver and one pair of socks." Jewels, silverware and the many suits belonging to the aristocratic Caballero were sold to pay the debts he had incurred in reconquering Santa Fe.

When the Marqués de la Peñuela was appointed Governor-General, he began a thorough restoration of the capital. The terraced Indian buildings around the plaza were torn down to make way for Spanish shops, houses and patios. In 1710 the slaves' church of San Miguel was restored by the energetic Marqués "at his own expense," as the carved beam states, and the parish church of San Francisco was rebuilt over the monastery begun by Friar Benavides in 1622 and partially destroyed in the rebellion.

The Indians appreciated the solid construction of the Palace of the Governors too much to destroy it. The Marqués repaired what damage had been done in the fourteen years of Indian occupancy and established himself in the Casas Reales behind the Palace walls. The Palacio continued to be the most important stronghold of the wide province. Within its salas the Caballeros carried on all the pomp of an isolated court with the colorful costumes and strict etiquette characteristic of Spanish rule. In the Sala de Justicia rebellious Indian chiefs were brought before Spanish authority, prisoners were condemned to the dungeon or sent up the hill to La Garita to be hanged, maneuvers were planned, secret treaties sealed and expeditions outfitted to carry Gentlemen-on-Horseback on still further trails.

The eighteenth century was the long era of Spanish colonization for the province. Military men were constantly busy with keeping the King's rule supreme, five thousand Spaniards against the unnumbered foes of roving Indians, beside the sixty populous pueblos. Padres went out unarmed to establish twenty-eight missions far away from the settlements. A site on the Rio Grande, named for the Duke of Albuquerque, in 1705, with La Cañada de Santa Cruz to the north, were the only Spanish towns in the entire province besides Santa Fe.

But up and down the Rio Grande y Bravo the seeds of Spain were sown in smaller clusters. Land could be had for the asking, in a petition to the governor, viceroy and king. The greed for gold persisted in the hope that the dry grants of land might hide veins of pure yellow metal. New Mexico became a patchwork quilt of Spanish grants. They were of odd sizes and, since the surveyor's compass was unknown, natural boundaries of trees, rocks and cañons were confusing in a land that was all trees, rocks and cañons. Adding to the confusion of the titles was the Spanish custom of dividing the land among the numerous children into narrow strips, sometimes only a half a mile wide on the river frontage but running back over the mountains for twenty miles. The vague descriptions of these thirty-five million acres were not to be settled until two hundred years had passed and another army of American conquerors came with their laws to establish the Court of Private Land Claims.

To the colonists of the 1700's it mattered very little if the holdings overlapped in the vast unknown continent. A Spanish grandee might ride for days on his own estate, larger than the state of Connecticut. From his hacienda he could look to any horizon and know that it included his grant from the King.

With such distances to cover, his horse was his most valuable possession. He was the Caballero, luxuriously mounted, owning great cattle and sheep ranges, and master of a home like a feudal castle, where a hundred peons worked at his command. By military force he had conquered his Indian foes, but the daily fear of raiding parties kept him and his horse on their mettle.

Settling the province, living on the frontier upon what provisions they could raise, molding a new pattern of life in the wilderness, could be accomplished only by men and women of great faith, vitality and resourcefulness. Time moved slowly, endured with a patience that is now called the mañana habit. It was in this century that the culture of the Caballeros took permanent root in a province so isolated that no other influence came in to change it.

II

Trails to Santa Fe

FOR two centuries Santa Fe had been a Spanish Queen holding court in a far castle. Romance was woven about her like that of a beautiful woman, drawing men of every race with the desire to possess her. Added to the lure of her charm was the potent hint that she was dowered with coffers of gold.

Like the roads to Rome, all trails led to Santa Fe. Authority centered here to make her fate the fate of the province. But being the hub of trails was an even more important factor in her story than the four conquerors who would command the country from her Palace.

Even time has not obliterated the first Indian trails of this land, though they were made in a dawn beyond our reckoning. They were not printed in sand but cut as imperishable records into the rim rock of mesas. So many generations of bare, brown feet followed them that the rock was worn hip deep. Later, naked, bronze-skinned men grew venturesome and, treading noise-lessly through primeval forests, left a faint path down to the tropics. This was the Turquoise Trail where northern Indians carried stones of life-giving blue to trade for gaudy mackaws and parrots. Parrot feathers and turquoise were, and still are, indispensable symbols used in Pueblo ceremonials.

But the primitive value of sky stone was to be out-rivalled by the dreams of gold. The Turquoise Trail became a traveled royal road as horses' hoofs cut into it to mark the Camino Real. This King's Highway was the oldest trade route used by white man in Amer-ica. Two thousand miles in length, it ran from Vera Cruz through Mexico City to Santa Fe. In the restless nineteenth century it was called the Chihuahua Trail, since Chihuahua was the clearing house for financial and military orders for the northern internal provinces.

Once a year a caravan left New Mexico to travel down this trail to the great fairs in Chihuahua and Du-rango. These conductas started from Abiquiu and Taos in the Rio Arriba and met in Santa Fe to gather into the long cavalcade a military escort, pack mules, burros, horses and more creaking carretas. The day of the departure of the conducta was officially pro-claimed one of the great holidays of the year. Country people came in from all the ranches to watch it start. On the way through the Rio Abajo paisanos gathered to marvel at its exciting, dusty progress and to give the cargadores more goods for the Mexican trade.

The conductas were officially subsidized to encourage

native industries in New Mexico. Heavy wagons were piled with cotton cloth and woolen blankets, beaver pelts, salt, turquoise, copper and gold. At the Chihuahua and Durango fairs, these native goods were exchanged for Mexican products and luxuries imported

from Spain and the Orient. Flowered "Spanish shawls," embroidered in China and shipped from Manila to Mexico for the Doñas of Castilla, were intercepted by the traders for the señoritas of Santa Fe. On the return journey the wagons were loaded with sugar, wines, tobacco, jewels and European silks. New Mexicans, inured to simplicity and hardships, craved these foreign fineries. Gold flowed easily through the fingers of the ricos for costly food and ornaments, but the large class of pobres were compelled to do without them. It was largely because of these luxury-laden conductas returning up the Chihuahua Trail that the new Santa Fe Trail prospered. American traders found a ready market for their unbleached muslin and calico, well below the Mexican prices, even after the 50 per cent taxes had been paid.

From Santa Fe the supplies were distributed over the trails that crisscrossed the wide southwest. Some went to the mines in Arizona and northwest Mexico, others went north to Taos to be traded for beaver pelts brought in by French and American trappers. Young Kit Carson was one of the trappers who suffered when styles in the American states outlawed high silk hats, and the price of beaver dropped until a pack of pelts was not worth the long winter's work.

Out of work, the trappers turned to new and untried lands in California. A hundred years after the missions had been established at Santa Fe, the padres had gone to California to start missions there. But it was not until traders and trappers started west that the Colorado River basin was really explored. The Spanish Trail from Santa Fe to the new pueblo of Los Angeles went north through Abiquiu and Colorado and crossed the swift stream at Moab, Utah, where the pack mules were forced to swim the river. Beyond were the Wahsatch mountains and the "Pah-Utahs, the greatest horse thieves on the continent." The sixty miles across the terrible desert was attempted in one day's journey or jornada, and woe be to any trader forced to stop in the choking white alkali sand. Only Digger Indians could survive in that desolation. In the spring when the Diggers were weak and helpless, they were hunted and brought to be sold in the New Mexican markets. Slave catching was an accepted part of the caravan trade, considered as lawful as hunting buffalo or mustangs.

The great incentive for packing to Los Angeles was horse-trading. New Mexicans loaded their pack mules with the only article of export in the province—hand-woven woolen sarapes. "Caramba," shouted the returned traders, "we gave only two blankets for a fine horse!" At that they brought back more horses than the blankets they had packed, for they had connived with the Mission Indians for stolen horses in the Tulares valley.

After the Spaniards' dream of finding gold came true in '49, foodstuffs were of greater importance to the growing population than hand-woven sarapes. New Mexican traders drove living blankets across the trail in great bands of sheep to be traded for horses and gold. The New Mexicans, in embroidered leather jackets and peaked sombreros, swaggered in the cantinas of Los Angeles. Sometimes they lost their year's profit drinking and gambling, sometimes they trebled their stakes, for the unquenchable love of gambling ran in the blood of every New Mexican. In the fifties the old Spanish Trail was abandoned for a quicker route to the gold state, going south by Zuñi or the Gila River.

In 1803 the expanding American boundaries crept closer to the long-held Spanish domain by the transfer of a section of the continent from France to the United States in the Louisiana Purchase. Across this boundary Spain and the United States regarded each other with distrustful eyes. In 1806 the two nations decided simultaneously to investigate each other's land. Lieutenant Facundo Melgares rode out from Santa Fe with a powerful, well-appointed army of Caballeros going almost as far east as Nebraska. He might have ridden farther if he had not heard an exaggerated report that an American military expedition was then penetrating the Spanish province. Lieutenant Zubulon Montgomery Pike and a few men had crossed Colorado. With youthful Yankee boastfulness, Pike named the mountain near Colorado Springs for himself, a greater monument to an individual than any other on American soil. Reaching the Rio Grande, which he professed to mistake for the Red River, he built a small fort on the west bank—the Spanish side. Melgares rode up to Pike's fort and took him as a prisoner to Santa Fe. Pike came peacefully enough, for it was part of his mission to get first-hand information about the famous Spanish capital. From there he was escorted to Mexico City to have his papers searched before he was sent back to the States.

Pike's account of his trip had the same effect as that of the earliest explorer, Friar Marcos. Again adventure

beckoned with the promise of gold in New Mexico—
gold to be found in mines and to be traded for quick-
profit merchandise with the rich caravans coming up
the Chihuahua Trail. But it was fifteen years before
the horse path was widened for covered wagons to begin their annual spring trips down the Santa Fe Trail.

Spain was no longer Queen of the Seas as she had
been when Cortés' horses conquered Mexico. Her
span of power had run its three hundred years, and she
was losing her colonial possessions. In 1821 Mexico
achieved independence from Spain under the leadership of Iturbide. Mexico was too much occupied with
her insurrectos to give thought to the provinces and
the provinces knew almost nothing of what was hap-
pening in Mexico.

On Christmas day in 1821 there had been the customary holiday greeting of "Viva España!" in Santa Fe.
The overdue mail stage arrived the next morning with
the news of Iturbide's victorious entrance into the City
of Mexico three months before. Facundo Melgares,
now governor, immediately made the official pronounce-
ment from the portál of the Palace of the Governors
and led the cheers of "Viva México! Dios y Liber-
tad!" The royal scarlet and gold banners of Castilla
were lowered and the green, white and red flag of
Mexico raised on the standard above the Palace. The
change of national symbols did not worry Melgares
and his officials. It had taken place without their
knowledge—so be it, they said, with a shrug of their
shoulders. They continued in office just the same, only

45

changing the name on the dotted line from **Spain to** Mexico.

The final phase of Latin dominion in the province, during the next twenty-five years of Mexican rule, had an epic quality. Like the transplanted roses of Castilla whose color is more golden in the few days before its petals fall, the last flowering was the most colorful epoch in New Mexican history. Every aspect of life in the province was accentuated in the dying flourish of Latin glory and the virile new influx of Yankee traders. Each profited to such an extent that quick-spent gold was plentiful for lavish living and mounting gambling stakes. With this impetus, old Spanish arts, such as weaving sarapes, painting santos, working in iron, tin and filigree, reached their peak in the decade of 1830.

The trails wandering into Santa Fe were the healthy arteries of trade flowing from the south, north and west. They had not penetrated eastward since the days when the magnet of gold at fabled Gran Quivira failed to materialize. But the trail was to be brought into Santa Fe from the east, seeking the wealth of the Spanish settlements.

During the sixty years when Santa Fe was the End of the Trails, she enjoyed an importance shared by few cities in America. Here the Chihuahua Trail from the rich southern republic met the Santa Fe Trail from the vigorous young nation whose irrepressible expansion was to conquer the continent. Either of the trails would have made a town important; both of them made it famous.

In the same year when Mexican independence was having its carnival in the New Mexican capital, a party of men in Missouri were completing their plans to bring three covered wagons to Santa Fe. Their leader was Captain W. H. Becknell, the "Father of the Santa Fe Trail." Other outfits had preceded him, but Becknell was the first to use the shorter, practical route. With twenty-one men he left Boone's Lick neighborhood in May and reached Santa Fe November 16, 1822.

The terrible hardships they endured on this journey would have stopped the plans of less hardy adventurers. Once they arrived in Santa Fe their joy and excitement were so great that they forgot that death had stalked them on the plains. They sold out the merchandise of their three wagons at the highest prices, returning east the following spring with five times their original capital. This was such a sensation that men of every class and age were eager to start on the next westward trek.

Within two years twenty-five wagons left Franklin, Missouri, in the spring in charge of eighty-one men. They took with them $30,000 worth of merchandise and returned with $180,000 in gold and $10,000 in furs. Chihuahua merchants saw disaster in such proceedings and influenced the Mexican government to prohibit the importation of certain goods and to place a 50 per cent tax on all American merchandise. But in spite of dangers, hardships and taxes the commerce of the prairies increased each year, as more and more

47

covered wagons wound their way down the Santa Fe Trail.

From the first spring days when restless men and eager boys joined the caravan setting off from the Missouri frontier, there was only one thought in the minds of all the motley group—to reach Santa Fe. The first call of "Catch up! Catch up!" started a pandemonium as the men hurried to catch their mules and oxen, corralled during the night in the circle of the wagons. Each tried to be the first to call "All's set." Above the uproar of hallowing at runaway horses and swearing at balking mules, of the rattle of bells, yokes and harness, creaking of wagon wheels, clanking of skillets and coffee pots, and trampling of many feet, came the cry from each wagoner of "All's set." "Stretch out," yelled the captain, as the wagons lurched into their appointed places. Then with a final look about, the deep-throated command of "Fall in!" started the white-hooded wagons on their long journey, following the faint wagon ruts.

Day after day passed in sleepy monotony in crossing the prairie whose far tawny expanse was only limited by the dome of the blue sky. But the teamsters woke up when a deep rumble shook the prairie, coming from a vast black mass moving close to the earth and sending up clouds of dust into the glaring sunlight. Buffalo! Every man leaped on the first horse he could find, chasing the huge bison and shooting them for fresh meat to be barbecued that night. or dried for "jerky."

The first signs that the wagons were approaching the New Mexico province were the dashing Mexican Ciboleros in flat straw hats, who had ridden east to hunt buffalo and tan their hides for robes to sell the traders. Many a Caballero had now become a Cibolero. The sport of merely riding a horse had given way to the practical purpose of chasing buffalo. Spanish horsemanship still had its glory however, for even Kit Carson and other mountain men who "ran meat" for a living, acknowledged that the Ciboleros were the best of the profession.

The shout of "Buffalo" was good news, but the cry of "Indians" struck terror to all men's hearts. Indians resented the destruction of their meat supply in the wanton slaughter of buffalo herds. They retaliated with savage raids, often planned for stealing horses. Swooping down on the lumbering wagons, riding their own mounts at break-neck speed, waving buffalo robes and yelling, they stampeded the horses and mules in the rear caballada and then drove them off.

The wagons quickly huddled together to protect themselves from flying arrows and tomahawks. Women and children were barbarously murdered or carried away as screaming captives. Men were scalped, disfigured and left to die. If American rifles succeeded in routing the marauders, Indians set fire to the prairie grass, consuming everything but the iron wheel hoops in the red race of flames.

Added to the terror of Indians was the terror of

49

thirst, for the trail across the parched plains was marked with hundreds of bleached human bones. Beyond was the grilling climb of high mountain passes, where the too heavily loaded wagons proved a cruel haul for mules and oxen. Sometimes they overturned, falling to eternity in the deep granite cañons.

The morning before the caravan reached the end of the trail, they stopped to "rub up" before they met the critical black eyes of the señoritas of Santa Fe. Frontiersmen washed the prairie dust from their faces and hardened hands, sleeked down their long hair with bear grease and put on their carefully packed homespun suits. As a final touch, each wagoner tied a fine new cracker to his whip to outcrack his comrades as they dashed around the Plaza in a hilarious, triumphal entry.

Stopping at Arroyo Hondo, six miles from Santa Fe, they repacked their wagons, piling each as high as it would hold, for the Mexican government taxed each wagon $750, irrespective of its amount of merchandise. Some of the empty wagons were hidden in hopes of getting them for the return trip, some were burned to destroy the evidence, some were sold to close-mouthed Mexicans. A wagon costing $150 in Missouri sold for $750 in Santa Fe, in spite of the wear and tear of the long haul.

They must hurry with reloading before the party of Mexican officials rode out to greet them. The long white snake of the caravan had been detected by lookouts on Atalaya Hill. Now the Mexicans rode up, with their jingling Spanish bits and bridles, their welcoming speeches more flowery as their keen eyes searched for contraband.

The lurching caravan pulled over the last hill and, at last, Santa Fe lay before them. At this signal shouts of "Viva Santa Fe! Viva Santa Fe!" burst from every throat. The green valley under the blue mountains looked fairer than any jewel to these weary wayfarers, and the whitewashed houses held for many the hope of home.

The dusty string of wagons rolled joyfully down the hills and into town. Cries of "Los Americanos!" "Los carros!" "La entrada de la caravana!" filled the narrow streets. After a wild circle around the Plaza, with whips cracking and horns blowing, the stage drew up with a flourish at La Fonda, disgorging its excited passengers and mail sacks.

So this was "Santy Fee!" It spread out in a maze of brown, box-shaped houses, low and flat-roofed. Mud walls running in any direction were golden in the dazzling sunlight and the long white portales drowsed in blue shadows. Dark eyes peeped out behind the iron bars across mica windows and hinted that the old gate to the patio might be left ajar in the moonlight. Eastern youngsters, timidly presenting a letter of introduction to the formal Papá, entered a spacious sala gratefully cool and dim after weeks of untempered sunlight. Striped sarapes rolled against the walls, brass candlesticks on long tables and silver-mounted saddles hung on pegs, gleamed in the scented darkness. Formalities over, host and house warmed to open-handed hospitality. Everything was foreign, with an illusive beauty that charmed the stranger for life.

In the Plaza, wagoners hurried to the customhouse at the northeast corner, to get through with Mexican taxes and meet the clamoring country merchants, gathered from placitas and cross roads for this great event of the year. Bolts of calico were tossed off the wagons into their eager hands, each outbidding the other for the gayest colors. Boys elbowed their way through the crowds. Women, walking proudly with eyes half hidden by their rebozos, admired these blond strangers who brought the thrill of new lands.

Every woman wore a rebozo, a scarf a yard wide and twice as long. On the streets it veiled her eyes, at home it clung to her shoulders. La Patróna's rebozo was of the finest striped silk. The peona's was of dingy cotton, never in the way in spite of her numerous duties. For the fandango, the muchacha twirled it over bare shoulders whose only other covering was a flimsy chemise tucked into a short, full skirt.

La Patrona's pleasures were fiestas and siestas. She was a night-blooming flower sleeping through the day in order to enjoy the night. Siestas made her eyes more brilliant by candlelight, but also encouraged early matronliness. Fortunately for her, hunger charts for flapper figures were unknown then.

Men's faces were fiercely mustached under glazed sombreros, heavy with metal embroidery. Their eyes glinted as bumptious Yankees whisked laughing girls away from their pelado lovers. The silver buttons of their tight leather trousers were unfastened to the knee to show the full white drawers. Short braided leather jackets swung out beneath the sarape, narrowly folded over the left shoulder. Their smooth, brown hands were sure at lovemaking, shooting, gambling and riding.

Democratic frontiersmen were astonished with the class distinctions between the rich and poor. The ricos, swollen with new wealth and power, were excessive in their merrymaking, drinking, gambling and graft. For them the day was divided between the serious business of eating and sleeping. A cup of rich chocolate and sugar-powdered sopapillas were brought to the Patrón's bed as soon as he wakened. Followed by a substantial breakfast at nine o'clock he rode about the hacienda for a couple of hours and returned to stave off hunger with a bowl of broth. At midday a heavy dinner was served with several kinds of meat, vegetables and a wine pudding. Succulent chile stews were scooped up with a folded tortilla, the skill of the tortilla cook attested by the thinness of this corn griddle cake. After dinner the entire hacienda relaxed in the daily doze. The special chocolate cook brought in the spicy, frothing chocolate and sweets at four or, if there were visitors, another cook offered a delicacy of brandy and fruit syrups that had been stirred constantly for three days as it simmered beside the coals. Languid talk and plaintive, extemporaneous love songs filled the twilight hours until supper. Before bedtime there was a nightcap of wine, brandy and spice cakes.

The pobres were so numerous that each was assigned her special task. They became more servile on their pay of from two to five dollars a month for a man, and fifty cents to two dollars a month for a woman. They were rarely paid these wages in money but had to accept them in coarse clothing and a few necessities. If the servant contracted a debt from his master, as he usually did, he was bound to work this out as a peon. Children of the destitute and orphans were sold into slavery, a healthy girl of eight being worth four hundred dollars. Indians, taken as prisoners or captured on slave-catching raids, increased the number of peons to hundreds working on the haciendas of the ricos for the nominal price of food and clothing.

For the pobres, the staple foods were frijoles, chile con carne made with jerked meat and stacks of tortillas. Thin corn meal gruel called atole was the hot drink in the days before coffee was imported. In spite of squalor and the barest necessities, every traveler commented on the unfailing happiness of the pobres. At least there was no unemployment nor overproduction to keep them awake at night.

Montar á caballo was the accepted mode of traveling. Ladies rode sidesaddles with long flowing skirts almost covering the horse. Men lost no opportunity to show off their high-spirited mounts and their own horsemanship. Occasionally the ricos drove over the rough roads between the haciendas in heavy coaches drawn by six horses, with postilions riding before and behind. Large, happy families of pobres were thankful to ride to town in ox-drawn carretas. The real transportation of the country was carried on by the small, dust-colored burro who hauled everything from firewood to country belles. Sometimes he could hardly be seen for children piled on from flapping ears to patient tail.

The haciendas were kept going by raising great herds of long-horned cattle, horses and sheep. Fields near the spacious manor houses were turned with a primitive plow made of a forked tree branch, and irrigated from acequias. The acequias also ran through the patios, bringing the only running water for the house to boast of a century ago. Corn was planted Indian fashion in little hills in the fields. Don Amado Chaves says that his grandfather brought home the first alfalfa seed, tied in a manta, as his home-coming present from Mexico. The alfalfa was planted in the vegetable plot near the house and the tender leaves were eaten as greens. He tells also that the first hard black wheat was found in the crop of a wild goose killed on the Rio Grande. The curious grains were planted and the seeds saved for future crops, but it was never popular because it was too hard for the women to grind on metates.

Humble country folk gathered beside the imposing walls of the west side of the Palace to sell their produce. In this Spanish market, mutton, beef and pork were strung on a line between two posts with ristras of scarlet chile and bunches of white onions decorating either end. Brown beans in baskets, bread and goat's milk cheese, melons, squash, corn, small peaches, wild plums and berries were heaped on braided mats on the ground before their kneeling vendors. In winter, wild turkey, venison and bear steak tempted the rico's purse. In summer, the fragrance of fresh cut alfalfa and prairie grass advertised a bundle of hay selling for twelve and a half cents, minus the blanket in which it was tied.

The Plaza was surrounded by a shaded arcade of portales, protecting the mud sidewalks and giving the banqueros a place to lounge. A few stores rose to a second story where the proprietors lived. During the siesta hours fat-jowled merchants dozed there in the pleasant shadows, drowsily scolding mocking birds whistling from bent amole cages or chattering Mexican parrots. Sunny hours slipped by unheeded for the only public timepiece in this land of Poco Tiempo was a sundial in the Plaza. Day ended when the copper bells in La Castrense rang out the Ave María and began with the matin call from the Parroquia de San Francisco.

The sleepy mud town woke up Sunday afternoons for the bullfight in the ring opposite La Fonda; or for numerous fiestas; or for the teatro, when a play, entirely enacted by men, was given on a temporary stage in the Palace or beneath the summer stars in a corral; and especially for the fandango sure to be given the night when mountain men whooped down the Taos Trail with their packs of beaver.

That day they had money aplenty from selling their

pelts, and they were eager to spend it on a spree and "fo-furraw." They were dressed up for this annual visit to town in new genuine beaver hats, Ute moccasins, clanking spurs and buckskin hunting coats, fringed and beaded and gay with quill and feather embroidery. Among the fringe there was black human hair—Indian scalps to check coups notched into the rifles.

That night awkward trappers danced to the primitive call of music from guitars and tom-toms. "Taos Lightning" poured down lusty throats by the gourdful to make mountain hearts beat faster. They snatched black-eyed girls in short skirts away from the jealous Santa Fe galanes. Before a Spanish pistol could be raised they fell upon the native, crashing him with chairs and tables, knocking out the candles, cursing in the dark mêlée. The fandango vanished.

The next day mountain men were broke. Fandango, monte, aguardiente, buying fo-furraw for Santa Fe muchachas, had cleaned them of even their red mules and silver-mounted Spanish saddles. They started back to a womanless life and hard trapping in the mountains. But the annual doin's in town had been worth it!

This flair of primitive lustfulness gave Santa Fe a far reputation. Raw frontier life came to a climax at the end of the trails. Prudish New Englanders, coming west to lay by a fortune, were horrified with the free license. The more horrified they were, the quicker they succumbed to it. Yes, even in those days "Santy Fee was different," an intoxicating mixture of races. Indians stripping men's souls naked with fear,

Mexicans clinging to the last decadent days of their glory, excitable French-Canadian trappers recalling the Vide Pouche, rawboned Americans surging with new power to grab western lands and gold.

Provincial law and order was still supposed to function in the Palace of the Governors. At this time it was noted for two decorative features. There were panes of real glass in the windows, brought with exceeding care over the Santa Fe Trail, and there were strings of Indian's ears festooned across the walls in the executive offices of Governor Armijo. Indians hung the scalps of their enemies at their belts. Mexicans retaliated by offering a bounty for Indians' scalps and ears, stringing them in dark sinister garlands.

La Fonda was the far famed inn at the end of the Trail. The stagecoach stopped there with a sudden, creaking bounce, and the passengers clambered down. The main entrance was on the corner of San Francisco and Seligman streets, much as it is to-day. Guest rooms rambled around to form a hollow block with outside doors on the street and inside doors on the patio. Along the southern side a huge gateway opened into corrals where wagons were unloaded.

At the bar, traders, trappers, politicians and soldiers met to pledge friendship and future adventures in champagne and potent Pass brandy from El Paso. In the ballrooms a baile was held the night the caravan came in, all classes mingling from the highborn señora in her fine lace mantilla to the peon in his flapping white pantaloons. Women as well as men smoked the cigar-

58

rito of the country as they danced, the women holding theirs in dainty golden tongs. Criadas brought a live coal to light them, for there were no matches.

Gambling tables vied with the blind fiddlers in drawing the crowd. Monte, faro, chusa, poker and dice were played with stakes of gold piled up on the tables. Women were devotees of the games, the fascination of the glittering goddess of chance often costing them their rings, brooches and even their rebosos edged with golden fringe. The passion for gambling was characteristic of the time, not only with cards but in betting on cockfighting, bullfighting, horse racing, lottery and tourneys on horseback such as El Gallo and El Coleo.

Don Agustín Durán, a customhouse official, was such an inveterate gambler that after he had lost his money, mules and clothes, he pawned himself in the excitement of the game. In the cold light of mañana he "confiscated" enough goods to redeem himself from his creditors.

The most famous gambler of the Mexican period was Doña Gertrudes de Barcelo, better known as "La Tules." Born a ragged peona in Mexico, she came to Taos as a comely young girl. Like every other courtesan, she soon made her way to the capital where her flashing eyes, luck and shrewdness gave her more influence than any other woman of her time. Her reputation of being the best monte dealer in the wide world helped her to lay away a fortune. When she attended the fiestas in the near-by placitas, four peons staggered

under her leather money chests. Not content with
tossing a handful of coins on the table, she scooped up
a fanega of pesos from her chest and challenged the
men to meet this bushel measure of silver.

Becoming the confidante of Governor Armijo, La
Tules ruled the province through him until her temper
and his courage ran short. Now she owned exclusive
gambling salas running through the entire block from
San Francisco Street to Palace Avenue, bordered by
Burro Alley. They were known far and wide for their
sparkling chandeliers where a thousand candles burned
through the night, and for Brussels carpets on the
plank floors. Carpets and floors were elegancies to be
found in few other homes in the province. Here balls
were held in one end of the long building, and monte
tables chained their victims in the other. Military
maneuvers were planned and political intrigues whispered in the private salas, while the music of the baile
deadened pistol shots—suicide or murder? Gossip
and scandal, love of money and love of women brought
generals, governors, clerks and peons together in this
outpost Monte Carlo, though they entered only at La
Tules' invitation.

She played politics as well as monte and loved to
block intrigues by her own wit. She aided the American troops when they arrived in 1846, and her salas
became their meeting place. They had reason to be
friendly with her, for she saved the day for Colonel
David A. Mitchell by loaning him a thousand dollars
to follow emergency instructions and send his troops

to Chihuahua. And Colonel Mitchell saved the night and social prestige for her by accepting her condition to escort her to an exclusive military ball.

Her beauty was finally lost under increasing years and weight, and she added a respectable marriage to her experience. Still commanding her gaming rooms in dignified obesity, a red wig and store teeth, she was an imposing money lender. Loving splendor and drama to the day she died in 1851, her will left exact instructions for the one thousand six hundred pesos to be spent for candles, high masses and prayers for her soul.

Through the tragi-comic drama of the Mexican period and the early trail days there was always one heavy hand that jerked the marionettes. The hand belonged to Manuel Armijo. It held a shepherd's crook when he was a ragged boy and cut out part of the flock to be hidden and sold for himself. It left greasy thumbprints on the few books the ambitious lad studied by the light of the camp fire. It knew its way into other people's pockets as the young political leader of the Rio Abajo. It smoothed the long feather in his hat and caressed the golden epaulettes on his uniform when he was governor of New Mexico. It was a large hand, traitorous to friends and country, cruel to enemies, soft to women, and always open to take "diligencia." It should have given an hombrón a better axiom for life than the one Armijo was most fond of quoting—"It is better to have the reputation of a brave man, than to be brave."

Taxes imposed to keep up the display of officials in the poverty-ridden province, with no help from war-torn Mexico, made the New Mexicans discontented. In 1837, when Albino Pérez was governor, an insurrection broke out in the Rio Arriba. Pérez met defeat from the insurrectos at the foot of the Black Mesa near San Ildefonso. He fled to Santa Fe, but the insurrectos overtook him the next morning, cut off his head and bore it around the Plaza on a lance. Joined by the Indians they killed other leaders, placing Don Santiago Abreu in stocks, cutting off his hands and feet one at a time, and gouging out his eyes. Then they made one of their own members governor, a Taos Indian named José Gonzales.

The brains which planned this revolt probably belonged to Armijo and Padre Martínez of Toas, a renegade priest who considered his own authority superior to the laws of his church. Armijo expected to assume the governorship. When he found that the insurrectos had chosen Gonzales, he assembled his forces from the Rio Abajo and marched on the newly taken capital and his former co-conspirators. Fortunately for him, he was joined by federal troops sent from Mexico, defeated the new administration, and was appointed governor for his loyalty.

Texas had broken away from the mother country, Mexico, and set up an independent government as the Lone Star State. Having tasted liberty, she was eager to strengthen it by adding the province next door and believed that New Mexico would be equally glad to escape from Mexican tyranny. While there was restlessness among the New Mexicans, there was a stronger hatred of the new conquerors, the gringos, and no desire to unite with them in Texas. In 1841 the Santa Fe-Texas expedition came up the cattle trail from Austin with papers in English and Spanish to offer New Mexico a sister's share in the new republic. The Texans were captured by Armijo. Their sick and starving condition unheeded, they were sent on the one thousand five hundred mile march to Mexico City, equalling the forced marches of Siberian exiles in its cruelty.

Obviously Armijo had no wish to come under the régime of Texas. He was a supreme dictator in Santa Fe whose rule was very satisfactory to the Mexican government. Hating the Americans, he was suave enough to foster trade over the Santa Fe Trail. He paid taxes to the Mexican government as well as the entire running expenses of the province out of tariff imposed on the traders. The entrada of the caravans not only meant news and merchandise and gayety in Santa Fe but pay envelopes for every official from alcalde to governor.

Besides the $750 charged for each wagon load of goods, the contraband articles smuggled in gave every official a chance for graft, politely called "making diligencia." Only the enormous profits the traders took "back to the States," and their knowledge of the New Mexican temperament made it possible for them to prosper under such conditions.

Fearing reprisal from the Santa Fe-Texas expedition Armijo took a vacation and turned over the province to one of his lieutenants. But he was succeeded in a short time by a new governor, Don Mariano Martínez. Armijo returned to Santa Fe to inquire of Martínez why Santa Ana had appointed him.

"Santa Ana wanted a change because the affairs in this province have been corrupt," Martínez answered. "He says there is stealing in every department from the governor to the lowest official."

"Por supuesto, that's true," Armijo agreed. "We have made diligencia all the way along by permitting illicit trade. If you call that stealing, I've been stealing all my official life and have the money in my pocket to show for it. But it doesn't make a change to put you in as governor, for you have been stealing all your life and haven't a dollar to show for it. Válgame Dios, which of us is best fitted to carry on an economical administration in New Mexico?"

The Mexican government evidently recognized Armijo's superior economic ability, for he was appointed governor again in 1845.

By July of the next year, Santa Fe heard positively that the American army was on the march over the Trail to capture the ancient capital. There was intense excitement as Governor Armijo called the Assembly in extraordinary session, voted a thousand pesos and gathered his tattered army.

Two couriers had been sent ahead, asking for peaceful submission to the United States, Captain Philip St.

George Cooke and James Magoffin, a wily Irish trader. There was the clink of American gold dollars in Magoffin's canvas bags and artful blarney on his lips. Armijo made his biggest diligencia the night he met these two Americans, though he left the meeting declaring that he himself would lead an army of six thousand men to vanquish the Army of the West.

The Americans were under the command of General Stephen Watts Kearny. Like de Vargas in a previous conquest, Kearny took every precaution to see that his soldiers molested no one along the route. He entered Las Vegas, made a long speech assuring the people that the United States had considered New Mexico her territory for a long time, and succeeded in administering the oath of allegiance without firing a gun.

Then he marched over the last lap of the Trail to Santa Fe, prepared for battle. He had heard that Armijo and his army would hold the narrow cañon at Apache Pass near Cañoncito, fifteen miles south of Santa Fe. This was a strategic point and could have turned the American army to seek a longer route if Armijo's threats had been anything more than the last puff of a braggart.

Armijo had threatened to hold the Pass and had assembled some of his ragged army. Suddenly he changed his plan and fled to his ranch at Lemitar with a hundred dragoons to protect his personal safety. He died there six years later.

The Americans, surprised by no guerilla warfare, made a peaceful entry into far famed Santa Fe by sunset August 18, 1846. The Stars and Stripes were unfurled into the glory of the setting sun, and a salute of thirteen guns was fired from the loma on the Santa Fe Trail. Instead of a night on a battle field, General Kearny slept quietly in the Palace of the Governors, now sheltering the fourth army of Conquistadores.

Santa Fe was essentially a Spanish town from the red earth of her presidio to her enormous power as capital of the province, for the short Mexican régime was only a slightly changed continuance of Spanish tactics. Yet at the moment of siege, her citizens forfeited their homes without one despairing cry of Latin eloquence or firing a single gun. Money talked. Economic advantage was more to each side than bursts of nationalism. For twenty-four years New Mexicans had reaped advantages of American trade on the eastern Trail.

And the United States, with little moral excuse for grabbing a weaker sister's property, took this opportunity for westward expansion. She was lured on by the same dreams of riches which had hypnotized Spaniards. When New Mexico, Arizona, parts of Colorado and California were ceded by Mexico to the United States in the treaty of Guadalupe Hidalgo at the conclusion of the Mexican War in 1848, the United States added one-third of its present area. But even her ambition of expanding the nation until it touched

66

both oceans, did not foresee the vast wealth the Southwest would bring her in the next century.

Though no battle had been fought for the conquest
of Santa Fe, the first thought of the American army
was to erect a fort to protect their new territory.   On
the mesa above the Spanish prison of La Garita they
built Fort Marcy, named for the Secretary of War.
Barracks of adobe, log blockhouses and ten cannon
commanded the peaceful green valley of the Rio Santa
Fe.

Santa Fe had been the end of the trail for Americans for almost half a century.   Santa Fe, captured,
became the halfway point for yet further western trails
to the Pacific and Oriental trade.   General Kearny
stayed in Santa Fe only a month and left with his
detachment for the occupation of California.

His somewhat unwilling guide was Kit Carson.   Kit
chafed under slow army regulations and besides he
had been on his way to Josefa and Taos.   But he faced
about and led the army to California.   This small,
unobstrusive, blue-eyed man was to play a leading part
in the American occupation of the West.   He carried
messages, too important to trust to any one else, from
Santa Fe to Washington, and gave the East picturesque
first-hand information about the West.   It wasn't as
exciting a life as his early days around Taos, and the
recognition of Presidents and Senators didn't mean as
much to his heart as his hard-won titles of Mountain
Man and Indian Scout.   But the old days were gone.
He served his country in new ways, never varying from

his old directness in Indian battles—"concluded to charge 'em. Done so."

Kit had womaned with two Indian girls. The Arapahoe bride died, and the Cheyenne woman gave him an Indian divorce by throwing his belongings out of the tepee. Then he succumbed to Spanish charm and married the beautiful Josefa Jaramillo. Charles Bent married her sister and the two families lived in Taos—at least Carson and Bent lived there when they were not trading or riding the trails.

Charles Bent had been appointed Governor of New Mexico to succeed the disgraced Armijo. Bent was one of the early Virginia pioneers who came over the Trail with his brother William. The thick adobe walls of Bent's Fort on the Arkansas had long been a sanctuary for traders escaping from the desert and Apaches.

No one knew better than Charles Bent the New Mexican temperament, yet he discarded caution when his life was at stake. Now that the American army ruled with military strictness the Mexicans regretted their supine submission to the conquerors. Gone were the days of diligencia, lordly ricos, easy life! Characteristically they started secret revolutionary plots and insurrections, with threats to kill all Americans and their sympathizers. It looked bad for the Americans, outnumbered sixty-five to one.

After three months of trying to quiet the insurrectos, Bent went to Taos to bring his wife and children to live with him in the Palace of the Governors. He found Taos in a tumult, harangued by Mexican and Indian leaders, and Taos Lightning flowing from every cantina. Hearing of a plot to kill Bent that night, his friends urged the Governor to return on the fast horses in his corral. Bent replied that he had no fear of an attack upon himself—weren't these people his friends and neighbors to whom he had given medicine, food and clothing when they were in need? Frightened by the frenzied yells and threats, Mrs. Bent and Mrs. Carson began to dig a hole through the adobe wall into the next house. As soon as the hole was large enough they pushed the children through and pleaded with Governor Bent to follow them. It was too late, for the rioters broke through the door, riddled Bent's body with arrows and scalped him. After two days the women and children were rescued by a friendly Indian, who dressed them as squaws and took them to his house.

Army officers put a noose around the neck of each insurrecto and appointed James C. Calhoun the next Governor. Calhoun had been the first Indian agent. His scanty knowledge was depended upon to settle the Indian troubles, the most difficult problem the Americans faced during the sixty years of the Santa Fe Trail.

Two years later Santa Fe was forgotten in the wild news that gold had been found in California, gold no deeper than onion roots underlying whole valleys and as rich as Spanish dreams. Men broke new trails in the mad rush to reach it. Breaking off the Oregon Trail was a quicker route than going over the Santa Fe and Spanish Trail. American migration, which might have enveloped New Mexico first in the westward wave, jumped over it to settle California.

But the white-hooded traders' wagons continued to come down the Santa Fe Trail. Free from Mexican tyranny the settlements on the Rio Grande were glittering rewards for men who dared to grasp them. Daring and the excitement of frontier life were as much a lure on the Trail as profits. Adventure and gold— no young man, Spanish or American, had been able to resist them.

By the time of the Civil War three thousand covered wagons rolled into Santa Fe, loaded mostly with factory cloth, dearly prized by frontier women. The wagons returned less heavily laden with wool and copper. Some of the wagon beds were soft with thick native wool mattresses. Hidden in the wool was a layer of shining gold nuggets taken from the placer mines at Dolores near Coronado's old camp. In 1885 the Santa Fe trade was estimated at five million dollars. Even in those days this was not an outstanding financial achievement. But the Trail business was important as a wedge driven into new lands to make way for later transcontinental railroads.

A few courageous women came over the Trail with their menfolks. Susan Magoffin is immortal for the diary of her honeymoon journey down the Santa Fe Trail in 1846. She traveled in a "Rockaway Carriage" in as much safety and comfort as her trail-hardened husband could provide. Other tenderfoot brides of German and Jewish merchants made homes in the dangerous foreignness of the Spanish settlements. Doomed women, like Mrs. White and Mrs. Wilson, were captured and killed by the Indians. There were also the usual camp followers, painted ladies who loved frontier excitement, easy money and lusty men.

French-Canadians, such as Ceran St. Vrain and Carlos Beaubien, had married into old Spanish families. Lucien B. Maxwell married Beaubien's daughter, who inherited the great tract of land known as the Maxwell Land Grant. Its extent must have been set by one of Armijo's lordly gestures, for its 1,700,000 acres made Maxwell the owner of the largest private estate in the United States. The hacienda near Cimarron was run with typical Spanish hospitality, and the solid silver on the long table was never set for less than two dozen guests. It is said that Maxwell kept from $50,000 to $100,000 as small change from selling cattle, sheep and grain. His bank was the lowest bureau drawer, and though the drawer was never closed, the awe of this Patrón was so great that not a coin was ever stolen.

Geographically New Mexico was looked upon as one of the southern slave states but she was admitted to the Union as a non-slave territory in 1850. New Mexico was, and continued to be, difficult to classify. She was neither southern, western nor northern. She was New Mexico, a sparsely settled, sunny province where Spanish traditions had taken root. She was content with her old form of peonage, differing from southern slavery

71

only in that peons were not sold on the open market.

When the Civil War threatened to rend the United States, the Southern cause was symbolized to New Mexico by Texas. The bitter antagonism between the Texas classifications of gringo and greaser and the Federal troops stationed in New Mexico drew the new territory's allegiance to the north. There were few decisive engagements in this distant land, but after the battle at Pidgin's Ranch near Glorieta, the Federal troops evacuated Fort Marcy, and the Confederates marched in to occupy Santa Fe for a month. Confederate strength was waning and by the end of the war the Federal Army came back to Santa Fe to remain until the end of the century.

After the Civil War, nation building pushed westward with renewed energy. Lawless border men as well as the ever present Indians preyed upon the trade caravans along the Santa Fe Trail. Railroads had come as far west as Chicago and then Kansas City. Now they would follow the Santa Fe Trail to make trade expansion safer. The American pulse was beating faster, calling for speedier transportation than slow oxen. Stagecoaches traveled day and night with many relays of horses, cutting the six weeks' trip from Independence to Santa Fe to two weeks and the fare from two hundred and fifty dollars to one hundred and twenty-five dollars. The Pony Express raced over western trails, and Francis Aubrey rode horseback from Santa Fe to the Missouri River in eight days. But with steam and steel time could be still further shortened. The iron horse came to supersede the Spaniard's caballo in the race to overtake the sun, as all of the great historical trails were traced with steel. Time was to be limited in a land that had been timeless.

Indians tried to stop this new supernatural monster by blocking the way with their own bodies. Unheeding, the black monster laid its ears back and ran over them. Pessimists argued that mountains and deserts were impassable, but the first engine wheezed over the high Raton Pass and into New Mexico in 1879. It belonged to the Atchison, Topeka & Santa Fe Railroad whose first intention was to connect those terminals. Having reached New Mexico, ambition again made the Spanish settlements only a stepping-stone to the Pacific. Surveyors contended that transcontinental traffic would be slowed down by climbing the five-hundred-foot grade to run through Santa Fe. Time was more important than sentiment, and the steel rails left the last fourteen miles of the Santa Fe Trail to follow the lower valleys on the push toward California. Santa Fe had given its name to a famous trail and railroad, but it was abandoned in the new hurry. A mountain spur connected it with the main line at Lamy Junction. The saying arose that people lived in Santa Fe but spent half their lives in Lamy waiting for trains.

Yet Santa Fe was to be the terminus of another railroad. The Denver and Rio Grande Western approximated the route of the old Spanish trail north and laid narrow-gauge tracks to connect Santa Fe with Denver and the rich mines of Colorado. Soon the

Chihuahua Trail was banded with steel as far as El Paso and the Mexican border.

The picturesque days of caravaning across the trails were over. No longer the hub of trails, Santa Fe was left high and dry in the mountains, to escape once more from too hasty, ugly progress. With a dreamy Spanish smile she settled peacefully against adobe walls, content to await mañana. But the siesta was never so deep but that at least one eyelid fluttered at the sound of politics. Railroads and industries might hurry by, but Santa Fe would remain the mighty seat where the political destinies of the country were settled.

While engines now pulled expensive freight across the plains, the trails were crowded with cattle. The Texas and Chisum trails ran from below the Rio Grande far up into Montana and the Dakotas. They followed the route of the early Spaniards and brought Spanish traditions to give color to another phase of western life.

For a century the horse had been important not because he was ridden but why he was ridden. The Caballero had become economically the Cibolero of buffalo hunting days. When "humpback cows" vanished, and domesticated cows took their place as the meat supply, the Cibolero was replaced by the Vaquero. Americans translated vaquero and took the title for themselves as Cowboy.

The world soon pictured all Americans as cowboys waving their ten-gallon Stetsons atop pitching broncos. The character of the cowboy with his dry humor, good sportsmanship and courage was typically American as it developed on the "lone prai-ree." But wherever boys of the Lazy T outfit or the X L Ranch punched and prodded cattle up the trails, they owed their equipment, tools, technique and even language to the vaquero from below the Rio Grande.

Lasso, lariat, cinch, morales, corral and ranch were Spanish words soon Americanized into everyday use. "Spanish bridles," bits, and spurs with clanking rowels had the value placed upon them long ago by Toledo steelsmiths. The cowboys' proudest belongings were a forty-dollar saddle and a ten-dollar hoss—both brought from Spain four hundred years before. His leather chaps had been shortened from chaparejos, the taps for his stirrup covers from tapaderos. His "cavvyard" was the mutilated term for the rear trail horses in the caballada. He learned quickly to throw the lasso, bulldog a steer and cook frijoles from his darker-skinned compadres and soon put his teacher out of the business.

The cowboy era had a short life but a long reputation. It was the last phase of picturesque frontier life and died hard, for we are loath to give up romance for robotism. It began soon after the Civil War when restless men searched for new adventures. The West was one vast open range where red cows and pinto ponies thrived and increased on prairie grass. Only the precious water holes had definite owners. But by 1900 there were too many wandering herds for grass and water holes. Barbed wire fences partitioned the range and in time flivvers patrolled the fences for the Cattle Industry, Limited.

In the wild and woolly days of the seventies, mining camps boomed in New Mexico as though they had sprung out of the red hills by rubbing Aladdin's lamp. Ranch houses were to be found on the uninhabited prairies, and cattle trails widened every once in a while into the main streets of straggling western towns. Cowboys rode in to shoot up the town, dance with the few school marms, and lose their pay to card sharps. Law became the cowboy code, simple and unfailing. Holding up the mail stage or occasional trains had artistic merit, but a petty thief paid for his lack of imagination by swinging from the highest limb. Horse stealing was a worse crime than murder. A placard in bold black type, and common enough in those days, was posted at Las Vegas, March 24, 1882.

NOTICE

TO THIEVES, THUGS, FAKIRS, AND BUNCO-STEERERS,
Among whom are
J. J. HARLIN, ALIAS "OFF WHEELER," SAW DUST CHARLIE,
WM. HEDGES, BILLY THE KID, BILLY MULLIN, LITTLE
JACK THE CUTER, POCKED MARKED KID
AND ABOUT TWENTY OTHERS
If found within the Limits of this City after
TEN O'CLOCK, P. M. *this night, you will be*
invited to attend a
GRAND NECKTIE PARTY
the expense of which will be borne by 100
substantial Citizens

Desperadoes like Wall Henderson, who always chose his victim's eye socket as a target, and the boy bandit, Billy the Kid, who killed twenty-one men before he was twenty-one, terrorized the country. Cattle rustlers drove off the rancher's cows and the feud between ranchers and rustlers continued for the ten bloody years of the Lincoln County War.

Bandits' holdups in the wild West were featured in eastern newspapers and reached the ears of the Washington government. The President appointed a veteran of the Civil War, General Lew Wallace, to stop the highwaymen. He arrived in Santa Fe just after the Lincoln County War had settled itself and the first railroad had become front page news instead of the rustlers' revenge. As governor, Lew Wallace found enough official worries in this raw, new territory, yet he had time to finish his famous novel *Ben Hur,* by working far into each night in his study in the Palace of the Governors.

The man who had the widest influence in these early tumultuous days of the Territory was Archbishop John B. Lamy. In 1850 this earnest French priest was appointed to a huge vicariate of scattered missions. He rode horseback for three months to reach his new headquarters in Santa Fe, and another two months to Durango to present his credentials to Bishop Zubiria of the northern Mexican Parish. With energy and consecration Bishop Lamy began to clean house in his frontier field, unfrocking faithless priests and inspiring

77

others to greater zeal in building up the missions. Teaching orders began schools, and Sisters of Charity started the first hospitals under his guidance. When he died, after thirty-eight years of unceasing effort, men and women of all creeds and races came to pay respect to this beloved missionary bishop.

The cattle trails epoch ended with the century. Nowhere were the "gay nineties" gayer than they were in Santa Fe. The army post, eastern politicians appointed to western plums, Spanish and pioneer families made life in the old capital comparable to that of a small kingdom. Cattle and mines kept plenty of money in circulation. The military band playing on the parade grounds, the whirr of roulette wheels, balls and champagne dinners livened the little town. A fringe-topped surrey and a pair of fast trotters were tokens of wealth. Heavy, ill-smelling hacks drove the stranger from the railroad station to the Exchange Hotel (the new name of La Fonda) through narrow adobe-lined streets, still suggesting Spain rather than the United States.

The Spanish-American War broke out in Cuba in 1898. Most of Roosevelt's Rough Riders who stormed San Juan Hill were cowboys from New Mexico, but there were rumors that certain Spanish families sympathized with Spain. Spanish traditions lived on, though an American government had repressed them for half a century.

In 1910 Congress at last acceded to New Mexico's long plea for statehood. Santa Fe, whose ancient authority had been supreme under Indian, Spanish and Mexican governments, now became the capital of the youngest state in the Union.

Soon horses were to shy at puffing horseless buggies honking along like terrified red devils. Automobiles had come, and country roads must be graded for speedier travel. The twenty years since statehood have been marked by a far-sighted development of state highways. They are remarkable in a state that is fourth in area in the United States, but whose taxable population is less than one medium-sized industrial city.

They are the arteries of trade for a new epoch as the Chihuahua and Santa Fe trails were for their centuries. Where the Camino Real was paved with Spanish dreams of gold, the modern highway is paved with oil—the gold of twentieth century Americans, found far below New Mexican soil. Where Concord coaches rattled over the Santa Fe Trail, motor coaches travel day and night to cross the continent. Santa Fe, cut off from main line railroads, is again a hub of modern trails. Climbing mountains and crossing deserts are no longer bugbears but are featured as scenic interest for jaded always-on-the-go Americans. Altitude matters even less to the next step in transportation, for airplanes soar like eagles over the land, only concerned with finding prairie landing fields. In 1631 the Mission Supply caravan made the journey from Mexico City to Santa Fe in nine months. In 1931 the same distance is covered by airplanes in nine hours. Time and highways have at last dissolved the isolation of New Mexico.

But no country can be known intimately from standardized highways, much less New Mexico. Where filling stations have brought conglomerate industrialism, native backgrounds have vanished. Indians have concentrated in their pueblos, intensified in the center of their ever dwindling fields. Spanish people have retreated to placitas tucked away in the folds of purple mountains. Even in Santa Fe, Spanish life is only the syncopated bass accompanying the shrill American treble.

But leaving the straight, level highways we turn off on twisting rutted roads to old romance. There we find unfrequented placitas drowsing in the sunshine, scarcely changed by the rushing centuries, for they seem to be under the spell of timelessness. Like desert chameleons the low, flat-roofed houses melt into the color of the background—adobes as red as the hills at Cienega, yellow as the mesa of Tierra Amarilla, gray as the dead backbone of clay at Chupadero.

Time goes backward as the road leaves the highway, suggesting the life of middle and earlier days. On the road to Chupadero I came upon a covered wagon pulled by two lean horses. There was no hurry, for a day had been allowed for a trip that a daring motor makes in an hour. In the distance I heard a Spanish song. Apples, my nose said, as I rode closer —yes, and gleaming onions and scarlet chile spilling over the wagon bed. Children's dark, gentle eyes peered around the edge of the wagon sheet. In the shadow of the white hood a woman cuddled a baby under her black shawl, and the man beside her sat with loose reins in his hands and a friendly smile under his mustache.

My horse passed the leisurely wagon. The road climbed unbelievably, up the sandy shoulder of the mountain to white clouds puffed out against the blue bowl of the sky. At the crest, clouds and sky receded for another world of mountain ranges cut by cañons. Far below, desert plains were shimmering golden sand. Around me the red hills were studded with dwarf evergreens. Above, the breasts of mountains flamed with yellow aspens until they touched the clouds and sky.

The road plunged down into a barranca. In the precious, watered green of a hidden valley Chupadero basked in the sunshine. A boy on a horse rode away from an adobe home where a striped sarape splashed its colors against a white portal. As he came nearer I saw long leather chaps, a leather belt and cuffs with shining brass studs, a wide sombrero set at an angle on a dark head. His brown face was young and his dark eyes inquiring, that centuries-old questioning look of his people as the stranger approached their country. It changed swiftly to smiling recognition. He was Pablo García. Our horses stopped for the customary greetings. Then Pablo rode on to Santa Fe, dressed up in his proud Spanish leather trappings. As the steady trot lessened, I watched the pony carefully climbing the hill, **Pablo** sitting easily in his high-horned saddle. Such a lone horseman on the trail had been typical of New Mexico for four hundred years. As Pablo was silhouetted for a moment at the top of the ridge, I thought of him as the last of the Caballeros.

III

Where Americans Are "Anglos"

THERE is only one place in the United States where
an American is not an American. In New Mexico, in
spite of being American territory for more than seventy
years, an American is an "Anglo" and a Spanish-American is a "native."

The reason for using these names touches a sensitive
spot in the body politic. Within the last generation,
the Spanish-speaking element of the state, still over
half its population, rebelled at being called "Mexicans"
and spoke of themselves as "Spanish-Americans."
Politicians were quick to flatter the fifty-five per cent
vote and immediately referred to them, in political
oratory at least, by the hyphenated name. Who then
were Americans? "We are all Americans," the Spanish voice asserted again, "but you are Anglo-Ameri-
cans." So now in every campaign you will hear the
New Mexican villages ring with the lauding of the

Spanish-Americans, while the Anglos smile unprotestingly as they are deprived of their full birthright.

To refer to the Spanish-speaking people as "natives," brings no reproach, for to the native belongs his
country. That is his innermost conviction—New
Mexico is his country. He is really neither Spanish,
nor Mexican, nor American, but New Mexican through
three hundred years of living upon the same soil, in the
same adobe houses and with the same folk customs.
He outnumbered the American immigrants sixty-five to
one when this territory was annexed by the United
States in 1848, yet his loyalty to our nation was demon-
strated in the World War when fifty per cent of the
New Mexicans who died in service bore Spanish-American names. If he prefers to call himself "Spanish-
American" that is surely his right.

The term "Mexican" has been in common use for
a century. Why is it suddenly so obnoxious? Perhaps
it is not sudden, but only recently has dared to become
articulate. It goes back to the days of the Santa Fe
Trail when the first swaggering Anglos found New
Mexico a Mexican state. They were the ones who
dubbed the natives "greasers," and were called in turn
"gringos salados" from the fact that strange freckles
appeared to have been "salted" freely upon their blond
noses. Much of the still present hatred of Texans and
"Mexicans" comes from the foray of the Santa Fe-
Texas expedition when the New Mexicans ousted the
cowmen and refused to become part of the Lone Star
Nation. Texans used the term "Mexican" with insult-

ing ridicule and, for almost a century, the native has never disassociated it from the suggested contempt.

Mexican nationalism, which withered in New Mexico, thrived south of the border line. To-day the Mexican is more insulted by being called "Spanish," than the Spanish-American is by being called "Mexican." The greatest compliment to pay any citizen of the southern republic is to call him an Indian, since the strength and virility, as well as the majority of the population there, is of Indian blood.

Santa Fe and Quebec are the only places in North America where the government is conducted in two languages. Where French is used officially in Quebec, Spanish is used in Santa Fe. Up to 1909, the reports of the territorial treasurer were printed in Spanish. The codifications of the laws of New Mexico are printed in both languages as well as the session laws passed by the state legislature.

The New Mexico Legislature, with its dramatic political fights, has always been bilingual. In 1929 the State Senate was composed of five Spanish-American members and nineteen Anglos, and its proceedings had the innovation of being conducted only in English. But in the House of Representatives the natives held the majority of twenty-five Spanish-American members to twenty-four Anglos, and the customary interpreters were busy translating all the business of the Lower House in the two languages. Every motion, every order of business, every wordy battle, every communication from the Governor or the Senate was paralleled in Spanish. The moment any member rose to speak an interpreter rose beside him, translating each phrase.

Good interpreters must be able linguists, for they must not only know Spanish and English well enough to translate the words instantly, but they must get the shades of meaning in each language. This may be used subtly to give the wrong twist to a speech if the interpreter is not of the like political faith. They not only echo each phrase, but mimic the gestures. Often an artful interpreter will make the best speech of the two.

You have only to listen to those two Armijos, Isidoro and George, to understand their able services. Though they have the same name, they are unrelated by family or temperament. Isidoro in his high gray derby and white tie is the dignified Spanish scholar, though his practical jokes are famous. George's head protrudes beyond his heavy shoulders as though he wanted a closer view of a ludicrous world. He has an actor's wit, using mimicry, buffoonery, drollery, with gestures which would make Charlie Chaplin envious. His stories are inimitable. He has the native audiences laughing with him until the tears run down their brown faces.

Not long ago a slow-tongued Anglo had to make campaign speeches. He said that he was a business man and not an orator and stated his platform with unqualified terseness. But his enthusiastic interpreter threw into the phrases the fire and melody of Spanish. The candidate stood like a solid tower, but the interpreter's arms flew out like windmills rousing the audience of Spanish-Americans and Anglos, who only needed to watch him to catch his enthusiasm.

The constant interruptions of an interpreter are disturbing to an out-of-the-state spellbinder. He finds another voice breaking into his soaring eloquence. But to the man who is accustomed to this translation the pause between phrases is used to advantage to build up a cannonading climax. The fortunate speaker is the one who uses both languages, making two separate speeches without interruption. Many of the Spanish-Americans begin with the old formality, "Señoras y Caballeros," and make their speech with all the grace of their native tongue, letting the interpreter put it into English, for the Spanish-Americans are born orators.

People who have looked in vain for farms and factories around Santa Fe often ask, "But what supports the town?"

The reply is "Climate, curios and politics."

And the greatest of these is politics.

The largest payroll in the oldest capital comes from state and federal offices. When a political job means bread and butter, it is of vital importance, whether the goal is the governor's chair or the janitor's basement. As one Capitol sweeper put it the other day, when he was about to lose his sixty-dollar-a-month pay check, "I have got to keep my job, amigo, I have a wife and nine children and we have only made the first payment on a Ford."

Politics is no cold science here, manipulated by an

awesome dignitary, but an all-pervading influence which penetrates everyday life.

To the Spanish-Americans a political job not only means family sustenance, but that which is as dear to Spanish pride—authority. An office, whether it is that of lieutenant governor or mayordomo of the acequia, is an honor for the family. A man's political strength rests upon his "influjo," upon how many votes he can influence, not by money as much as by family connection. In a country where families run from ten to twenty-five children and children's children this influjo is treated with proper respect.

For many years elections in New Mexico were settled by the Patrón system. The Big Boss, who owned Spanish land grants larger than the state of Rhode Island, employed hundreds of sheep herders, vaqueros, peones. Unable to read or write and uninterested in affairs beyond the home range, they voted according to the orders of the Patrón. This influjo of controlling unvarying hundreds of votes was a large part of his feudal power. He used it for the most part wisely, bringing back political plums for his hacienda and henchmen.

When the votes fell below the necessary strength he is said to have voted his sheep, the Patrón with the biggest flocks having the advantage. A Patrón from one of the sheep counties once phoned up to the Capitol to ask how the election was going.

"How has your county gone?" headquarters asked him.

"How many votes do you need?" he replied.

"About two thousand."

"All right," the Patrón promised, "I'll send them up to you in the ballot box to-morrow."

To-day the Spanish-American has had Anglo schooling, peonage has vanished, and he is a more intelligent voter. But there is still a trace of that instinct which looks for the protection of a Patrón.

Never yet has there been a campaign in New Mexico when the race issue has not been raised. Each party assures all comers that they are the best friends of the Spanish-Americans. Anglos have been known to incite race riots, hoping that by rousing the disgruntled natives the solid vote might flop to their party. This has brought about a newspaper sentiment for race solidarity, trying to awaken race consciousness.

With fifty-five per cent of the vote, why don't the Spanish-Americans control the state? For one reason, they don't and probably never will vote as a race. It is to their credit that they are, first of all, American citizens, divided into American political groups. They have never yet banded together as a solid antagonistic race. Most of them are as staunch in adherence to party as Hoover and Smith, though there are many of both races in both parties who lend uncertainty to political prophecies by jumping the fence to run this year with the sheep and next year with the goats. New Mexico leaders are notoriously broad-minded, campaigning from one platform and then the other in succeeding elections. Jealousy among themselves of their own leaders is another reason which prevents Spanish-Americans from sticking together. While they may follow Patrónes more than theories, they follow their own Patrón only until his strength becomes too dictatorial and then they desert to another of their rising sons.

There was some question as to how woman's suffrage would succeed in New Mexico, since the Spanish-Americans are conservative and fully believe that a woman's place is in the home, waiting upon her master. However, when they realized that the women doubled the family's vote, every girl, every crippled grandmother, every woman who was blind, lame or bedridden was hauled to the polls in all the glory of bannered election cars.

The first election after equal suffrage became the law, one Spanish wit who was running for sheriff tacked a "Votas para las Mujeres" placard on a broom, raised it aloft and marched to the polling booths at the head of thirty-nine black-shawled women. They were going to see to it, to the fourth generation of cousins' aunts, that the family would be honored with an office.

The result is that the Spanish-Americans not only urge their women to vote, but are proud to put them up as candidates for office. Four Spanish-American women have served capably as secretaries of state. The first woman to act as governor in the United States was Mrs. Soledad Chacon, then Secretary of State, who filled the governor's office temporarily in 1924 while the acting governor was out of the state.

Women have proved themselves to be as clever politicians as men. More than that cannot be said, for to the Spanish-American, politics is a lifetime game, played with the unceasing keenness of a gambler and with the love of drama which the interplay of factions emphasizes in isolated mountain placitas. These black-shawled women know more about intensive organization and house-to-house canvassing than the League of Women Voters will ever learn.

One important politician is a little old woman with a quiet, rosy face. She follows the ancient calling of midwife. On her rounds among her patients she naturally talks politics, along with the casual conversation which gives the physician time to study her patient. If she cannot persuade a woman with her good party arguments, she looks at her wisely and shakes her head. "You don't believe what I tell you of Juan Ortiz, my daughter? Bien, in three months more you will send for me. Then we shall see if I can come!" On election day seven of the biggest cars and fastest drivers are turned over for her use. She keeps them busy, going from one precinct to another, for she knows each family's politics and not a possible vote escapes her.

Voting polls are a disgrace to Santa Fe, and the secret ballot is a farce. Electric voting machines are unknown and unwanted. The law allows the blind and illiterate to receive help in marking their ballots, printed in long sheets in Spanish and English. From the number who receive help from eager ward workers, most of the population must be both blind and illiterate.

As for the secret ballot, in the state capital you step up on a box at the schoolhouse window and call out your name while the three men inside the room inspect the poll books to see if you are registered. Given the ballot you step back into the sacred precinct of the booth, with three flimsy canvas sides and the fourth side open. Two or three workers may push into the booth with you, ostensibly to help with the marking and perhaps to see if you are voting as you have promised—after a little sideline persuasion. If the voter is sufficiently cowed by the ward worker, the worker will mark the ballot and hand it in himself. If not, you approach with your folded ballot and climb the box again. There is no ballot box in sight. Your ballot is handed over the high window sill into a hand whose inky thumb mark may identify your secret vote. You trust to the three bipartisan counters that your ballot, your precious American secret ballot, lands in the ballot box and is later counted.

This unbelievable condition is the fault of both Anglo political parties. Until they both desire to have elections conducted in at least an outwardly fair and just manner, in compliance with the laws of the state, New Mexico will continue to have a reputation for corrupt political practices.

Spanish is not only the preferred language for getting votes in such large counties as Taos, Rio Arriba, San Miguel, Socorro, Valencia, Mora, Sandoval and Santa Fe, but it is the common language of every other phase of life. Along the narrow winding streets of Santa Fe you hear quite as much Spanish as English. Traffic signs around the historic Plaza are painted in both languages. Many advertising circulars are printed only in Spanish for distribution among the large part of the population of the oldest capital. Plays in Spanish are presented by local Spanish literary societies or by troupes from Old Mexico who find an enthusiastic welcome for their native tongue. Catholic churches and Protestant missions have sermons in both Spanish and English, while in the mountain villages the services are entirely in Spanish. Language students find that these sermons offer one of the best ways of accustoming the Anglo ear to Spanish rhythms.

For this Spanish is the old court language of the seventeenth century, preserved in its medieval usage and color like a fly in amber The crest of the wave of Spanish culture in the new world broke upon the high mountains of New Mexico and crystallized there. Scholars say that New Mexican Spanish is almost archaic in its unchanged purity. However, it does not belong to the sibilant speech of Castile, but to the softer cadences of Andalusia, for southern Spain was the homeland of the majority of Colonials who settled in New Mexico.

There is, of course, the native patois where "donde" has been shortened to "onde" and where "lado" has been elided to "la'o." No direction is complete without that characteristic pointing with the lips and chin. "Allá," with a little pursing of the lips means, "Just over there," while "A-llá," with an oblique pointing of the chin, tells you that it's "wa-ay over there." Or as the little boy shouted, who was trying to guide his father in backing out a load of alfalfa, "Poco P' allá p'acá, Papá,"—"A little over there by a little over here, Dad."

A few purely New Mexican words have been coined, such as "estafeta," for post office. Many Spanish land terms, like cañon, plaza, cienaga, mesa, arroyo and acequia have crept into common Anglo use. Words pertaining to horses have been Anglicized so long that we have almost forgotten their parentage.

There are nine weekly newspapers and one illustrated monthly magazine published in Spanish in New Mexico. These differ from other foreign language periodicals in the United States, for they are not a lost link between the immigrant and the fatherland. They are concerned wholly with the news of their own country, New Mexico, its politics and local interests. No matter which political faith they follow, all of them are unanimous in their desire to preserve the Spanish language, and they rise to Latin fervor in the battle cry for "native supremacy."

This does not mean, however, that the reading matter of the Spanish-Americans is entirely confined to Spanish periodicals. One morning I was standing under the portal in front of a Tienda Barata in Tierra Amarilla when the mail stage rattled in. Tierra Amarilla is a village growing out of the mesa of "yellow earth" in the wilds of Rio Arriba County and probably one of the most remote spots in America to-day. The stage delivered one Denver paper, three State dailies, one Spanish weekly and the Congressional Record to a fine old Spanish-American gentleman. That afternoon his country store became a meeting place for the rancheros who sat on the counters cracking piñones while the translated news was read aloud by Don Francisco.

A recent law requires that all public schools in the

State shall be conducted in English as the language of instruction. Fortunately, most of the high schools offer a "foreign language" elective of Spanish where this indigenous tongue has practical application. Its importance as the coming commercial language with Latin America has already given native sons coveted positions in the diplomatic service and foreign-relation offices.

The older generation appreciates the courtesy of

95

being addressed in their native tongue. Their old brown faces light up with the pleasure of finding an Anglo "simpático," and not by so much as a flicker of a smile would they show the discourtesy of laughing at your "kitchen Spanish." The younger generation, however, are proud of being able to answer your stumbling questions in their best school English.

State law provides that all court proceedings must be conducted in English, but in almost every instance in northern New Mexico they are also translated into Spanish. Sessions of the district court take the place of a Grand Opera engagement in these far-away county seats. In Taos the Plaza is crowded with horses tied to the hitching racks, and covered wagons stand side by side at the cobblestone curb. In the bed of the wagons there is a ration of alfalfa for the horses, and ranch eggs, hens and honey to trade at the store. Gayly striped blankets are folded over the wooden seats in front, but the family has deserted them to attend court.

The opening of court is the big day. In the ten o'clock sunshine of a bright June morning an olive-skinned gentleman stands before the courthouse door on the Plaza and cries:

"Oigan! Oigan! Oigan! La corte del distrito está en sesión."

("Hear ye! Hear ye! Hear ye! The district court is in session.")

Knots of country people, chatting before the store, break up to hurry toward the courthouse. They file into the long narrow room and take their seats just as an interested audience packs a theater. Twice a day, with night sessions sometimes happily added, this audience packs the court room to standing room only as long as the session lasts. Anglo artists, artists' wives, writers from near and far, dudes and paisanos crowd the room for the entire length of the two-a-day run.

Every order of the court, every question, cross-question and reply is translated into Spanish. Many of the officers of the court are Spanish-speaking, most of the jury. And good jurymen they are too, not worrying about the business they have left for jury duty, but thoroughly enjoying the drama of each case.

We think of the Spanish people as being emotional, yet a native court room audience is far less emotional than an Anglo one. I was in the court room in Taos recently when a sensational case came up for a preliminary hearing. It was one of those triangles which offer melodrama in a theaterless mountain village. A woman had lighted her cookstove one morning, when the lid suddenly hurtled through the air, striking a child. Then the stove blew into a thousand pieces, bruising the woman.

"A man dropped dynamite down the chimney the night before," the neighbors said, having their own theories. No motive could be found for the man's action, since he bore no grudge against the woman. As always it was "Cherchez la femme." "She is an

97

enemy of the lady he lives with," the neighbors smiled wisely, ignoring his unimportant legal wife and six children.

Spanish-English, Spanish-English, the testimony went on. The accused rose to testify. No gay dare-devil Don Juan this, but an old man whose white hair and mustache made a blur against his brown skin. Tears ran down his cheeks as he sought to prove his innocence. Almost every man, woman and child there was either a friend or relative of the principal wit-nesses. I looked at them to see which were on the side of the old man. Their faces were eager, interested as they would have been at a movie, but unmoved by either anger or pleasure at his story.

Other witnesses testified in Spanish, translated into English and still the friends and relatives were but interested observers. The court adjourned to the next room to take the testimony of the woman and child. They had recovered from their injuries long enough to have been up and around for some weeks. But in order to play their parts realistically to-day, they had been brought in on stretchers and lay with sheets pulled over them. The crowd watched, interested but silent.

The court came back to the court room. The old man was bound over to the grand jury. The court adjourned. The crowd filed out. There were no cheers, no hissings, no photographers, just the pleasant news in low-toned Spanish that the case would come up before the district court in six months for a return engagement.

Another generation may put on a radio-talkie of the vanishing Spanish-Americans. It will tell of the colorful bygone days when an American was only an Anglo. Conditions are changing swiftly in the country of the Spanish-American since motors have invaded its isolation. We are coming to value the Spanish charm of living leisurely just as Anglo competition has gained some headway in this land of Poco Tiempo.

Spanish songs which serenaders still sing in the placitas are the swan songs of dying racial contrasts. Perhaps the native newspapers and politicians raise their voices louder because they see that the growing influx of Anglos will wipe out their majority. With English taught in all the schools, the coming generation will have no reason for bilingual legislatures and courts. Intermarriage will fuse the Spanish-American with the Anglo so that there will be no need for awkward hyphens. Even New Mexico will be a state of standardized Americans.

IV

The City of Contrasts

MODERN Santa Fe is the City of Contrasts. Every day the newest bumps into the oldest. Winding narrow lanes twist into broad paved streets. This morning a huge commercial bus, the last word in motor equipment, stops to let a pack train of burros, laden with kindling, file leisurely by. A white Rolls-Royce, looking like an animated bathtub, swerves sharply at the corner to avoid hitting a covered wagon whose driver sings out in melodious Spanish: "du-RAS-nos, me-LON-es, ce-BO-llas, chi-le."

The fragrance of harvest time brings the housewife hurrying out to the wagon to clamber on the axle, and peep over the high wagon bed into boxes of peaches, round green melons, shining white onions, and strings of scarlet chile. In Spanish they bargain over prices. His price drops a little and she raises her bid. He hands her a lard can filled with small sweet peaches for the price they both knew she would pay from the beginning. But it has been an interlude in human relations for which some have time in Santa Fe, but that has been lost elsewhere in our hurried and impersonal chain store marketing.

Three knocks at my door this morning announced the blind Tamale man. He had no sooner left me some tamales, "passed you a good day, señora," and stumped off, than a high voltage salesman rang the bell to insist that a house could never be a home without an automatic refrigerator.

A beautiful new home on the Camino includes all these newest inventions in a huge mechanically equipped basement. Yet across the road from this house any sunny morning you may see native women washing as their grandmothers washed—the clothes boiling in a tub raised on four stones over an open fire.

Up Cañon Road there is a new schoolhouse. It is a joy to the eye in its American-Spanish architecture, and a joy to the children in its modern playground apparatus, its modern ventilation and lighting, its modern desks and books. Not a hundred yards away there is a flat piece of ground overlooking the river. There are no weeds on it for its mud has been carefully packed and hardened and brushed. When the children come out for recess, they watch goats driven round and round on the yellow wheat spread over this primitive threshing floor in just the same way that Boaz threshed his wheat when he discovered Ruth getting away with his profit more than two thousand years ago.

The Plaza is still the heart of Santa Fe. There the contrasts of daily life are brought out amazingly in the three races who pass and repass through this open square weaving the pattern of the town. Trees and grass have made it an oasis from the surrounding red sand hills. On its benches, old men move from shade to sunshine as the year progresses, cracking piñones and talking politics in the tongue that retains the pure flavor of the medieval Spanish spoken by the Conquistadores.

Indians stand on the street corners offering to sell you silver rings or black pottery, drawn out of the folds of the bright striped blankets wrapped around them. Cowboys thump along the sidewalks in their ten-gallon hats, gaudy checked shirts, high boots and spurs. "Dudes" imitate them in an outfit which shrieks its novelty. Business men rush along in a hatless hurry. The bells chime and black-shawled women flow out of the arched doors of the Cathedral and down San Francisco Street like whispering shadows.

At night the dim light in the twin towers on one corner of the Plaza silhouettes the uneven rails of a ladder which might be pulled up as a protection against marauding Apaches. The pursuit approaches. It is a motor stopping long enough to take gas from the red filling station beneath the belfry.

In the moonlight the Plaza looks like a nine-o'clock town soundly asleep in the darkness of its ancient buildings. But on Galisteo Street or up Cañon Road the bailes are just beginning. A Spanish orchestra whangs out jazz tunes, sharp-eyed Mamás are seated around the benches outlining the sala, and the door is crowded with dark-skinned youths each waiting for a chance to dance with the señorita of his heart. In another part of town a Hindu philosopher may be revealing esoteric secrets to his ardent followers, or the artists on the Camino may be putting on a party. Any Saturday night you may hear the wail of a velorio, a shooting scrape, the drifting notes of a ukulele or the thickened song of a borracho lurching homeward.

Fashions of different ages suggest other contrasts. In the rooms of the Historical Society in the east end of the Palace of the Governors there are the saddle trappings used by Don Antonio Lucero de Godoy in

the reconquest of Santa Fe in 1692. The leather is tooled, embroidered and cut in fancy shapes. Near it is a grandfather bicycle with its huge front wheel and lofty seat. The solid wooden wheels of an ox cart stand against the wall. Not far away there is a stagecoach which journeyed over the Santa Fe Trail and a dilapidated hack which was society's conveyance two decades ago. A group on horseback comes around the corner of the palace, girls in trim breeches and fluttering scarfs riding English saddles.

Outwardly Santa Fe has become a tourist town where you may see the western craze in all its phases. Americans have added their folk ways to the customs of two other races, equally as amusing and primitive if we stop to look in the mirror.

Yesterday a tall, bald-headed gentleman from Ohio strutted in and out of La Fonda in a skin-tight brown sweater with a silver concha belt outlining the dinner bulge between his knees and chin like a flotilla of warships sailing around the equator. From his neck dangled a resplendent necklace whose silver squash blossoms, in Indian symbolism, are a token of virginity.

The first sign of "going native" in a stranger in Santa Fe is the tendency to discard his derby for a wide-brimmed sombrero to suit the wide open spaces which he has just "discovered." Next he barters with an Indian for a silver ring set with a barbaric stone as blue as the western sky. When a man once gives in to adorning himself with jewelry his competitive instinct arises and he determines to have the largest turquoise for his ring, the widest, most savage hammered band for his bracelet and a clanking silver belt of conchas which would have been the envy of the armored Conquistadores.

The second day a man feels like a pioneer and buys a cowboy outfit for the part. He appears in a ten-gallon Stetson, a checkerboard flannel shirt, riding breeches and high-heeled boots. To this he adds a leather holster, even though the western code now forbids him to pack a gun. However he usually has one stowed away in the pocket of his car to be ready for the holdups and cattle thieves, which only happen in western yarns. Oh, yes, he drives his car. The cowpony is seldom seen in the picture, savoring too much

of reality. But the cowpuncher's outfit stays on him
from dawn until bedtime, and some of them sleep in
their spurs at first just to keep up that old tradition
that a cowboy goes to bed with his boots on. I even
knew one youth from Boston Tech who gouged out
the floor beneath my sewing machine, wearing his nine-
inch spurs while he was concocting a costume for the
Conquistadores' Ball.

What the well dressed man wears "out in the cow
country" would give an Easter egg some startling sug-
gestions. For it isn't just one color or two, which
satisfy these modern Don Quixotes, once they have
broken away from the conventions of tweed. There
must be at least three or four colors to get a start.
Take the matter of shirts. One may be white, the
next blue, the next pink, the next purple and the whole
belted into the corduroys under an Irish green and
black flannel plaid that sets off all the rainbow hues
where the unbuttoned collars turn back.

Like most styles these multi-ply shirts had their
origin in utility. In the good, bold days it was thus
that a gentleman carried his wardrobe. There was once
a famous lawyer who had to make his two months'
circuit of the upper counties on horseback. One day
a shying bronco pitched him off and broke his arm.
When the nearest doctor rode over to set it, he had to
cut through twelve shirt sleeves before he came to
the fracture. The lawyer explained that it was winter time, and when he dressed up for the baile Saturday night, he just slipped a new shirt over the ones

he was already wearing. It didn't much matter about the fit, for you remember that shirts buttoned down the back in those days, and if they became too bulky to button the long-tailed speaking coat hid them anyway.

In Santa Fe it isn't the women who vibrate to western scenery—it's the men. Rarely do you see a woman in a tall Stetson, and never does she don those outlandish leather divided skirts affected on Hollywood locations. It may be that women are too conventional to break away from the season's silhouette, but it is probably because Paris offers such a quick changing display of queer cuts and colors that women have every opportunity to satisfy their love of variety without adding masquerade costumes to their wardrobe trunks. But they deck themselves with such trinkets as Indian and filigree jewelry and that feminine lure of Spanish shawls and combs.

While women don't "go primitive" as easily as men, the garb of the female cross-country motorist is one of the reasons why people shudder at the name "tourist." A wheezing Lizzie stops before the Palace of the Governors, packed from ground to roof with children, dogs, pots, pans, chairs, mattresses, springs, bedding and bird cages. Babies, bottles and bananas spill out as Ma emerges to "see the town." This usually means a trip to the nearest grocery for a box of crackers. Ma weighs about two hundred. Filling station by filling station she has discarded regular clothes and made herself comfortable for the trip. She bulges in large khaki knickers, a sleeveless blouse, nude silk stockings and high-heeled slippers. Over a frousy gray bob she has pulled the ultimate triumph of a net boudoir cap.

Freak clothes are a phase of the nomad mania—a vacation urge to escape from home and home conventions. The gypsies have dressed their part picturesquely but there should be a Twentieth Amendment to prohibit women wearing khaki the same shade as leather complexions.

The West has always been a man's country. Being master of it, he brooked no ridicule for his riot of colors or raiment. Nowhere in the world is there a more picturesque figure than the Indian with his red and orange striped blanket, a green fillet wound around his long black hair, the tails of his purple shirt flopping over his calico trousers, silver bracelets, silver necklaces, blobs of turquoise fastened through his ears, and more turquoise and coral strung around his neck. Following the law which nature sets—and the flapper upsets—for female birds and beasts, the Pueblo mother is inconspicuous in her serviceable dark blue slip-over and has to satisfy her decorative sense with a little jewelry and half a dozen petticoats, whose red and white embroidered edges come just below her short skirt.

As for the cowpuncher, he swaggers about in boots stitched with bulls and butterflies, silver spurs, vivid shirts and neckerchiefs and fancy chaps while the drab forlornness of the ranchwoman is proverbial.

Yes, it's the men who lose their inhibitions in Santa

107

Fe and have a chance to be the potential desperados which every man thinks he might have been. He has reached the land of enchantment where men are still half-gods. He is part of the he-man frontier, the last stand of brawn and not brains. Of course it would be cruel to suggest that a real cow person rides over his ranch in ordinary pants and a battered fedora. As long as satin breeches, brocaded vests and lace ruffles have been taken away from him, a man must have one place left in the world where he can cut a romantic figure.

Besides that, like an advertised brand of clothing, western togs make old men feel young. The stage is set for the eternal boy who likes to dress up and play pirate. Youthful repressions are no longer restricted to Roman striped ties. The Santa Fe Fiesta furnishes the time and place where every man joyfully turns back to the beckoning past. A New York attorney regained his youth last year by winding a broad yellow sash around his middle-aged spread, and his friend from Chicago made merry in a tasseled sombrero and a beaded vest hung with elk's teeth. Not for a fancy dress ball did they put on these costumes, but for the entire three days of the Fiesta.

The artists and writers adopted this western garb long ago and abandoned the velvet jacket and flowing tie of their Parisian student days. To-day, by his looks, you can't tell whether an artist is an automobile mechanic, a cowboy or an Indian. Besides giving them a chance to revel in color, these clothes have the incomparable value of wearing longer for less money. It doesn't matter if they bag at the knees, and a daub of paint here and there adds to the color combinations.

Take Witter Bynner strolling down the Santa Fe Trail from his home on the Loma in a scarlet flannel shirt and Mexican sandals, or Sheldon Parsons driving his roadster in a ten-gallon sombrero with his whiskers waving above a knotted green handkerchief. Or Gerald Cassidy's Irish smile beaming above a purple Navajo blouse. Or Carlos Vierra in a campaign hat dear to the heads of all Rough Riders. Or John Sloan happy in a mauve velvet shirt, more precious since it has faded to a soft tone. They add local color to the streets of Santa Fe. And then, in astonishment you may meet Eugene Manlove Rhoades in a plain brown suit and an old brown hat. If any man knows the cow country, it is this writer of cowboy stories. Perhaps he has lived in New Mexico too long to "go native."

Even the Fred Harvey system, which prohibits men from coming coatless into the other dining rooms along the Santa Fe Railroad, has given up its rule in happy-go-lucky Santa Fe. At La Fonda men in shirt sleeves, velvet blouses and khaki find no waiting steward to thrust them in odd-sized black alpaca coats such as are provided even in the heat of Needles. The Santa Fe Railroad has been a pioneer in saving the colorfulness of this country. Now it revives the picturesqueness of the Pony Express in uniforming its stage drivers in gay velvet shirts, neckerchiefs, tall sombreros and a leather holster over the hip, and its couriers in Navajo blouses and jewelry.

Clothes refuse to conform to regulations here. It is not likely that dress suits will have more than a biennial airing from the moth balls. In 1927 Governor Dillon refused to buy a dress suit for his own Inaugural Ball. It almost started a fashion for appearing in sheeplined coats, since the Governor had been a sheep man. Finally feminine persuasion induced him to compromise with a dinner coat.

At dances any and every variety of dress may be seen, from long pants caught up over high-heeled boots, velvet shirts and corduroys, puttees and rangers' olive drab to gray business suits and the black and white Tuxedo. No one feels ill at ease or unconventional unless it is the lone man in the stiff, bulging bosom. The only fear is being too dressy.

There is one occasion when a dress suit is required— that is when you are on the Volunteer Fire Department, and the alarm strikes terror over the quiet town. At least to the stranger one February night, it would have seemed that the entire force wore regulation dress suits to fires. The siren shrieked into the evening just as dinner parties were assembling before a Charity Ball. Hostesses were deserted. As always, every one rushed to the fire. The second truck was crowded with volunteer firemen in dress suits. The fire hose gushed over them and smoke blackened their white linen as they surrounded the burning building. The onlookers cheered. Some thoughtful neighbor provided coffee when the fire was out, and after hot water, soap and a change the dinner parties were resumed.

To belong to the Volunteer Fire Department is a social privilege. One must be unanimously elected from a waiting list to fill a vacancy. The Volunteer Fire Chief has a brass pole extending from a trapdoor in his bedroom closet to his garage below. His helmet and coat hang like a fire horse's harness on a convenient peg. He has a standing bet that his car can beat any other to the fire.

The alarm starts to sputter. Business conferences are left with decisions in midair, and doctors and attorneys shift their responsibilities to some one else. There's a chance to make every small boy's dream come true by racing through the streets on a red engine.

Another unique volunteer organization in Santa Fe is the Women's Board of Trade. While they do not make the racket of a red engine, their long fight has been equally valiant for the town's safety. Before the twentieth century began, a small group of women leagued themselves together as a Board of Trade, the only time women have used such a name in the United States. They became the Town Mothers, taking over the care of the Plaza as their garden, and making Fairview Cemetery a peaceful green refuge instead of a desolate sand field. Their work included aiding the sick and destitute. They started and have kept going the Public Library. They baked cakes, washed dishes, gave charity balls and Plaza fêtes to carry on their activities. Those were the pioneer days when neighbor nursed neighbor, sidewalks were loose boards, Father was busy and Mother knew best how to run the town. But Mother grew tired of assuming all the worry, and lately Fathers have taken over much of the civic responsibility.

Old-timers regretfully watch the changes which have lost friendly familiarity in formal acquaintance. But the changes were bound to come with a growing population and have brought some compensations. Santa Fe still remains that rare spot where worth is counted more in personality than in dollars, where swank is taboo and luxury of little importance.

In the old residential capital official titles are so common that it is a distinction to be a plain "Mr." There are enough "Generals," shortened from ex-adjutant-generals, ex-attorney-generals, ex-surveyor-generals, to make an army post blink. Governors, judges, colonels, rival Kentucky.

Drawing upon almost every state in the Union and many in Europe for citizenry, its small-townness is lost in a cosmopolitan freedom. People find anything they want here from study and siesta drowsiness to gayety and whoopee. They enjoy themselves more perhaps because they lack city amusements and are forced to make their own entertainment.

Climate is one great factor for settling here permanently. Dry, pure air and sunshine flooding mountains and valleys are Santa Fe's greatest asset. In spite of New Mexico's reputation for baking deserts, high altitudes insure cool summer and dazzling winter days when the snow melts before there is chance for skating or tobogganing. Sunlight has come to be considered nature's best remedy. "Tuberculosis" is not whispered as a dread scourge but as a passing malady soon overcome with rest and care. This leads to the comment that "sick people" are round and rosy, while "well" ones have not as much time to acquire suntan.

For the majority, the old town is still guided by the western slogan of "Live and Let Live." Not taking upon himself the rôle of his brother's keeper, it matters very little to Santa Fe what his brother does. The placid and the passionate live as they please. Queer people become queerer against the limited background and everyday virtues are only headlined in obituary notices. Unconventionalism serves its purpose as conversation, making a good dinner table story and a marvelous tale to take back East. Neighbors abide peaceably side by side, as they have done for three hundred years, and it is only the newcomers who must have forty acres to protect their privacy.

Personal freedom, like many other evolutions here, has been attributed to the artists' colony. However, by knowing the stirring history of Santa Fe, one would surmise that such an atmosphere had always been characteristic of the isolated western capital. "Howdy, stranger" was the old-time greeting, with no inquiry as to whether the name was an alias or why he couldn't go "back home." That western acceptance of face value has led to many amusing and expensive incidents of presentable strangers "doing the town" and skipping before their bills were paid. Church deacons have gone elsewhere with more legal funds than filled the collection plate they carried for long pious years, and painted ladies have been honored guests at tea parties until their night life was discovered.

Painters, writers, sculptors, dancers, drawn from a varied background of the world's art centers, come to Santa Fe for a two-day stop-over and remain here to build their homes. After that they become a hardy, thriving element in the life of Santa Fe. They not only add the bohemian note of studio life but give freely of their time and effort to make this a vital place to live. They accept in full measure that town consciousness which makes Santa Fe unique. They are as interested in paving and sewers, elections and talkies as the business men. Being articulate, their opinions are sometimes more effective than their number.

Ask them why they came here, and they will tell you that they wanted to escape city crowds and enjoy freedom and simplicity. Some will add that they were attracted by the lines of the mountains or the vivid colors of the landscape. They know well enough that the only man who has dared to use the real colors of a sunset is the maker of picture postcards, and that not one canvas nor one poem can reveal a whole country. Away from schools of painting and writing they become individualists who seldom pull together or approve of each other's work. Being unsatisfied with human limitations, they are restless experimenters with art and life.

No matter how divergent their standards, each is sincere in seeking to express his viewpoint. Entertainment is the goal, varying from entertaining one's own pet theories without much monetary appreciation, to entertaining the public with a return of good sized pay checks. If they are modern painters, they see the primitive lines in people, mountains and house tops. If they seek the picturesque, here is the setting.

If they are "Rough Writers," their motto is "When in doubt, bleed the hero" in accumulating wordage. They fulfil their goal by giving readers the thrill of vicarious experience. Then there are the highbrows who sweat to eliminate words, counting one word satisfactory when it suggests ten, and one line of poetry worth a novel. There are journalists who revel in colors and odd customs, novelists who suffer with their brain children, researchers who delve into myths and forgotten languages and essayists who analyze the American scene.

It is this variety which is the best indication of a living, growing town. It brings in the art disputes of Paris, Peking and Peoria to knock out any local ruts. It furnishes standards in Indian and Spanish poetry to measure by. It takes from Santa Fe pictures, poems and characters that meet with world acclaim and leads to the prophecy that American arts will have their real birth in the Southwest.

That prophecy is based not on what the world brings to Santa Fe but what it gets from the locale. It goes back always to the fact that the Indians live here and are the first American artists. It is a theory of environment, suggesting that those who live near the earth partake of earth forces.

What the world brings to Santa Fe varies as much as the traveler. There is the farmer who shakes his head over desert wastes and says: "Why do you need roads when there are no farm products to bring to town?" There is the motorist who counts his trip by the speedometer, the number of punctures and the price of gas. There's the woman who only remembers a town by the talkie she has seen there. There's the middle-aged couple who are suffering pilgrims on a tour of "Seeing America First." Ma says: "Pa, let's go up to our room and read that last instalment in the *Western Story Magazine*. My feet hurt and I'm all tuckered out traipsin' around this mud town." There's the lady poet who raves, "My psyche is stirred by the infinite rhythm of these mountains, by the pulsing beat of the dear Indian tom-toms."

There's the dude who bargains with an Indian for a turquoise necklace set in jet. He doesn't know that the "jet" is a melted phonograph disc, but he beats the Indian down from his price of forty dollars to twenty-seven fifty and offers him a ride to town to make up the difference. Says the Indian when he is on the front seat:

"Umh—Cadillac!"

"You know Cadillac, John?" says the dude, thinking "John" had never seen a motor before.

"Yes, I ride Cadillac in Detroit, Rolls-Royce in London, Hispano-Suiza in Paris, but I like Ford best. I travel everywhere with Indian show."

And when the dude exhibits his necklace in town he finds the dealers' price is fifteen dollars.

These contrasts are the high lights of modern Santa Fe. In primitive surroundings it savors of sophistication; in a mechanical age it cherishes imagination; in the youngest state it is the oldest capital in the United States; in an English-speaking nation Spanish is used as much as English; in a republic it has grown around the only royal palace.

It is one of the few important towns in our expanding nation whose population has changed very little in the last century. With ten thousand inhabitants now, its census figure has only doubled in a hundred years. It is interesting that so small a town could have won fame in a nation where bigness is the talking point. But Santa Fe is larger than the three-mile limit in every direction from the Plaza. Its sphere of influence embraced all the land west of the Mississippi, and that great territory centered its life in the capital, where races and cultures crystallized through the centuries.

The chances are that it will never be an industrial town. It will remain a city of homes, where people have time to enjoy beauty and sunshine and ponder the ways of life instead of rushing madly through them. If its influence is to remain vital, it must produce ideas which will be of benefit in education, government, art and health. Its significance in the past has been due to the fact that it drew upon these sources. Ideas have always been its maximum production, fought over with arrows, cannons and words until they achieved definite results.

On account of its isolation in being sidetracked by railroads for fifty years, Santa Fe has escaped that flood of boosting standardization which makes the bigger and better Main Street in Minneapolis the same as the bigger and better Main Street in Dallas. Through its slow growth, it has remained individual. Its development has been as natural as the native way of adding on one adobe room at a time until the house surrounded the patio. Real estate has increased in value without any boom. Its vitality has never been exhausted by artificial advertising, nor its character lost by a desire for "forty thousand by 1940." Although good highways and motor travel are making it a pivot again, its only slogan is "The City Different."

V

Pueblo-Spanish Architecture

STRANGERS coming to Santa Fe feel that they have stepped unexpectedly into the Old World, leaving the United States somewhere behind a tawny mesa. They find in her old buildings romance, color and quaintness, so eagerly sought in Europe. Moreover, these are genuine. There is no need here for papier-mâché façades or fake cliff dwellings. Any mound or cañon in her vast front yard reveals a civilization older than Rome. History has dowered her with a medieval palace and clusters of native homes built by the three races who met here at the end of their trails. They left their records in an architecture that is so primarily American that to-day it seems foreign.

This native architecture has two sources—the pre-Columbian pueblos and the transfusion of Spanish design. Since Santa Fe was the City of the Caballeros, her palace, churches and homes were dominated by Spanish tradition, but they were also fundamentally influenced by the Indian.

Pueblo communal buildings and the modern skyscraper are the only original ideas which America has contributed to world architecture. It is interesting to note that the newest phase is now adopting the basic elements of the oldest. As in many other forms, modern art is returning unconsciously to the first principles of the ancient Americans.

The terraced Pueblo apartments and the skyscrapers were both affected by the necessity for concentration. Though the Indians had plenty of land, their people were concentrated in a few community buildings for protection against attacks by their enemies. The skyscrapers rose story upon story because land was scarce and ground rentals dangerous to the pocket book. Both of them were built up from a massive base in simple vertical lines. Both cut the exposed construction of flat walls with contrasting irregular planes. The set-back relief of skyscrapers is only an elongated version of the pyramidal roofs of a pueblo, giving the light and symmetry which the Indians found essential long ago. The difference between them is more a matter of skin than of skeleton—the surface treatment of sharp angles in tall machine-made forms against the rounded lines of lower handmade walls. Perhaps when the skyscrapers are old enough, they too will mellow with age.

But in spite of the fact that Pueblo houses and sky-scrapers have grown along the same lines, Santa Fe is frantically opposed to having high buildings spoil the low sky line of a Pueblo-Spanish town. Other cities may point with pride to eighty-five story steel giants, but the oldest capital has passed an ordinance prohibiting buildings from climbing more than three stories. The charm of the Plaza would be lost with a Woolworth skyscraper towering over the long, flat Palace of the Governors.

Here we turn back to the first source of American architecture in the pueblos. Those pyramidal apartments, housing three hundred to five hundred inhabitants, grew out of the earth long before their architects knew that there were any people beyond the four mountains marking their world corners. Being primitives they knew only those fundamentals developed from cave dwelling necessities. They were not hampered by classic traditions of Rome or Greece, France or England. They built for need and permanence. Since their builders were innate artists, their homes became part of the environment. They reflected the rise of mountain peaks against the horizon in their ascending steps and the color and form of the earth in their materials. They followed nature's disregard for accurate angles, using the pleasant inexactness which no mathematically planned structure can have to-day unless it varies consciously along natural lines. The first roundness of corners was made by the stroking of Indian hands and finished into flowing, plastic lines by wind and rain. With only the simplest materials they depended upon the proportions of sun-baked masses against deep shadows and honest craftsmanship to achieve lasting beauty.

For their walls they made forms of skin and cotton cloth, filling them with mud just as we pour cement to-day. They were plastered then and now by women. Their bare palms smoothed the mud, leaving faint curving lines and a slightly uneven surface. This is the prototype which is exaggerated in the corrugation of modern dappled plaster. Since the mud finish was renewed every spring, the walls stood as dry and firm as stone. There was no dampness to crumble the adobe. Their thickness was arrow-proof and insured warmth in winter and coolness under the summer sun.

Pine and cedar from the surrounding forests provided sturdy rafters or vigas for the ceiling, extending beyond the house wall in uneven lengths. The flat roofs sloped slightly for drainage with some of the vigas hollowed out into guttered canales. Over the vigas they placed pine branches, or aspen saplings laid at an angle to the vigas in "herringbone" fashion. Over this a thick layer of earth was tamped down and rounded over the wall line. These flat roofs made terraces in front of the second, third and fourth story apartments. The only stairways were ladders which might be pulled up to protect the higher apartment dwellers. The windows and doorways were small. Little light penetrated through them to the middle rooms, which were used only for places to store grain and skins. The interiors were whitewashed with the native gypsum, yeso, for the Indian made the most of light-reflecting surfaces and never darkened the interiors with earth-colored plaster.

These great apartment units were the castles which the Conquistadores told of seeing in the Seven Cities of Cíbola. It was no wonder that cities rising out of the desert should have seemed marvelous to wayfaring soldiers. At Cicuye, the original Pecos, they found ten thousand inhabitants living in many storied buildings, grouped along well-planned streets and plazas. They had not made their entradas into a wilderness, but into a land of walled cities where people had already developed a high type of architecture and agriculture.

The Caballeros set out at once to establish their own towns where they could maintain the rule of Spain, They were soldiers, priests, explorers and farmers and, only by necessity, builders. Spain seldom created any art for her time and energy were occupied in keeping her military power supreme. But she incorporated the arts of subject nations and encouraged their flowering.

In this distant province, the padres and soldiers were forced to turn architects to build their fortress-palaces and churches, conscripting native labor and materials. This resulted in a design based on the grandeur of Spain, taking on an even greater beauty in their homesick remembrance. Its practical application had to be worked out in indigenous construction. Indian laborers

123

followed the padres' plans but built in their own fashion. Both worked with patience and a deep love of beauty and created a new form equally as interesting as either of the originals. Each left his stamp upon the new architecture. The Indians gave it sculptured mass, plastic lines and indented doorways. The Spaniards added the nave and transept in the form of the cross in their churches and the fortress compound in their one-storied palaces.

From the exterior, both the Pueblo community buildings and the Spanish citadels had the appearance of solid mud bulwarks to protect men in the wilderness. But with the Spaniards, the outer walls and rooms were only a thick shell enclosing courtyards. The Spaniards lived on the inside of their hollow squares, while the Indians lived on the outside steps of their mud pyramids. The two types varied in plan with the needs of two races, since every detail of this frontier architecture had its first reason in necessity. For either, ornateness was as impossible as luxurious living. The simple forms reflected the bareness of the desert and its magnificent proportions.

The colonists who had set forth from Andalusia found a heartening resemblance to the homeland in the blue mountains and tawny deserts of New Mexico. They built their homes in the new country much as they had in the old. The soil had the same clayey consistency which was used for the plebeian brick in Spain and her African colonies. The Conquistadores taught the Indians to mix the mud with straw, cut it into bricks and bake them in the sun. Adobe bricks were an easier method of building, and the new ways overcame the old puddled walls.

With the cross and the sword the Caballeros brought along their love of art. Carving was part of their inheritance. Their tools were few and crude, but they sufficed to fashion pine and cedar into some semblance of Spanish carving. Indians were set to work with planes, chisels and knives and incorporated their own symbols into the European plans. Heavy doors, lintels and vigas took on this curious mixture of pagan and Christian art. Corbels were hewn in the silhouette of scrolls which came from the acanthus leaf design capping Roman columns, but they bore the Indian symbols in the gouged carving on their flat surfaces. Spindles had been used for window bars in Aragon, but no lathes were available in the new province. Slats of square cross sections of pine were notched and champered by the Indian workmen to give the effect of window bars. Later flat strips were carved into curving lines which simulated the profiles of spindles, painted in bright colors. There was a saying in Spain that window bars absorbed the heat of the sun and kept it from entering the room. In New Mexico wooden bars were doubly treasured for keeping out the sun and the Comanche.

As we have seen, city plans for the New World were drafted in Spain. The Caballeros obeyed these royal ordinances as rigidly as though the King were in the country instead of being separated from his colonists by a continent and an ocean. Palaces were built according to official specifications, and churches followed ecclesiastical authority. While church and state intermingled in ruling the land, the two types were never intermingled in architecture. Domestic plans had their own treatment, distinct from the other two.

Royal buildings showed the frugality of an outpost capital in a province too impoverished and distant to permit any luxuries. They were planned for permanence and substantial ruggedness. The dimensions of the official salas reflected the pride of Spanish spaciousness in their size and high, raftered ceilings. Windows and doorways were squared for the simpler construction of barricading doors and bars. Arches, characterizing the later Californian buildings, were seldom seen in this first right-angled Spanish architecture, for adobe bricks could not be used safely in more than a five-foot span. Occasionally the inside ends of the zaguán, opening into the patios, had the pleasing contrast of a narrow arch.

Although the missions built in the pueblos followed ecclesiastical plans, they responded more easily to the natural design of Indian laborers. The end of the church behind the high altar bulged in a solid primitive mass like the beautiful lines of the church at Ranchos de Taos to-day. The roof was supported with long vigas set into the walls with corbels. The front was a high whitewashed wall, ending in a terraced outline surmounted by the cross. The plain surface of such a façade, as the mission at Tesuque, was relieved by a wide opening for the doors and by niches at the top where old copper bells hung.

The missions bear a strange resemblance to the geologic forms of the country. There is an eroded pink mountain near the purple funnel of Embudo which looks as though it might have been the original design for these temples of earth. Its sheer wall has the vertical surface of a façade. Its height breaks in weathered shelves which gave form to the Indian's altar and the padre's church.

Other missions were planned on more elaborate lines, such as the churches at San Felipe, Santo Domingo and Acoma. There splendid balconies jut out above the door, and high towers rise at either side. At the tops, these sturdy campaniles taper into rounded caps pierced with four cone-shaped openings. Within these conical arches the bells are silhouetted against the turquoise sky. Adobe walls surrounding the Campo Santo carry the flowing lines of the earth construction back to the earth again.

Santa Fe has only two official buildings remaining from the early Pueblo-Spanish days. They are the San Miguel Church and the Palace of the Governors. Probably neither would be recognized by a Rip Van Winkle Conquistador if he should wander back into his City of the Holy Faith to-day. Three centuries have necessarily changed them. San Miguel has been strengthened with stone ramparts and topped with a new wooden tower. However, the back of the church bulges out into the winding street with the old primitive look in its heavy walls. The interior preserves the choir loft, carved vigas and corbels which men glorified into a place of worship so long ago.

Three centuries have also changed the Palace of the Governors. Age has shrunk it in width and height. Where it faced the Plaza Mayor in a four hundred foot stretch, now the Plaza and the Palace are only a block long. Where its towers rose like giant sentinels at either end, there are enclosed one-story corners to suggest past stateliness. Where its courtyards and Casas Reales covered acres, there remains the fragment of one placita bounded by the double row of rooms. Yet these rooms were the cradle of the oldest history in the United States. They were official salas from whence royal rule spread over a vast province in New Spain. The story of Santa Fe and the Southwest was written within these venerable walls. The preservation of the Palace of the Governors has kept intact one of the most important monuments on the Western continent.

Some twenty years ago Santa Fe passed through the dangerous age. She hesitated between accepting the wrinkles and gray hair of advancing years or of having her face lifted and becoming a flapper grandmother town. Fortunately she decided that the buildings of a town were the features of its face, and that age expressed in architecture added to her personality. The decision was not made without a struggle, however, for the herd instinct of building every American town alike was strong in those American pioneers who had come in with the railroads to make a new center out of an old Spanish capital.

It was consistent that archæologists, who had been attracted to the Southwest on account of its antiquity, should have been the first to plead for the preservation of the ancient Palace. After the new Capitol had been built three blocks south of the Plaza, the Palace of the Governors was deserted as the seat of government. The rooms which had been used by Indian chiefs, Spanish Hidalgos, Mexican generals and American governors became private offices. The building showed signs of neglect. In 1907 the legislature passed an Act converting it into the Museum of New Mexico, saving it as a shrine for posterity.

In 1908 the Archæological Institute of America chose Santa Fe as headquarters for the School of American Research, and was provided with offices in the Museum. This focused here anthropological researches in North, South and Central America, as well as bringing new interest to the surrounding southwestern field. It was one of the most significant steps taken in the development of modern Santa Fe.

The Museum and School of American Research not only attracted scientists who studied the country from the prehistoric cave dwellings to the living Indians but later made it possible for artists, writers and musicians to find hospitality within its walls. With the Art Museum, built in 1917, it has encouraged all educational resources. Its pioneering paved the way for widening interests which led to the Indian Arts Association, the

Department of Anthropology in the State University and the new Rockefeller Laboratory. The prehistoric area in Santa Fe's front yard is so vast that it invites investigations in many lines. Men such as Adolf Bandelier and Charles F. Lummis devoted a lifetime to studying it, but in spite of the expeditions covering the past fifty years, even the sites of its ancient ruins are not yet thoroughly explored.

In the army days, following the American occupation in the middle of the nineteenth century, the Palace had been brought up to Victorian standards with jigsaw cutouts over its porch and wooden casements for its doors and windows. In 1907 these were torn off, and the Palace was restored as far as possible to its original dignity. Heavy posts and carved corbels held up the vigas of its long portal as they did in the days of de Vargas. Sometime the enclosed ends of this portal may be raised to the height of the old towers which once guarded the presidio. The thick arrow-proof walls were replastered with mud and sand. Muslin ceilings were discarded so that the old rafters might be seen, and the flat roofs were made weather tight. More than two hundred and fifty loads of dirt were taken off one room at the western end, showing that in past centuries summer rains were overcome by dumping a sackful of earth on each new leak.

The Palace has lost one of its decorations of a century ago, for strings of Indians' ears are no longer festooned upon its walls. But the narrow glazed windows, which attracted curiosity for hundreds of miles, still give it the air of an armed fortress. They look out upon the Plaza Mayor and the inside placita where trees and hollyhocks are reminiscent of the gardens of the Casas Reales. The rooms enclosing the placita on the north serve as laboratories for the museum staff and studios for visiting artists.

The eastern end of the Palace is used by the State Historical Society for exhibits of every era in New Mexican history. Here are stone idols from the mountain shrines of the sun worshipers, Spanish paintings on buffalo hide, copper stills, the proud, brass bed of Governor Manuel Armijo, a portrait of Kit Carson, and the bust of Lew Wallace beside the chair he used while writing the last chapters of *Ben Hur* in this building. Period rooms suggest the days of the Spanish colonials. A fine reredos from the church near Talpa shows the soft blues and pinks of vegetable dyes used on the wooden panels in the primitive pictures of the saints. The State Library joins the north and south walls. It includes valuable New Mexicana, books of the history and archæology of the Southwest and special collections, such as the Fink Library, said to be one of the most complete linguistic collections in the world.

A long vista of doorways, molded by mud and sand, extends through the many rooms of the Palace. In the central rooms, facing the placita, cases set into the thick walls exhibit potsherds, bone implements, war bonnets and feather prayer holders found at Puye and the Rito de los Frijoles. The murals above them depict scenes

131

in those cliff dweller cañons, from the time when little
fires showed that the honeycombed walls were inhab-
ited by cave men and women to the lone Indian gazing
at the ruined homes of his ancestors in the waning
moonlight.

The dungeon where traitors were thrown into the
Spanish prison has become a locked closet for rare
manuscripts. The fortress now houses miniature mod-
els of Bent's Fort and the walled pueblo of Pecos.
Skulls still grin from the walls, but they bear peaceful
scientific labels telling whether they were low or high
brows and whether their mothers flattened the babies'
skulls by strapping them to cradle boards. Cannons
and iron bars in the central doorway have been replaced
by a "Public Entrance" welcome. The old Sala de
Justicia, where Indian witches were tried and young
Zebulon Pike protested his geographical ignorance, is
given over to the records of New Mexico soldiers of
three races who took part in the World War. Battle
cries and martial music may be mute to-day in the somber silence of an ancient treasure house, yet the Royal
Palace is still recording history.

During the ten years after the Palace of the Governors was restored, artists began to form an art nucleus
here. This led to the dream of many broad-minded
citizens to build an Art Gallery which would encourage
this new phase of American expression on the old soil
which had produced Indian Art. Through the zeal of
Director Edgar L. Hewett, and the late Frank
Springer, to both of whom Santa Fe is indebted for

years of faithful devotion and future vision, the plans for the Art Gallery were begun. Contributions from friends over the state were matched by the legislature. The ground, which had been occupied by army barracks and later given to the Santa Fe schools, was donated for the new building.

What better model could there be for new art than the Pueblo-Spanish missions of New Mexico, the oldest

in the United States? Details of six of these Franciscan missions were blended together in the plans for the Art Gallery. Two of them were gaunt ruins but enough of the proportions were left to reproduce them and allow their influence to go on through future generations of builders. Old materials gave way to fireproof steel and brick, but girders were hidden in the high ceilings and sharp angles rounded in the likeness of primitive walls.

133

The great towers and balcony were inspired by the church at Acoma, one of the finest examples left us today and fortunately restored by sympathetic hands. The massive doors beneath it, with the carving and smaller set-in door, are like those at Santa Clara. The corner nearest the Plaza, with its jar-shaped doorway and indented porch above, was suggested by the mission at Santa Ana. The ruined walls of Pecos were raised again along the northern side. With tree shadows playing over its rough pink plaster and hollyhocks nodding beside the Laguna façade at the northeast corner, it is one of the most satisfying bits of architecture to be found anywhere. These details are drawn together with stepped sidewalls rippling down from the roof to the set-back terraces. Some are whitewashed like outer living rooms, some are a part of the earth-colored building.

It is not the reproduction of these details which makes the Art Gallery notable as much as the spirit which created it in following the Indian's traditions. Its sculptured symmetry, plastic lines, terraced walls, the variety of its composition and the contrast of shadowed doorways and dark vigas jutting out beyond the hand-smoothed plaster, give it a feeling of gradual human growth. There is no stiff plumb line here, no parallel repetition of arches, no blueprint exactness of utilitarian angles. Instead, this Cathedral of the Desert seems to have roots which go deep into the soil, of the same color as its surface.

The building surrounds a patio whose portales make

a shady cloister. A bronze tablet set into the south wall is a memorial to Alice C. Fletcher whose lifelong friendship with the American Indian gave her enduring fame. The entrance hall is given over to a display of Indian Arts where pottery and textiles may be studied by modern designers and students.

The galleries have space for two hundred pictures, new exhibits being shown every month. Since taxpayers own the building, the Museum offers any artist the use of exhibition space for a limited time, making it the only free gallery in the United States. Its scope is broadened with a no-jury, no-prize system. Many Southwestern paintings have their première here, afterward being exhibited in larger cities and Europe. The Museum also owns a valuable permanent collection of paintings and drawings, generously given by visiting artists or donated through friends of Southwestern art.

Upstairs the spacious room on the north is used by the Women's Museum Board. The ceiling has split aspen saplings set between the vigas in the traditional herringbone pattern. Carved corbels and vigas are set off with color in the gouged designs, and carried on in the native furniture of the long refectory table, chairs and cupboards. Bright cushions in the deep window seats, a terraced fireplace in the corner, church candlesticks and copper bowls filled with flowers make this room inviting for teas and informal lectures.

In the gallery opening off the women's room are the paintings of Donald Bouregard, a young artist whose future promise was cut short by his early passing. His sketches had been selected by Frank Springer for the murals for the St. Francis Auditorium. After Bouregard's death, Carlos Vierra and Kenneth Chapman were chosen to complete the murals. They are episodes in the life of St. Francis from the time of his boyhood inspiration to found his Order in Assisi, and his influence upon Santa Clara and her Sisterhood, to the distant work of his followers, in the Franciscan missions of the Southwest and Central America. Vierra's fine mural at the end of the transept shows Columbus and his son at the door of a Franciscan mission and the Spanish galleons which were then the dream ships of the great discoverer.

The St. Francis Auditorium is like some old chapel converted to new uses. Its flagstone floor, uncomfortable wooden pews, altar platform and the high ceiling of the transept carry out the atmosphere of an early mission. Life in the twentieth century makes it a community center where plays, lectures, concerts and school contests are given. When only part of the lights are turned on against the high vigas, and the corbels are thrown into the relief of light and shadow, it takes on the mystic quality of the faith of those Franciscans who struggled to build temples for the worship of God in this far land.

The Palace of the Governors and the Art Museum stand out as examples of the old and new-old architecture. The first is the earliest type of Spanish government house, built according to royal mandates on simple but dignified lines of a palace-fortress. The sec-

ond is a throwback to those days of high creative culture which sprang up through the needs and dreams of
men in an isolated environment, a combining of Indian
symmetry and Spanish plans.

The restoration of the Palace of the Governors led
the way to a renaissance of these authentic types. Fortunately Santa Fe realized the value of her heritage in
time to save it. Too often, American progress has
come hand in hand with utilitarian ugliness to destroy
an ancient setting.

Many new buildings have followed these old lines
with an interesting variety which shows that the form
is still plastic. Opposite the Art Museum a business
corner has been successfully adapted to this type. The
buildings for the State School for the Deaf, to the
south of town, are effective contrasts on more formal
lines. The post office claims the honor of being the
only federal building in the United States whose plans
conform to local architecture. Its long arcade and
high towers fit into the scene as they face the rise of
the Cathedral. Sunmount shows excellent examples
of outside stairways, patios, balconies and wrought
iron grills used for a modern sanatorium. La Fonda
with its terraced mass and patio is a worthy successor
of the first famous inn at the end of the Santa Fe Trail.
Even its five stories rising gradually at the back, carry
out the lines of a pyramidal pueblo and overcome what
might have been a mistake in height by its well-planned
bulk.

One characteristic bit of Spanish architecture which

was much used in Santa Fe a century ago is seen now only in old houses down on Water and San Francisco streets. Yet of all types it would be most easily adapted to modern business needs. It was the straight walled two-storied adobe surrounded with upper and lower railed porches. The square sides made the most of ground space for stores and offices and the double porches carried on the Spanish feeling. They were the New Mexican sisters of those balconies whose picturesqueness is the charm of creole cities. In New Orleans as well as in Santa Fe, they were first planned by Spanish architects. These two-tiered portales were once the outstanding Spanish note of the buildings surrounding the Plaza. In time they may be replaced there to restore the character and unity which was the pride of this historic square.

The civic spirit of keeping true to traditions is growing in Santa Fe. The sentiment of old principles of construction is the cornerstone for the majority of modern builders. It has proved its worth not only in deeper appreciation of the sources of the country but in added dollars. As Charles F. Lummis once said to me about the future of Santa Fe, "We can't do business on sentiment, but we certainly can't do business without it."

VI

Old Castles in New Spain

A SPANISH proverb says "Whom God loves He
gives a house in Sevilla." Here it would be changed
to "Whom God loves He gives a home in Santa Fe."
Modern America may be the country of the homeless,
but in this ancient town there is an overpowering urge
to own an old castle in New Spain. People who have
prided themselves upon being as rootless as goldfish
are the first to succumb to that desire to have "a little
place in Santa Fe." They cannot resist buying a few
vigas, an old door and a blue blanket. In a few months
the second state of Santa Fe-itis shows them building a
red mud house on the red hillside. The first of May
no longer means a restless searching for high apartments at higher rents, for now they are watering their
own Spanish iris in their own placita. Gone are the
days of letting the landlord fix the leaks. They even
enjoy sessions with the plumber, sinking their pipes
three feet underground below freezing depth, and

painting their bathrooms a riot of color. It shows that Americans are home lovers after all, if leisure, space and pocketbooks permit.

The one essential for a home in Santa Fe is that it must be interesting. This has been as successfully achieved in two rooms as in twenty. There is no goal of luxury here nor of building a house that is bigger and better than the Joneses. But there is a criterion that a home must have personality and that it should conform to the architecture of the country. Those home builders who have had the courage and patience to follow traditions have added greatly to Santa Fe's old-world charm.

Such houses are inherently right in this setting and climate, yet they would be as out of place on an Illinois prairie or a Boston suburb as a Burmese temple. Most of America needs to find an architecture which is as indigenous to its locality as the "Santa Fe Style" is to Santa Fe. Perhaps the gaudy experiments of imitating Venetian canals, Mediterranean villas and Tudor manor houses which have sprung up inconsistently over our country from Oregon to Florida will result in creating some type that is truly American. Santa Fe has set an example, not of copying, but of adhering to that which is authentic for itself.

With the testimony of historic buildings constantly before us, architecture is a vital topic here, discussed at wedding breakfasts and clubs as avidly as baseball or prohibition. To the purists, the one unforgivable crime is any deviation from tradition. To the average home builder personal comfort comes first and architectural traditions second. To the artists, there is a satisfying beauty in flowing lines and a form evolved from environment. To the union mechanic, there is jaw-dropping disgust for the disrespect shown for plumb lines and fractions of inches. One carpenter expressed his consternation loudly when he cried, "Up in Seattle I make a line true and straight, but here I work on mud houses and now my eye is all crooky!"

There is no place in the world where a man feels as competent to build his own home as in Santa Fe—and does it. . . . Watching the native dig up his backyard, mix adobes and lay them up in mud seems child's play. But the native has inherited a knowledge of his materials and tools through generations of experience, leaving the wind and rain to be his master sculptors. He needs no cellars, attics, furnaces, electricity, no heating except the corner fireplace and often no plumbing. But the modern American must have all the nationally advertised innovations.

It is this inability to simplify life or architecture which results in the knobby-headed strays of the "Santa Fe Style." Simplicity fools the unwary and is as hard to imitate in a lowly adobe as in a Paris gown. Many awful examples advertise this amateur botching. Bad as they are they show a spirit of trying to keep Santa Fe in character and only a lack of understanding in how to accomplish it.

The lucky person finds an old adobe and "remuddles" it, or, failing to find one, builds a new home along traditional lines. He is never so pleased as when the passing tourist refers to his new home as "that old ruin." He feels that he has achieved the tranquil spirit of age which makes his home seem part of the ancient earth. If he has invested in experienced technical advice, modern comforts aid in preserving an "atmosphere" which is yet sufficiently warm.

The charm of these Pueblo-Spanish houses lies in simplicity, sturdy building and suitability to site and exposure. With little exterior decoration they depend upon the contrasts of sunlight and deep shadows and the form and color of adobe clay for interest. There is much humanness in the inconsistency of natural variations and the direct, honest craftsmanship of their construction. They are witnesses to that litany of the desert, "Sun, sand and silence."

A great impetus was given the home building urge at the beginning of the Santa Fe renaissance twenty years ago when a group of business men, artists and archæologists became its spokesmen and started a competition for "Santa Fe style homes." From that time the oldest capital recovered from the red rash of brick bungalows which had spread over the United States. It came of age in an appreciation of the types of homes which had been found best suited to this land during three hundred years. They had developed along lines which were distinct from ecclesiastical or official buildings.

Three types of domestic architecture have come down to us in their chronological sequence—the

Pueblo, the Mexican and the American-Spanish. They
are seldom found absolutely true to type for the needs
of men have overlapped since the days of the first
Americans. In each we find resemblances to the others,
like the faces of mothers and daughters. In the Indian
villages to-day there are houses of the Mexican type,
while all adobe houses bear some kin to their pueblo
ancestors. New Mexican houses varied more than any
others found in the Spanish colonies, for they were so
much influenced by the Indian architecture of the
Pueblo country. This distinguished them from the
Spanish-colonial found in Florida or California.

While modern inventions prevent the pueblo type
from being carried out in the same primitive fashion
the Indians use, it is the basis of all subsequent native
architecture. Certain elements have been derived from
it which give even new homes a distinct pueblo character.

The outstanding features are the terraced stories
piled up into picturesque masses and the free use of
line and form. Second and third stories stepping back
from each lower story remind us that the Indian was
influenced by his environment to build houses like mountain benches ascending shelf by shelf to the rim rock.
These terraced masses compose into symmetrical form,
heavy and broad at the base and narrowing into
lighter lines at the top. The width of the fireplaces,
jutting out beyond the housewall at the corners like
low ramparts, gives the base lines added broadness
where they flow into the ground. The modern desire

for a high sun deck, offering wide vistas of mountains and sky, has left out the walls of the upper story, framing the square open tower with corbels and lintels. Though they are an American combination of superimposing a belfry top on a communal dwelling and may not please the purists, they comply enough with the pyramidal lines to remain harmonious.

With the handmade construction of walls, openings for doors and windows have no right-angle lines but take on the curves of Indian jars, rounding in to the simple casings. These openings are few and narrow, leaving bold unbroken planes of earth walls. The arrangement is varied by intersections at odd angles and by contrasting planes. Every line has its human deviation, whether it is the roof swaying slightly toward the center, or the walls bulging in a weathered curve. It is this modeling of adobe clay, molded by hands and carved by wind and rain, which gives the pueblo type its chief characteristic of plastic form. It is as different in treatment from the geometrical modern house as an Indian olla is from a matchbox.

These ollas are used as the Indian's chimney pot and are one of the few decorative details of the plain exterior. Like the whole architecture, details have their origin in necessity and not in ulterior decoration. The painted pottery jars are set into the chimney top, the bottom smashed out of the ollas and the smaller ones fitted into the larger until a protected draft is assured. They give an amusing, unexpected finish to squat mud chimneys. The estufas, mud ovens shaped like beehives, might also be considered decorative details since they contrast conical forms against the pyramidal houses. They are built not only on the ground but on second and third story roofs, serving as family fireless cookers. They were probably introduced by the Spaniards when they first taught the Indians the secret of binding adobe into bricks with straw.

Since the pueblo type is the natural exponent of native materials and climate, sunlight and shadow are depended upon as the great decorators. Massive walls stand out with sculptured boldness against the deep shadows. Vigas pierce the outside walls in uneven lengths and give the play of dark slender lines on sun-soaked adobe surfaces. Rounded openings become silhouetted patterns against the bare wall spaces. Ladders ascending from story to story catch the sunlight on their bleached frames and leave striped shadows below them.

Although ladders are the only stairways in adobe pueblos, the stone and mud communal houses such as those at Acoma and Walpi cut steps into the wing walls to ascend from story to story. The kivas, the sacred council chambers half under and half over ground, have broad stately steps with an adobe staircase bounding them in irregular saw-tooth lines. These primitive steps, used on the interior as well as the exterior, have been the inspiration for modern stairways, achieving a unique, satisfying beauty.

On the interior the ceiling is supported with vigas showing the crude smoothing of round rafters. Pine branches, boards and thick layers of cinders and mud make them weatherproof, though sand and rain sometimes sift through. More recent ceilings have replaced the pine branches with wide boards or filled the space between the vigas with white plaster. Door and window sills are as deep as the thick walls with a rounded indenture outlining the casement instead of mitred corners.

Walls, glistening like snow with their yeso finish, are accented by the bright colors of striped blankets spread over the bedding rolled into a daytime couch and the gala dance kilts, skins and sashes hung over a pole swung from the vigas—the only closet for fiesta wardrobes. The Indian's decorative sense makes use of a clay imbedded with tiny flakes of mica, called "tierra amarilla." This "yellow earth" is melted in water and painted on as a deep border outlining the floor and openings, and ascending over the fireplace in those terraced steps which symbolize the sacred altar. Against the whitewash this golden frieze gives the impression of a rich metallic luster.

Mud houses use mud not only for walls and roofs but for floors as well. These mud floors become almost as hard and durable as dark cement when they are mixed with ashes and tamped down while wet. They are sprinkled each morning and swept with a small broom made of wheat straw.

The primitive fireplace is not only a necessary but an architectural feature of each room. They are most often built into a corner with a raised hearth and cone-shaped opening. The hood rounds from the center toward each wall, and the mantel varies from a single shelf to several shelves terraced back toward the chimney. Corner fireplaces are so much prized that where a corner of the room is not available, a side wall is built out like a graduated screen and the fireplace nestles into the corner, with an olla of mutton stew simmering in the ashes. Occasionally there is a long chimney hood extending from the ceiling over the entire end of the room with places on the two-foot hearth for several pot fires and daylight penetrating through the many-storied chimney vent.

A small recess was scooped out of the wall beside the entrance to hold the prayer meal bowl. Upon entering the door each visitor took a pinch of the sacred corn meal to scatter in the six directions as a blessing upon the house. The Spaniards enlarged these holes in the wall to make niches for saints' statues. Sometimes they were lined with tierra amarilla and used as nooks for yellow oxalis, bright leaved coleas or the trailing green of the Wandering Jew. Later they became wall cupboards, protected with spindle doors and painted on the inside with vivid contrasting colors.

The Mexican type of domestic architecture goes back to the great manor houses of past centuries, the center of life on haciendas in Old and New Mexico. They were one-storied groups of rooms built around patios. They rambled over a great area in a land where holdings ran from horizon to horizon.

The Caballero's home was his castle. As in

Spain, this type of dwelling grew out of a need for home defense and turned a bare, uninviting fachada to the invader. It dispensed with even native shrubbery which might hide a sulking Apache. Set into thick, arrow-proof walls the small windows were barred on the outside and the wide entrance was barricaded with heavy solid doors. This opened on the zaguán, a covered passageway dividing the house and wide enough to permit the family coach, ox-teams and silver-saddled horses to be driven through it into the patios and corrals. The Patrón and his guests did not need to open these big gates but used a smaller door set into them. This small door within the door was the Spanish version of the "needle's eye" of Biblical times, too narrow to permit the rich young man and his camel to pass through it after the city gates were closed at sundown.

As cold as Spanish pride on the outside, hospitality was equally warm on the inside, once the guest was invited to enter the zaguán. All the joy, beauty and outpost luxury were lavished on the inner salas, patios and sunny portales. The patios were more often called placitas in New Mexico, meaning a small family plaza, and later a neighborhood where the houses of several families clustered together. Acequias ran through them, watering the cherished roses of Castilla and the cottonwood trees, whose green branches arched over the open patio, providing a grateful shade. Water was precious in arid gardens and while it gurgled on its way through the banked ditches it was seldom used lavishly. A well with a pointed roof took the place of fountains and pools, with a hollowed log beside it as a watering trough.

The rambling plan of the haciendas was due to rooms, added on from generation to generation, for sons who brought their brides back to the paternal home. They took heed of the Spanish proverb which warned them that one roof could never support the talk of a mother and daughter-in-law. Apartments for the newlyweds were built on to the father's house, enclosing the privacy of a new patio. Beyond the family patios and the servants' quarters there were cedarpost corrals for oxen, horses and sheep.

As in any feudal country these manor houses depended upon hordes of peons to keep them running. After peonage was abolished, the manors were divided into smaller private dwellings. The feeling for protection still demanded adjoining house walls. The houses were built flush with the street to the property line in plain, unassuming exteriors. The families retreated from roadway dust and noise to the living rooms and walled gardens in the rear. Sons continued to settle upon the paternal land and built their new homes at almost any angle in the back yard.

You will see these long house walls bounding Cañon Road and clusters of pinkish-yellow adobes climbing the foothills. There is a delightful lack of formal planning about them that carries on the old sense of a large, happy family. On either side of the river the hills are benched off with river boulder terraces before adobe houses basking together in the sun. On the terraces grow small peach orchards whose pink blossoms are never to be forgotten against the blue May sky. Later those Aztec flowers, dahlias, spring up in a profusion of shades and foliage. In the summer twilights neighbors sit on their doorsteps and sing old folk songs back and forth to each other. At Christmas there is a tree and a miracle play in which each man, woman and child in the placita has some part.

These humble descendants of the manor houses are characterized by one-storied rounded lines of adobe curling over the roof and melting into the earth. The low foundation of cobblestones shows no break between house and earth, for years of snow and rain have washed down the adobe to cover it in a broad flowing base. They are so much a part of the landscape that they almost seem to be mounds of earth hollowed out for human habitation. They are the growth of the soil, profoundly influencing people who live within and near the earth.

Simple as these earth walls are, they offer great variety in color and texture. The color is always in harmony with the setting, for it is of the same soil as that beside the doorway. It may be as rusty red as the hills at Cienega, as golden as Tierra Amarilla, the gray-brown of plowed fields, or the rich cream at Taos. Fresh mud coating gives the walls a smooth new texture, six months' weathering brings out a million tiny cracks like the wrinkles of an aged, interesting face. Wheat straws mixed with the mud produce the textile quality of a golden-threaded fabric.

High adobe walls run back from the house and around the garden like protecting arms. They tie the house to the landscape in long undulating lines, and contradict that charge of being "as ugly as a mud fence." Nothing is more satisfying in Santa Fe than these "mud fences" with apple blossoms or stately hollyhocks nodding above them. Sometimes they parallel the curve of the horizon in their rain-washed contours, continuing the handmade look of this Mexican type house. The high walls are intriguing with the glimpses of gardens beyond them. Their gates are a delightful surprise with spindled doors set into the frame and the adobe wall banked above it in a terraced outline. One of the famous gates is that leading out from the church wall at Sanctuario, shadowed by old cottonwood trees growing along the bend of the acequia.

The most notable addition which the Spanish gave to the adobe house was the carved lintel, corbels and posts. These bracket-capped columns are lineal descendants of those found in Spain in wood or stone. They mark the line of Spanish conquest from New Mexico to Panama. The posts, called puntales, were peeled logs brought in from the forests and smoothed with sand to a fine texture. In Spain the scroll-cut corbels were called "zapatas" since they resembled huge wooden shoes, but in New Mexico, where wooden shoes were unknown, they were called "soportes," supporting the heavy, carved lintels. This T-shaped frame fitting into squared lines is as typical of the earliest New Mexico-Spanish architecture as the arches are of the later California missions.

The first break in the barricading walls was an indented porch, looking as though the wall of the middle

front room had been knocked out and a frame of lintels, posts and corbels set in its place. The feeling of an open living room was carried on in the white or pastel-tinted yeso finish of the three inner walls, contrasting with the outside adobe plaster. Sunlight and shadow were balanced in this deep recess and the sun-baked exterior.

Doors and lintels offered the only opportunity for ornamenting the plain fachada. Spanish carvers wrought rosettes, crosses, names and dates into heavy doors like those at Sanctuario and Santa Cruz, or chiseled panels into the thick wood. Sometimes hand-hewn planks were the only decoration, pegged together with wood, running up and down or from corner to corner in a simple design. Before hinges were used, the door turned on wooden pivots fitting into holes in the casing. Later broad iron hinges added another decorative note, nail heads were studded in geometrical patterns, and moldings fitted into panels to simulate carving.

Spanish love of color, inherited from the polychrome Moorish tiles, made use of bright paint to add joy to the earth-hued fachada. Blue, red, orange and green are gay notes in doors and windows. Sometimes several shades are combined like a garden bouquet, the result of many half-filled paint cans. Blue is preferred to other colors and is so predominant that a blue door has come to be a symbol of the country. Virgin Mary blue is most loved because, perhaps unconsciously it is the satisfying complement to yellow adobe, and consciously because its celestial hue is the shade of Mary's robes.

As in Spain, further color is supplied by windows full of blossoming plants. Every sunny exposure has its red and white geraniums, purple-ruffled petunias and brilliant leaf plants. It does not matter that the flower tins still bear the labels of "Pure Lard" or

"Tomato Puree," since the flowers attract all the attention. The native housewife is as proud of her window gardens as many a man is of his orchid conservatory. She exchanges cuttings for the fresh fragrance of pink Martha Washingtons, but her treasures are the odd native plants grown by her grandmother. These may be tecolotes, named so because the mottled gray-green leaves remind one of an owl, or deditos, another member of the cactus family whose thick spiked leaves stand up like the fingers of a hand. During the summer, tubs of pink oleanders are set under the portal, with a background of white walls and the note of turquoise doors and windows under the long shaded portal. Roof gardens flourish too, a cactus or a yellow daisy sending its roots down into the dirt roof in saucy security high above the road.

In the interior the rooms have a clean, monastic frugality with candlelight gleaming upon whitewashed walls, deep windows and doors, dark-raftered ceilings and simple home-carved furniture. In the old days such luxuries as gilded mirrors, prints framed in solid silver, carved statues of saints, and rich brocades stood out against the uncrowded background.

One of the most beautiful rooms I have ever seen was in an old native house in the quaint village of Cordova, north of Santa Fe. It was stripped of all luxuries but the proportions of the long sala were proof of a proud, wellborn race. Steps led from the road up to the double paneled doors, and the mud floor was scooped out to form another step into the room. An adobe banco ran around the entire room with bright Chimayó blankets spread over the bench like a brilliant striped frieze against the white walls. With this seating for many guests the only furniture was a table and two chairs. The vigas were brown, and gleaming with the patina of age.

Our hostess had an old-time grace in her long black calico dress and shawl as she sat explaining that the family liked this sala for its cool, fresh air and the view of the valley and mountains through the windows and open doors. Her gentle face reflected the quiet and peace of the room and spoke of a people who had never allowed poverty to destroy their true dignity.

Building on from year to year involved many different floor levels with one or more steps leading up from room to room. This broke the flatness of a one-story plan and offered the variety of vistas through raised doorways. Where a higher elevation permitted it, a flight of steps with a carved rail or a balcony projected into the living room.

Carved grills were silhouetted against windows and inner doorways. Smaller spindled doors were fastened over shelves built into the walls, or used for trasteros, the high china cupboards. Closets were unknown, since the clothing and linen were stored away in huge carved chests.

There is a peasant quality about these Mexican adobes similar to that found in Spain and Mexico before the day of ornate architecture and gold-filled carving. Conditions in a far outpost simplified living, and that simplicity made it beautiful. This Mexican type is more original and true to Santa Fe than either the pueblo or the American-Spanish.

To-day all the native crafts of the country find their right setting against the rough finish of these creamy walls. The blue and faded rose, violet and brown of old Chimayó blankets hang beside arched doorways or are thrown over deep couches and chairs. Far away mountain villages have given up spindle beds, carved chests and grooved beams. Candlesticks and vestments have been rescued from ruined churches. Tin candeleros, gayly painted tin frames, and bultos set in wall niches repeat the romance of the country. In a modernly equipped adobe radiators are hidden behind carved grilles, lighting fixtures are encased in wrought iron or tin candelabras, or sunk into the walls in wells of light. The corner fireplace with piñon logs standing upright as they burn against the fireback adds a unique decorative note to the living room, bedrooms, and even the bathroom.

However, adobe houses had to be remudded every year since the rain washed off the mud coating from roof to ground. With more time than anything else life provided in the old days, and many women's hands to smooth the plaster, this was considered only a necessary part of the spring house-cleaning. But when the hurried Americans came in, they demanded a more lasting finish. With transportation quickened by the new railroads they used brick cornices, lime plaster, wooden casings and tapered columns as a more durable exterior on the native adobe.

This last phase of native architecture has been given many names—the Santa Fe-Spanish, Spanish-colonial and American-Spanish. The name Santa Fe has been associated with the renaissance of Spanish architecture in the Southwest chiefly because it had its first revival here, though fine types of old buildings are found as well in Taos, Chimayó, Cordova, Galisteo, old Albuquerque and Las Vegas, Las Cruces, Juarez and on to Mexico.

Spanish-colonial suggests the more ornate type of buildings found in warmer Spanish colonies. It also has the confusing sense of colonial English architecture, while the term, as used here, generally refers to the time of the Conquistadores. American-Spanish seems to come nearer explaining this outgrowth of additions made, after the American occupation, to the old Spanish lines of form and color.

Lime and brick were native materials as well as adobe. Deposits in the foothills along the Santa Fe River offered the necessary clay for the first brick plant which was started here about 1870. Later it was taken over by the State Penitentiary and has continued as a profitable industry for convict labor ever since.

During the decade from 1870 to 80 life was quickened by railroads penetrating this remote western land. It was also the day of the red brick fronts of the Victorian era. The fashionable blush spread even to this frontier capital where imposing mansions of the

eighties rose of imported red brick, and the less pluto-
cratic contented themselves with street veneers of
native brick. Even the pobres added brick cornices
and window casings and plastered the adobe walls
with native lime.

It is said that the brick cornices were Italian innovations first used here by masons building the St. Francis
Cathedral. However, they were following Spanish
traditions, for the counterparts of these houses were
found in Spain and north Africa where brick carried
out the same red trim and use as hip-rounded tiles.
Lime plaster was much used in Spain in gleaming white
or colored to cream by adding water strained through
manure heaps. Here white lime plaster was invariably combined with the brick cornice, since the water
seeping under the bricks gutted out the adobe.

In New Mexico the mechanical age was heralded
with brick plants and planing mills. Where adobe
had washed away around doors and windows, wooden
casings now protected them inside and out. The casings were cut to taper slightly toward the top and
were joined above with a pointed pediment. Window
bars gave way to wooden shutters, painted in bright
colors. Windows grew wider and more numerous
until there was a merchant who boasted that his new
store had "windows every damned where."

The rounded logs for portales were turned out from
the mills with boxed bases and tapering lines which
needed no corbels to support them. Instead of being
a recessed porch bounded at either end with the rooms

of the house as in the Mexican type, the portal now became an outer piazza built entirely outside the house wall on one or all sides. Since many of these portales extended on to the street, a low railing kept burros and urchins from invading them. Under the portales the wall had a smooth finish and was tinted lemon yellow, turquoise, pink or white, continuing the old feeling that the portal was an open living room. They were the nearest approach to the American front porch but even so native families seldom sat there to watch the world go by. They still preferred the privacy of their own enclosed patios.

In spite of the additions of mechanics and newly annexed sources, the American-Spanish house retains much of the original flavor of the native architecture. It is only a more permanent finish to respond to climate. Brick cornices and lime plaster reflect the Spanish treatment. Their sharp corners become softened with age and the sag and bulge of settling adobe walls give even brick casings an undulating line. Painted shutters, doors, windows and portales add happy notes to the fachada. The house plan is still one or two stories with varying levels of the cornice where the flat roofs drain to the southern exposure.

Of the three types of domestic architecture, the American-Spanish is most easily adapted to modern living. It has had an added impetus from the Spanish building fad of the last decade. It is like the house of some "rico" who has brought back ideas and treasures from Spain and Mexico. Its high ceilings still keep the old vigas in dark lines against the rough sand plaster, tinted white or cream. Delicate iron grills show their tracery against windows and patio doors. Wrought iron finds its place in curtain poles, hinges, flower brackets, and lighting fixtures. Spanish carving is seen in beams and furniture, with heavy wooden doors displaying heraldic motifs as well as fantastic birds and beasts. Priceless vargueños, those writing desks with carving, inlay, secret drawers and iron hasps, have followed the old trail from Spain to Santa Fe. Along with them came torcheras, chests, chairs, leaded lanterns, tapestries and brocades to hang behind mirrors or paintings. Even the patios have sometimes lost their informal planting and are patterned after Castilian gardens with clipped hedges in geometrical designs, potted carnations, and a center fountain, to bring old-world formality to these castles in New Spain.

Polychrome tile imported from Mexico, gives a Mexican note to these houses. Used for panels, friezes, step rises, fountains and tables their gay colors are effective against the plain walls. Floors are laid with black and white Mexican tile or the red Spanish tile, as well as brick set in old patterns or the large flat slabs of native sandstone. Mexican glass, pottery and weaving add bright peasant colors to the dinner table. Chairs and benches, both of painted wood with rush woven seats and others of leather, are typical Mexican furniture.

These importations from Spain and Old Mexico are in keeping with the historic background of Santa Fe. They emphasize its Latin sources without adding an unrelated, artificial note. The gamut run in domestic architecture from the primitive pueblo to the formal Spanish allows a wide range for individuality. This insures Santa Fe against future monotony while keeping true to her own genuine evolutions.

VII

Spanish Trails and Sanctuaries

THE picturesqueness of narrow streets, winding in
and out around adobe houses, is one of the lingering
memories of Santa Fe. They are as crooked as the
meanderings of a burro, turning off the straight path
here and there to nibble at prairie grass. Warm adobe
walls of houses and gardens flank them on either side,
leaving no room to widen the twisting lanes. Where
the walls stop, masses of tall gray-green chamisa and
yellow roses of Castile border the way with three
poplars growing just where they should and a woman
walking demurely in her long-fringed black shawl to
complete the picture.

These streets were at first faint paths threading the
earth, made by barefoot Indians coming over the hills
in long easy strides on the north-south trail between

Pecos and Tesuque. Conquistadores followed the paths, plowing through the sand along water courses with Spanish stallions, solid-wheeled wagons, colonists and dusty, long-gowned padres. Caravans coming up the Chihuahua Trail and over the long haul of the Santa Fe Trail wore the paths through the wilderness into wagon roads. Railroads traced them with lines of shining steel. Now the highway department grades them for cross-country motors and city fathers seal the roads within the city limits with cement.

But in spite of the paving, the streets wander as inconsistently as a woman's fancy. There is seldom a clear view one block ahead. Here the old Santa Fe Trail turns to the right swooping down a hill and past an arroyo, then it turns to the left to pass the house of a rico and the San Miguel Church, with still another bend before it reaches the Plaza. In places the roads are not wide enough for two cars to pass. You must wait and honk your impatient horn until the delivery boy ends his backdoor chat. Some of them are still innocent of sidewalks and leave the pedestrian scurrying from the middle of the road when a motor races by in a cloud of dust. Adobe houses under a clump of old trees jut out as though they were the end of the road, but the road unexpectedly curves past them and follows its own waywardness.

Santa Fe's Main Street is an indication of its differentness from any other "Main Street" in America, though it is no wider than those of Sevilla or Rome. San Francisco Street, the "calle principal," begins at

163

the Cathedral, passes the Plaza and runs into a bottle neck that slows up Main Street traffic. Head-on collisions are only avoided when one has learned to drive in the spirit of the country—poco á poco. What matter if two minutes are lost at the end of the day?

It is the traffic cop who has difficulty in persuading strangers that in Santa Fe they must do as the natives do—and likewise a warning never to be too sure that the wood wagon ahead will always turn to the right. One street sign gives its advice as "Slow and Blow." Those who have not yet been steeped in the feeling of infinite time provide speed fines for the city government, for the traffic cop displays no inertia. His warning toot stops many a motorist from making California in a two-day hop.

One morning he pursued a Ford running out of town like a jack rabbit. His siren did not slow down its wild flight, and at last Benny Chavez pulled up alongside a worried girl.

"Don't you know you're going too fast?" Benny shouted.

"No, I'm not going fast enough," the girl began to weep. "My sister is on her way to Lamy in an ambulance, and she's forgotten her pocket book. I'm trying to overtake her."

"Well, you'll never make it in that. Put your bus over on the side of the road and jump in here," said Benny with a Castilian gesture. "We'll catch her."

The postman walks through three hundred years of history as he delivers letters on streets bearing ancient titles. Even the names on the letters suggest the old-world note, addressed to some Spanish Don in the shaded Spencerian flourish still used by children who have left the old placita years ago to work in crowded cities. The imagination of the local postman must be more stirred than the city carrier with only an algebra problem for his daily round—X is to 20463 West 115th Street. In Santa Fe the streets are not unemotional numbers on a straight meridian line showing where "Q" crosses "13," but weave into daily living the significance of the past. Too often these street names are the only memorials to those Spanish and American pioneers who molded the drama of this country.

There is De Vargas Street, Oñate, Don Diego, Don Felix, Don Cubero, Otero, García, Delgado, Ortiz, Martínez, Sena, and the American period with Selby, Carleton, Marcy, Jefferson and Garfield. There is the remembrance of Spanish roots in Barcelona Road, Cadiz, Sevilla and Avenida Andalusia. There are those that trip the English tongue such as Cerrillos, Castillo, Galisteo. From saints' names, such as San Antonio Street, San Francisco, San José, San Rosario, one may turn the corner into the prosaicness of Manhattan, Kentucky, Santa Fe Avenue or Allendale. He is lucky if he finds street signs with these odd names, for many a stranger drives in back yards looking for "the road to Las Vegas."

The Alameda keeps true to its Spanish traditions as a public walk and drive along the river. On one side willows and cottonwoods bend over the river banks, and on the other the long walls of Loretto convent and the Bishop's Garden, once the beauty spot of Santa Fe, give it an air of cloistered seclusion. Water Street derives its name from the fact that it was the river bed of the Rio Chiquito whose stream turned the mill wheels on the site of the present Montezuma Hotel.

Another road which has a watery title is the Acequia Madre, named for the mother ditch whose winding course it follows. During the spring and summer the acequia runs full, with children paddling and sailing sticks under its little bridges, and barelegged men with hoes guiding the precious irrigating water over their alfalfa fields from the smaller "daughter ditches." In winter the banks along the road are a red hedge of willows and a frosted silver when the pussy willows come out. Later goldenrod, Michaelmas daisies and clematis grow close to the running water, and old gnarled cottonwoods provide a shady lovers' lane. Two cars can hardly pass where it twists around an adobe placita, and burros and babies scramble up the banks. The homes built along the Acequia Madre have fortunately preserved the picturesque character of this lane.

If you are an adept at sharp corners you may turn from the Acequia Madre into the Camino del Monte Sol and the artist colony which spreads out over the loma. It was once known as Telephone Road when wired poles were a marvelous innovation, but the artists restored its original name as the Road of the Sun Mountain. Adobe walls, golden in the morning sunlight, flank each side of the Camino, broken only by interesting gateways through which you peep at gardens and studios.

Cañon Road runs parallel to the Acequia Madre and has three names in its six-mile length of following the Santa Fe River. Leading down from Santa Fe Cañon it is Cañon Road, retaining much of its old time flavor; the middle part was named for the Captain-General Diego de Vargas and passes the San Miguel Church, which with the oldest house dates back to the settlement of the Tlascaltecan slaves in the original Barrio Analco; past the railroad tracks it twists again and becomes Agua Fría road leading to the village of that name three miles away.

The north side of the Plaza, beyond the Palace of the Governors, was always the scene of military glories. In the days of the Spanish Presidio it was known as the Realito, the place where the lesser royalty lived back of the Casas Reales. With the first wave of Americanization this section was taken over for army headquarters, barracks and officers' homes. The streets were renamed with patriotic fervor for the war presidents, Washington, Lincoln and Grant. These broad straight streets, planted with shade trees, are a contrast to the winding, sunbaked Spanish roads. They point to that difference in racial temperaments between a folk-made zigzag and the formal exactness of surveyors' compasses.

Grant Avenue ends with the Bridge of the Hidalgos across the Arroyo Mascarros, a sandy wash that becomes a turbulent river with summer cloudbursts. "El Puente de los Hidalgos" was named in memory of those Spanish noblemen, like Don Juan de Oñate, whose titles of Hidalgos were bestowed upon them for discovering the Province of New Mexico and holding it for the Crown. Beyond the bridge on the crest of the hill, a large cross is outlined against the blue sky. This is the Cross of the Martyrs, dedicated to the fifty-one Franciscan friars who lost their lives in bringing Christianity up the Trail into a pagan land. It has become a meeting place for community devotions with anthems rising around it in the dawn of Easter morning and a long procession winding up to the Cross of the Martyrs for vespers before the Fiesta begins. Tucked away in a cañon back of the cross, the Fiesta Bowl has made use of a natural amphitheater with tawny sandhills, the purple range of the Sangre de Cristo and puffy white clouds for its backdrop.

The highway beyond the cross is the old route to the upper Rio Grande Valley, the trail of Indians going to Tesuque and the northern pueblos, of conquering soldiers in coats of mail, of caravans from the mesa towns in the Rio Arriba, of fur trappers from the high mountains north of Taos. Curving over the hilltop it forms one leg of the horseshoe-shaped "Circle Drive" which runs along the Divide for a few miles before it turns back again to Santa Fe.

The view from the Divide is one of the most beautiful panoramas in the world, with its ever changing colors of blue and rose, silver, green and violet. It lies under the sun in an expanse of one hundred miles to the far peaks in Colorado, only a shade deeper than the blue dome of the sky. The valley in the center is caught between the high ranges of the Sangre de Cristo and the Jemez, a shimmering land where a silver trickle of the Rio Grande flows along the foot of dark sloping mesas, and the intense sunlight paints purple shadows on crumpled salmon cliffs. The road dips down into the greenness of the Tesuque Valley with its apple orchards, summer homes and adobe houses perched on the red foothills. The last ranch house was an inn for stagecoaches. A bell hung in the adobe tower to summon travelers from a stroll in the orchards for the final seven miles of the journey. During the wait, fresh horses had been harnessed so that the stage might dash into Santa Fe with whips cracking and passengers clinging to the sides as the heavy coach careened around the Plaza.

Two miles farther north a road turns off to the left to the interesting pueblo of the Tesuque Indians, and beyond that to the pueblos of Santa Clara, San Ildefonso and San Juan with Spanish hamlets and ranchos huddling close to the "Big and Fierce River."

Lincoln Avenue stops after its two block length at Kit Carson's monument and the Federal Building, first intended for the State House. Its solid gray stone walls were constructed with that hope for permanence the nation was trying to secure, not only here in the Indian country but in the nation after the rupture of the Civil War. A simple sandstone shaft before it is dedicated to Kit Carson in memory of the doughty scout who braved the dangers of scalping knives and ambush attacks to bring important messages safely through to Santa Fe.

At the end of Washington Avenue a road up the hill leads to the Garita and Fort Marcy. Half-ruined adobe walls are all that remain of the chapel, a last refuge for traitors condemned to hang in the Spanish prison. The Garita was a diamond shaped prison with towers at the corners but the walls have melted down now into a mound of earth. American soldiers went beyond the Garita to the highest level of the mesa to build Fort Marcy. Earth breastworks which once hid the mouths of cannon, are level enough to-day to form a drive around the brow of the hill, but a feeling of military defense persists in the shape of the embankments and old arrowheads buried in the dust.

This vantage point gives a comprehensive view of Santa Fe, spreading up and down the valley and protected by high wind breaks of mountains. The old town lies in the hollow of a giant's hand whose curving fingers are the Sangre de Cristo and the mysterious Jemez to the north and west while the hollow palm spreads out to the shaded blue of the Cerrillos, Ortiz and Sandia hills far to the south. Pinkish-yellow roads trickle down into the valley from the sandy loma on the other side. Adobe houses hold their footing up to the mouth of the Santa Fe Cañon to the east. Down toward Agua Fría poplar trees stand guard around the ranches like tall green sentinels, and farther south motors make a trail of dust to the descent of La Bajada. Only twenty miles, as the crow flies, you may see White Rock Cañon as a cleft in the Jemez and, beyond, the Rito de los Frijoles where the cliff dwellers' homes once honeycombed the tufa cliffs. Sunset from Fort Marcy is a divine theatrical pageant lighting up heaven and earth.

Hillside Avenue twists around the base of Fort Marcy, with unexpected, picturesque views of quaint adobes and cottonwood trees, and new homes whose terraced gardens flourish on the slope of the hill. Hillside finally winds its way into Palace Avenue, given its title because it runs east from the Palace of the Governors.

The original deeds for the houses in the first block beyond the Palace bear seventeenth century dates. One of them, the Prince home, retains its green portales, dating from the days when portales bordered the four sides of the Plaza. Governor and Mrs. Prince refused to tear down their long porch, when the modernizing fever swept Santa Fe thirty years ago. These portales point the way to-day to restoring the Plaza to its original setting and perhaps even to restoring the adobe wall around the Indians' capital. The Prince home, famous for its entertaining and the rare collections in its reception rooms, still beguiles the passer-by with glimpses of patios through old doorways. Next to it is the Sena Plaza, the old manor house of the Sena family built around a spacious courtyard. It has been remodeled into a business block now, filled with offices and craft shops.

Palace Avenue became the "best residential street" in the nineties, its stately houses and fine trees still reflecting a gracious Victorian dignity. It not only boasted the first brick house which was built in Santa Fe county, but still has a haunted house whose peeling gray paint, crooked locust trees and deserted rooms are all that any treasure-seeking ghost could ask for.

Forty years ago small town standards recognized no social status for any one daring to live south of the river. There were few bridges across the stream, and two blocks south from the Plaza was "so far out of town!" But "Tenement Row" was built soon after that, just over the river on College Street. Its clapboard walls and plumbing were the latest luxuries and the élite sought it then as they do the newest apartment houses to-day. Social standards forded the river and took a geographical jump. Most of the building from that time on has climbed the loma south of the Rio Santa Fe.

College Street, named for St. Michael's College for boys, is the entrada of the Old Santa Fe Trail, where covered wagons wound down the hills and at last entered Santa Fe. Outside of paving this twisted road, it has been changed little since motors have taken the place of caravans. Here you may see a deserted old manor house with many courtyards given over now to

172

repair shops. Near it is a delightful Spanish home with patios and gardens secluded behind high walls and wrought iron gateways. At night, the adobe houses under the loma huddle together like a herd of camels asleep in the darkness. Only a glimpse through a high narrow window of a candle burning before a shrine against a white wall reminds you of people living within the silent, peaceful clumps of clay.

Parallel to College Street, Don Gaspar Avenue presents one of those contrasts which keeps Santa Fe interesting. It runs straight up the loma from the Plaza with shade trees and modern brick and stucco homes. The one native element in it is the name Don Gaspar for Don Gaspar Ortiz, who gave a right of way through the corn fields for the street. Don Gaspar was the Piñon King, buying the little brown nuts gathered by the natives from the trees dotting the foothills and selling them at a good profit in Mexico City.

Unfortunately, New Mexico's State House and Governor's Mansion were built before the revival of native architecture. In that Victorian period people lived in adobes through sufferance and not through preference. Accordingly the Capitol and Territorial Governor's home were built on the then-fashionable Greek and Colonial lines. While they are good examples in themselves, they are hardly consistent for an ancient capital which had built its own Spanish palace half a century before the Pilgrims succeeded in importing Colonial columns to New England. The great seal of New Mexico above the Capitol portico shows two eagles, the American eagle in the background with arrows in his talons and the Mexican eagle of Montezuma in front, standing upon the legendary cactus with a rattlesnake in his mouth.

All roads lead back to the Plaza, like arteries which feed the heart. Santa Fe could not be the "Villa Real" without this open square around which every Spanish town was built. The Plaza has been the setting for all the acts in her illustrious history from de Vargas standing in the Plaza to receive the hostile Indians as his subjects, to Lindbergh seated on the folded top of an automobile as he was driven around the town. Half a century ago a picket fence enclosed its park with hitching posts where vaqueros might tie their pinto ponies. A low coping has replaced the fence, now offering a hurdle for bronco Fords. The benches along its shady paths are filled with those who lack almost everything but time. To the efficient American hustler these banqueros are an inexplicable phenomenon, drowsing through the summer day, talking politics, cracking piñones, happily watching the world wheel around the Plaza. To the foreigner they are the only Americans who enjoy life. As Ernest Block said, while he was writing part of his symphony, "America" here, "In New York people rush from subway to subway; in Chicago they tear from Elevateds to taxis; in Los Angeles they race through the air in planes; but in Santa Fe I see people who *do nothing;* they leave me alone so that I can work. They sit and talk here or they just sit. Thanks be to God that I have found one place in America where men can do nothing!"

But when the Conquistadores' Band plays on Sunday evening beneath the summer stars, the Plaza is filled with eager life, boys and girls circling around in opposite moving streams, and singing as the band plays "Adelita," small boys tweaking skirts, black shawled dueñas sitting on the benches waiting for the last piece which stirs the blood like the grand exit of a circus.

The monument in the center of the Plaza is famous for two mistakes. Commemorating the victories of the Civil War in New Mexico, it is the only place in the United States where the term "Rebel" is carved into stone and where February is spelled with only one "r." The end of the Santa Fe Trail is marked with a stone map, the last of those markers erected by the Daughters of the American Revolution every ten miles along the entire route of the Trail from Missouri to Santa Fe. A bronze tablet set into the east wall of Seligman Brothers' Store reminds you of the pioneer merchants of the Trail days, when dusty travelers climbed down from the stagecoach to purchase supplies from the original Seligman's store. Another monument stands in the Plaza as a record of uncounted time. It is a large stone tree stump, brought from the Petrified Forest near Los Cerillos, a reminder of those ages before men made trails in forests that turned to stone.

San Francisco Street runs down from the Cathedral of St. Francis into the sunset. A long remembered picture of Santa Fe is this ancient thoroughfare in the evening light: at one end, the western sky a blaze of fiery color; and at the other, the Cathedral and the mountains behind it bathed in the reflected radiance until they glow like rose quartz. To the north, the Sangre de Cristo Range and the clouds are stained with the crimson which gave them the name of the blood of Christ. Shadows fill the street where people are hurrying homeward, banqueros quit the Plaza, and only the mysterious stain rests upon the Cathedral towers as the bells chime for vespers. San Francisco Street settles into evening peace after the noonday hustle.

American ways have invaded this calle principal, bringing such rapid changes that old landmarks are being torn down as I write. Little shops under long, rickety portals have been replaced by up-to-date stores and new theaters. Yet within the sound of talkie programs there are paneled doorways where ristras of chile still advertise Spanish cafés. In the window of a Tienda Barata there are such native wares as brown sugar cones of piloncillo, freshly-ground blue corn meal, lumps of yeso ready to be baked and mixed with water to whitewash walls. An old curiosity shop is packed to its dark roof with sarapes and drawn work, Indian jars and strange, staring santos.

It is hard for these native shops to relinquish their place in the sun for the lower end of this street has long been a Spanish market. When the American occupation took over the market place on the west side of the Palace of the Governors for army barracks, the

176

market moved to San Francisco Street. Up to a dozen years ago, covered wagons drove in to the corner at Galisteo Street and lined up side by side Saturday mornings to sell peaches and melons, hens and lambs.

Across the street was Burro Alley, a rendezvous for burros and wood vendors. When the leñadores had sold the loads of split piñon and cedar, a hundred burros were turned into the corral on Burro Alley to wait

for their masters. Sometimes the burros drowsed through the afternoons with long ears and heads drooping, sometimes they started a wild stampede with loud brays, kicking and biting.

But their masters were too pleasantly occupied to pay attention to the burro corral. With the few reales earned from the wood sales they sauntered off to buy a skirt-length of black sateen, a pail of lard and a sack of flour for the family in the mountain placita. Near

Burro Alley they were sure to meet other compadres. Why not have a drink of mula blanca and roll a few brown paper cigarettes? Then, squatting on their heels in the shade of a portal, there was a game with much-thumbed Mexican cards and gossip of the plaza before evening came on. Finally the leñadores rounded up the burros in the corral with resounding whacks and "het-choo-choos," tied on the flour and lard, jumped in an empty wood saddle and started home laughing and singing at the first winking stars.

Burro Alley once bounded the famous gambling rooms of Doña Gertrudes de Barcelo. It was here that "La Tules" lived and held her mighty court, in salas that ran from street to street. Monte, roulette, faro and poker had their exclusive tables where every one who could obtain an invitation, from priest to peon, bet on the wheels of chance. In her later years La Tules was a familiar figure waddling up San Francisco Street each morning to deposit her bags of gold. Santa Fe mourned the day when the last salas of La Tules were torn down to make way for display rooms. Now shining motors stand at the corner where coaches-and-four used to wait through the night.

Agua Fría Road, across the river from San Francisco Street, is the last bit of the town to remain as little changed as possible by modern conditions. It is here that you step into the Old World, an ancient settlement leading its own life, tranquil, unspoiled and apart. Off the beaten track time and space are relative, for it is still a century away from the disturbing honks on the Plaza. Mocking birds sing in amole cages in the moonlight, a wistful love song drifts in the darkness as some youth twangs his guitar not far from the window of his love, or a fight with gleaming knives adds another insult to a long standing feud. Willow trees droop over the road and an acequia gurgles along beside it.

The high path called Alto is part of it, a forgotten way above the river bed. It is little known to any save artists who sketch the old house with the dark green portal, tall poplars and mountains back of it, and the sandy yellow slope of the river and silver gray chamisa bushes in the foreground. Even the air seems under the spell of silence, drugged with dreams and sunshine. Where the adobes face each other across the narrow way a blue door opens into a patio. There children shout to a goat perched on a high wall to remind you that this is still a mischief-loving world.

Like Rome, Santa Fe is a city of churches, with five Catholic places of worship to four of the Protestant faith. The Episcopal, Presbyterian, Methodist and Baptist churches conform to the modern buildings found throughout the United States. They have been erected within the last eighty years, since the American annexation, when Protestant missionaries journeyed out to the far western field. Most of the Catholic missions in this large diocese were begun soon after the padres arrived in the seventeenth and eighteenth centuries and are historic monuments of those early days.

The church of Our Lady of Guadalupe offers one reason why the parish spreading out along the Agua Fria Road has sustained its old life. The communicants need not cross the Plaza to the Cathedral for they have their own church, a focus of life for the large community. Baptisms, funerals and weddings in this chapel are part of the sorrows and joys of the neighborhood. Carnivals in the padre's garden, Spanish suppers in the Parochial school across the street, a procession in honor of the Virgin of Guadalupe in December are common bonds cementing the folk customs of this parish.

Though its high walls were built only a few years ago and the original architecture changed after a recent fire to look more like a California mission, this quaint church has about it the atmosphere of a provincial church in France. This is partly due to the stately trees planted around it long ago by French priests and to the cloistered seclusion of the stone walls. These walls, donated by the late Archbishop Jean Baptiste Pitaval, are more of a memorial to the stone mason than to the French Bishop if the cornerstone set into the arched gateway is left to tell the tale. It reads "J B P. Erected by Louis Napoleon, 1918."

Framed by the tall poplar trees, the old doorway is further embellished by a panel of Mexican tiles picturing the Virgin of Guadalupe, the patron saint of Mexico. When one comes from the sunshine into the dim interior of this church there seems to be, at first, only a myriad of candles twinkling before the high altar. As the eye grows accustomed to the dimness, the old carved corbels and vigas set into the thick walls trace the high ceiling. Above the altar is a copy of the original painting of Our Lady of Guadalupe, which first appeared miraculously upon the blanket of the shepherd Juan Diego in Mexico. Beside it are age-darkened oils, brought here in the days when this church was built in the last decade of Spanish rule, more than a century ago.

Across the river in the sandy plain west of the town is the church of San Rosario, said to be part of the chapel of General de Vargas when he established his camp there after the reconquest of Santa Fe in 1692. De Vargas had brought with him the statue of his patron saint, "La Conquistadora," Our Lady of the Conquest. She traveled in state all the long way up from Mexico in her own solid-wheeled wagon, a moving shrine to inspire the soldiers to retake the City of the Holy Faith from the pagan Indians. After Santa Fe had been regained, de Vargas vowed that his success was due to her intercession in answer to his prayers, and ordered his soldiers to build a chapel in her honor at the camp, saying "When a Lady has come to stay among you, she must be housed." The statue of "La Conquistadora" was placed in a side chapel of the Cathedral years ago, but she comes back on a yearly pilgrimage to San Rosario to keep de Vargas' vows and spends a summer week in her first home. San Rosario is a simple adobe church whose bareness

181

reminds one of that first chapel built under the stress of war and siege. Before it lies a dreary, unkept cemetery whose life-sized marble statues and iron railings wound with faded paper roses remind you of campos santos in the hill towns of Italy.

Beyond it is the National Cemetery where New Mexico veterans of every American war are buried. The uniform white headstones stand out in military precision against the green sod. Across the road is St. Catherine's Indian School, an order established by Mother Catherine Drexel of Philadelphia for the education of Indian children in the West and Negro children in the South.

The Cathedral of St. Francis of Assisi is the head of one of the most extensive dioceses in the United States. The sacristy is part of the ancient parroquia in the monastery founded by Friar Alonzo Benavides in 1622. Under the inspiring zeal of Bishop Lamy, the present Cathedral was begun in 1869 and built of native yellow sandstone along massive Romanesque lines. While its spires have never been completed, the towers and church have an impressive dignity. Bishops Lamy, Salpointe and Esquillon, the pastor of the Cathedral, are buried under the high altar. To the left in the Sacred Heart Chapel is the statue of "La Conquistadora," her complexion still an unwrinkled pink and white, though she is more than two hundred years old. She wears an azure robe, a gauzy veil and orange blossoms and it is said that she has an extensive wardrobe in the cedar chest, often replenished by the faithful women who attend her. The chapel to the right with its carved beams is dedicated to that favorite Saint, San Antonio. On one wall hangs a picture of "Christ in Gethsemane" painted by Pasquale Veri in 1710.

Back of the high altar and entered through the sacristy, if one of the good padres will unlock the door, you may see the "museum" and one of the finest reredos in America. It was taken from the old Military Chapel, La Castrense, which stood in the middle of the block on the south side of the Plaza until 1844. As services had not been held in the Castrense for some time, there was talk of using it for a court room, but Don Donaciano Vigil, governor at the time, refused to have business conducted on holy ground. Bishop Lamy sold the building to Don Simon Delgado for a store and used the money toward building the Cathedral. The reredos bears the inscription that it was the gift of Don Antonio Marín del Valle and his wife who placed it in the Castrense in 1760. Unfortunately the "museum" is too small for a full appreciation of the graceful proportion and fine carving on this high stone altar back. Perhaps some day it will be given the perspective its beauty deserves. Among the figures in its panels are the gallant San Juan Capistrano in armor, who was with the Christian army, St. James (Santiago) on horseback with his raised sword, and the Virgin in high relief. A little color left on the stone suggests that the figures were originally painted. On the other walls are old Santos de tabla, rescued from ruined churches, and paintings dating from the ecclesiastical schools in Spain. Primitive bultos, a Nativity Group of the Three Wise Men riding an elephant, a horse and a camel, a crib of gold lacquer and jewels, and a wistful madonna with upraised hands stand on top of a case whose glass doors protect brocaded vestments and altar hangings.

Two cracked boards set into the east wall of the small room mark the only known graves of the early frailes who came to New Mexico with the Conquistadores three hundred years ago. The other fifty-one were martyred and lost in spreading the gospel to the Indians. Padre Zarate died at Picuris in 1632, and Padre de la Llana was buried a few years later within the great mission he built at Quarai. This was one of the cities that died of fear, and when the Indians deserted it, they took with them to Tacique the remains of the beloved padre. A century later that pious governor Antonio Marín del Valle made a pilgrimage to rescue the bones of the padres and moved them again to a final niche in the thick adobe walls of the parroquia.

Within the gardens of the convent and academy, where College Street begins its twisting way, the Loretto Chapel is a little gem of Gothic architecture. A golden statue of the Virgin gleams high above the slender spires, and her halo glows with lights during the twilights of May and October—the months of Mary.

Two blocks beyond this, up College Street, San

Miguel rests in its venerable dignity, the oldest church standing in the United States. It was built about 1636 as a place of worship for the Tlascaltecan slaves of the Barrio Analco and almost destroyed by the Indian rebellion of 1680. When de Vargas reconquered the province in 1692, it was hastily restored with the aid of the Tano Indians who were then living in Santa Fe. The Marqués de la Peñuela completed the repairs in 1710, "at his own expense," as the old beam carved with his name bears witness. Its outer appearance has changed many times within the past two hundred years, but the back of the church preserves its old solid lines. The stone buttresses in front, propping the ancient walls, are almost hidden by the Trees of Heaven with their scarlet flowers and deep shadows.

A sign on the door bids you "Ring Thrice" for admission to this oldest church, since it is used now as a chapel for the students of St. Michael's College and is only open for public worship on St. Michael's Day and Holy Thursday. The white-haired Brother who slides the inner bars and unlocks the doors contributes to the old-worldliness of this shrine. He shows you the treasured bell with the Spanish crown forming the handle by which it hung and invites you to touch the clapper against its thick sides. Mellow tones ring out in the silent chapel, for votive offerings of silver and gold were added to the copper when it was molded long ago in Spain. He points out the historic beam placed there by the Marqués de la Peñuela, the dim choir loft above it and the carved corbels and beams.

The light from high windows finds tiny cracks in the whitewash and unevenness where the heavy adobe walls have settled through three centuries. On either side of the altar there are old paintings gouged with holes where flying arrows were aimed at those who sought sanctuary here during the battle with the Indians for the reconquest of Santa Fe. A highly colored print of Da Vinci's famous painting of St. Michael and the dragon has the place of honor in the center. Turned columns, whose spirals were carved with crude tools, rise behind the church candlesticks and lacy altar cloths. In 1704 the remains of Captain-General Diego de Vargas were buried in this church, fulfilling the request of the great conqueror to lie "under the platform where the priests stand to say mass." Near him is another sepulcher, that of Padre Juan de Jesús who was buried in this holy ground in 1694.

Up De Vargas Street, beyond the church and the College grounds, a deserted cemetery reminds you of the many men and women who have lived and died through the forgotten centuries in Santa Fe. It is said that when the graves were eight deep in this God's acre, the new campo santo was started at San Rosario. Here the charred gate, mournful trees and headstones fallen over in the weeds give all the settings for a ghost story on eerie moonlight nights.

So many influences have been at work in forming the old town that I have been able to describe only a few

186

of them. Public buildings are largely impersonal in the history they tell of a town's growth, but every house along the narrow streets has its story, a composite of the stories of all the people who lived in it. Each is a human document, scorched with Latin love and temper, scarred with the greed of white conquerors, and made even more dramatic in this ancient setting of romance, intrigue and mystery. For there has never been a time when Santa Fe did not resound to some thrilling story, unbelievable anywhere else, but taken at its sly face value here as a part of the life of the country.

There, for instance, is the unpretentious house of a witch woman who was murdered because of her black magic in running the cards and the fortune she had tucked away. Here is a manor house turned into modern apartments, but keeping true to the traditions of stately salas where generals met to sign secret treaties, and the tilt of a Spanish comb or the flirt of a fan was an international affair. Here is a tumbled-down adobe where even the poorest native will not live because it is haunted by the moans of a son who drove an iron spike through his mother's head. Here is a door with a bullet hole where an assassin aimed too high in the darkness. There is the "Bank Saloon" turned into an innocuous candy shop, and former gambling casinos that now advertise soda pop and hair-cuts.

What a review it would be if all the famous characters, ancient and modern, could come back to walk the streets of Santa Fe again—a mincing Don in a long cape who had a Bluebeard's reputation for mysteriously disposing of his wives; courtesans who flaunted their profession; gamblers with diamond studs; trappers with bundles of pelts; zealous missionaries and soldiers striving to change the world. They have passed into tales of "Those Days" but their lives have formed and colored the town.

VIII

When the Saints Play

THERE was a time when Saints took a day off from
heavenly intercessions to play with mortals. It was
in the centuries of long ago when jollity was part of
religion instead of being sternly divorced from it.
Then laughter, as well as prayers, rose as incense to
God in grateful enjoyment of the Father's blessings.
Both were essential to the many happy fiestas sprinkled
through the calendar.

Life was not regulated by union hours into a five
day week, nor into religious observance which sliced
an hour out of Sunday for lugubrious sermons. Work
and play overlapped with that Latin insistence that

work must never be allowed to interfere too much with the joy of existence. Life and religion dovetailed the happenings of every day to give each other deeper value. So affection for some special guardian saint was increased by vespers in the twilight before the saint's day and a long community fiesta the following day and night. Saints' statues, carried out of the church and around the plaza for an airing, added no solemn note, for the saints were good friends who liked laughter and merrymaking.

New Mexico has been called the Land of Mañana —it might as truthfully have been called the Land of To-day, for the philosophy of enjoying Hoy Mismo —this very day—permeated the country. Mañana was that nebulous to-morrow into which one shoved work and worries. The native believed, and continues to believe, that he lives to be happy to-day—not that he must slave to-day in order to be prosperous twenty years from now. To-day is filled with God's sunshine, to-morrow may never come; if it does, it is that shadowy time when the Lord will provide children to succor old age. Improvident? Perhaps! It is a question of racial outlook as to whether to-day or to-morrow is more important.

With this philosophy of enjoying to-day, fiestas garnished each month with gala days. Work was neither so competitive nor important but what it could be abandoned for a few days when the community played together in happy pastimes and enduring faith.

We moderns have standardized life into cut and

dried blocks of work and vacation with little over-lapping between. We have made it a serious business of working to gain luxuries and leisure and a more serious business of enjoying them after we have gained them. We have set aside Memorial Day, Independence Day, Labor Day and Thanksgiving with the official proclamations of national holidays, giving patriotism a preponderance over religion.

But to the Spanish colonials church and state were one. Patriotism had its outlet in constant warfare with the Indians instead of firecrackers and long-winded addresses. Frequent vacations were times to go a-visiting. Father left the farming, Mother closed the blue door behind her, and the whole family piled into the wagon to drive over the hills to a neighboring fiesta. There was always a friendly roof for shelter, room for many pallets on the mud floor and a never-empty stew pot to feed the guests. Things were evened up when the same simple hospitality was returned at a later fiesta. This love of pasear was mostly confined to villages only over two mountains from each other, for the wagon progress was slow and a long trip down dangerous trails offered no lure for hitch-hikers.

When Santa Fe was the royal city of the province of Nuevo México, this combining of church and play was an integral part of community life. Americanization has divided them now into separate manifestations of church services at one time and carnivals, county fairs, cowboy rodeos and Indian shows at another.

But in Spanish-speaking villages up and down the

Rio Grande and the Rio Chama, far enough away
from the railroad to escape Americanization, old fiesta
customs are almost the same as they were in the days
of Castilian glory. Outside of jazz, played unconsciously with a syncopated accent, and soda pop and
jim-crack stands brought in by enterprising Americanos, fiestas in these forgotten villages might well be
those enjoyed by the Conquistadores. For traditions,
transplanted to this far virgin soil long ago, are like old
apple trees bearing the same small, red apples year
after year with few new graftings. They have changed
less on these isolated mesas than the same traditions
which originated in Spain, where the fecund life of a
whole nation constantly creates new patterns.

Every month has its fiesta in some tiny village, perhaps to celebrate the day of their patron saint, perhaps in honor of the Big Brother Saints who are universally loved. There is, for instance, the feast in
honor of Señor San José in far-away Las Trampas,
June 6, another at Chimayó, July 25, San Lorenzo's
Day at Peñasco, and a Matachines dance at Bernalillo,
August 11. There are others at Códova, Truchas,
Taos, and horse races at Tierra Amarilla and Galisteo
to make one believe that a plumed captain-general
might come riding over the hills at any minute to take
part in the merrymaking. These fiestas are home-
coming times, unadvertised for tourists but known far
and wide to friends and relatives who drive over steep
mountain roads in covered wagons and rackety Fords
to renew home ties.

This summer, when we were stuck in the mud just out of Peñasco, we blocked the way for a big car headed for the village. Two black-haired youths got out to help us and soon mother, two daughters and two babies left their automobile, picked their way around us in the mud and hurried on the half mile to the settlement. They could wait no longer, for they had spent five days on the road in order to be in time for the fiesta in their old home. They had lived in Utah seven years, and now they were returning for a visit, in the prosperity of a shining motor and lace-trimmed dresses. Joe, of the sleek black hair and eyes, and the toothbrush and gold fountain pen sticking out of his pocket, confided that he would meet his novia at the baile that night and marry her before they started back to Utah. The fiesta and a childhood sweetheart drew them back to the mountain village, home ties stronger than movies and a seven-dollar-a-day job in the Mormon mines.

It is like peeling off a thin veneer to find the native pine beneath to see one of these old-time fiestas at Agua Fría, almost within the city limits of Santa Fe. If the parish of Our Lady of Guadalupe is a century away from the Plaza and the present, the village of "Cold Water," three miles beyond, leaves off a hundred years for every mile you travel down the rutted road. Here is a rough rock encircled with a tumbled-down fence to mark the spot where Governor Pérez was beheaded by the Indians in the revolt of 1837. Here are old deserted houses where some family has left no children to claim the land. Other adobe homes are snug and prosperous near the bank of the acequia where green trees shed puffs of white cotton. There is a portal of faded turquoise and a peaked well stoop almost hidden behind pink hollyhocks. Passing beyond it you see an old man sitting against the wall in the sunshine, his cane propped between his knees and his

mongrel dog asleep at his feet. Farther on, in the village, there is the home of a wood carver who fashions saints out of knots of piñon or carves the silhouette of the patron San Isidro driving the oxen around the field for the poor farmer. Here are wagons coming down the road filled with wide-eyed children, and burros with wood circling their mouse-colored bodies like peacocks' tails.

The plentiful cold water at Agua Fría gave reason for the last stop of the Spaniards who followed the river from there to Santa Fe. It was but a little respite, for they were within sight of their goal. The road bends under a clump of alamos whose green branches make a frame for the high pate of Baldy and

the range of the Sangre de Cristo flowing down at
either side like the drooping shoulders of an ageless
Buddha. While these trees may not have been even
seedlings in the days of the Conquistadores, the vista
of mountains under the branches always reminds me
of how grateful this view must have seemed to weary
soldiers.

But where the water supply for growing Santa Fe
is conserved in three reservoirs, there is only a trickle
left for Agua Fría. The gardens and orchards have
shrunk to small fields, a line of green cottonwoods and
a hedge of feathery gray chamisa. Agua Fría is now
a village of wood vendors. Cords of green piñon and
cedar dry before the houses in high resinous stacks
waiting to be split and sold in Santa Fe. The modern
highway westward follows the level prairie to the south
and the village of Cold Water continues its old customs in undisturbed obscurity. Its roads do not invite the stranger for they are cut across by acequias
and flooded where the water has spilled over.

That is of no importance, however, to Chopita and
her mother driving in to San Juan's Day fiesta in a
sagging old buggy which her father has difficulty to
keep from overturning. Chopita's face is round and
smiling for is she not wearing her new yellow-pink
taffeta dress with a turquoise ribbon around the waist,
silk stockings a shade lighter than her husky young
legs and elaborate slippers bought only last week in
Santa Fe from the Tienda Alberto? Even her straight
blue-black hair has been bobbed above her chubby neck.

A que sí, she has planned for months on this Big Day, June 24, the fiesta in Agua Fría—a city compared to the remoteness of her father's ranch.

There are Josefita and Carmencita walking down the road in their new store dresses, carrying their new slippers to save them from the ten mile walk over the mountains. "Qué hay, nita?" Chopita shouts to them. There is no room in the one-seated, one-sided buggy to ask them to ride, but the girls don't mind walking. They are happy though hot in the June afternoon sun, hurrying on to arrive at their aunt's house before it is time to go to vespers.

The old adobe church is crowded in the twilight with men standing on one side and women on the other. Their voices join in the low surging chant of Ave María and rosaries slip softly through the fingers. Candles gleam on the altar and those in tin sconces along the walls light up the Stations of the Cross.

After vespers quiet men and women file out of the church doors. Through the darkness the flat roofs are outlined with luminarios, homemade lanterns made with a candle set in sand in the bottom of a paper bag. Beyond the ruddy bonfires burning around the campo santo there comes the music of guitars and violins, for musicians are walking down the starlit road, playing as they go. The crowd follows these Pied Pipers to the dance halls. In a few minutes the baile is in full sway with dancers making the most of fiesta revelry and music far beyond midnight.

The next morning they meet again at mass. The

196

modern church spire rises toward the turquoise sky, an incongruous note above the primitive mission and the adobe walls around the campo santo. Inside the church there are garlands of bright paper flowers and red Christmas bells festooned against the newly white-washed walls. The saints are decked out in gala silk dresses and strings of gold and pearl beads. At the end of mass San Juan is lifted from his shrine and carried out for a tour of the Plaza in the fresh June morning. An old man pours gunpowder out of a beer bottle into an ancient flintlock musket and fires it in mid-air to ward off any lurking evil spirits. In spite of his fixed wooden stare, San Juan is no longer a solemn saint but a friendly soul who enjoys the fiesta promenade in the sunshine to celebrate his birthday.

After he has returned to his niche, there is visiting from house to house, neighborhood gossip and talk of weather and crops. Chopita joins other country girls at the gay stands of the Americano peddlers, tempted with tawdry trifles at the wheel of chance and soda pop and cracker-jack. They giggle, whisper and nudge each other when a group of boys passes, but Spanish etiquette forbids any twosing. After a dinner of tempting Spanish delicacies there is a laughing, chattering hurry to find places beside the road to watch the Correr el Gallo.

The feast of their patron saint, San Isidro, is always celebrated in Agua Fría in December, but the birthday of San Juan Bautista, June 24, and San Pedro's Day, June 29, offered a good reason for a summer week of merrymaking. There was horse racing for St. John and cock-fighting for St. Peter, for St. Peter was credited with having a special sympathy with game cocks since the dawn when the cock crew thrice above his head. Now the two sports have been combined in the Correr el Gallo, or chicken pull for the fiesta of St. John.

There is the alcalde going down the road with a chicken struggling under his arm. Every one leans forward to watch him bury the cock in the sand until only the red eyes and flapping comb are evidence of the frightened bird.

The boys are ready on their horses, their wide sombreros set tightly on their heads. The pinto ponies have sensed the excitement of the day and rear and plunge so that it takes more minutes to get them back of the line. A gun is fired and off they go, racing down the road toward the speck of cock's head sticking out of the sand. They have gone too far and turn back, twenty horses piled up in a dusty scrimmage. They lean far over their high pommeled saddles with their horses tearing along at a gallop to clutch at the sand. Finally José swoops to the ground, grabs the cock by the neck and twists it as he swings it over his head with a shout. He wheels his horse for a get-away but the crowd is after him, yelling and spurring their ponies. They overtake him, Antonio snatches the cock away and the pursuit turns after him. One grabs a wing, another tail feathers until only the dismembered carcass is left to the victor. They ride back to the Plaza, eager to try their luck at other gallos buried in the sand until the hen roost gives up its last strutting master.

After the Gallo races were over, we sought the shade of some alamos for a picnic lunch and a siesta. When we returned, the village had an unexpected foreboding stillness, sharper than the drowse of a lush June afternoon. Down the twisting road, lined with sunbaked adobes on each side, people congregated in a haunting hush. The scraping music from violins and guitars drifted out of an open doorway, but it was at the house across the road where the crowd had gathered. Some one whispered that a visiting girl from a nearby rancho had been run over by a wild automobile. Through the screen door we could see a padre moving about in his priestly robes and candles burning. Women crowded inside the room as the Last Sacrament was given, and the men outside sank on their knees in the dust. Laughing Chopita had had her big day. The priest came out, a German Franciscan with a yellow straw sailor surmounting his long rope-girdled gown. The men questioned him as he started his car back to Santa Fe. Then they sauntered across the road to the deserted dance hall. "Pobrecita!" they murmured —but life was short—on with the dance.

In a few minutes the hall was a maze of couples stalking out the one-step. The vigas across the wide white room were covered with flowered wall paper and the posts were wound with cheesecloth. The orchestra sat on a high platform at one end, a blind fiddler accompanied by a guitar and an accordion. Farther down the road another baile vied for fiesta patronage with the whine of popular jazz ground out of a phonograph.

Most of the boys were coatless, collarless and their shirt sleeves, held up with gaudy elastic, were rolled above their elbows in preparation for the strenuous work of a hot afternoon. Their soot-black hair, cut bowl-shaped by the village barber, rose in stiff wet pompadours above sloping Aztec foreheads. The village vamp was there, her popularity attested by the rills of perspiration streaking the lavender powder on her face and neck—and the city girl, her sophistication bought at the price of city men, supercilious of the country louts but distracting them when she deigned to dance. She had that Latin knack of making her dark suit look chic. The majority were typical Spanish girls, their soft black eyes looking out of oval faces at a happy, innocent world.

Mothers and children sat on the benches, never tired of watching the dancers. One group was the family of the red-headed man whose progeny ascended from a carrot-topped baby in a pink hood and green ribbons to older daughters whose Titian hair recalled some ancestor in far Andalusia.

The orchestra played on and on through the warm afternoon and night, interrupted now and then by fist fights and a flash of knives outside the door. Gun shots startled the dancers. Police dated the "nice, quiet dance" with one man killed and three severely wounded. A hot Latin quarrel over some trifle started it, but too much mula blanca was the real transgressor. Hastily the weary parents gathered up their daughters and drove home, planning for the next fiesta.

Early in September, Santa Fe has its fiesta. It differs from the purely native fiestas in that it reënacts one of the most dramatic episodes in Spanish colonial history with the combination of Spanish folk ways, Indian dances and American carnival. With the exception of our Puritan Thanksgiving Day it is the oldest historical celebration in the United States, a focus of the romance interwoven by three races during the past three centuries.

The fiesta began in the year 1712 when the Marqués de la Peñuela issued a bando commanding the town to commemorate the reconquest of this province by Captain-General Diego de Vargas in 1692. The Marqués was the D. A. R. of his day, restoring the oldest church at his own expense and insisting even then that Santa Fe should take an active interest in her history. He saw that the reconquest of the Holy City, a perilous feat of only twenty years before, had all the essentials of a stirring drama. Such pageants, depicting the martial glories of the mother country, were highly popular in Spain. Here in this isolated province, a historical fiesta would inspire the colonists toward greater zeal in subduing the Indian country and give them that typical Spanish outlet for national feeling in drama. The Marqués set the stage with de Vargas riding up to the city walls in resplendent armor, velvet cape and plumed helmet, accompanied by his soldiers and brown-gowned padres. There was the tense moment of the captain-general entering the gate of the hostile pueblo, relieved when the cross and the scarlet and gold banners of Castilla were again planted before the Royal Palace.

After more than two centuries the same drama thrills us with its crisis. The fiesta begins with Sunday vespers in the Cathedral and a solemn march in the September twilight for a community service at the Cross of the Martyrs. The way is marked with little bonfires burning along the road and a thousand lighted candles held in the hands of men and women winding up and down the hill in the dusk. Above, the Milky Way reflects the twinkling tapers, and big stars burn in the quiet night-blue sky.

The next morning de Vargas once more rides in on his silver saddle to reconquer the Villa Real. The cross and royal banner are planted before the Palace of the Governors as they were in 1692, and the Alcalde in his brocade satin coat reads the ancient edict for the two hundredth time. The return of de Vargas to his camp outside the city, followed by soldiers, padres and war-painted Indians, is a signal for the merrymaking to begin.

The fiesta needs no artificial scenery, for the Plaza and the Palace of the Governors furnish an unequalled stage setting. The historic park, no longer a battle field, is gay with banners of all colors waving through the trees. Crowds in costume throng through it in holiday saunterings, stopping now beside a blind fiddler seated on a bench and then following gay troubadours and joining in the chorus of the yard-long verses of "Adelita."

The Historical Pageant is followed the next day by the Hysterical Pageant giving full reign to the artist colony's ingenuity in caricaturing every issue in village life from Detour Buses to the Painters' Dream of selling pictures as fast as oil stock. The native people enter into it with the zest of their happy Latin temperament, dressed as buffalo hunters with raised spears, followed by high wagons whose two solid wooden wheels creak loudly with every turn. Trailing them are long lines of women in the gay flowered dresses their grandmothers wore. The Hysterical Pageant is the highlight of the Pasatiempo, inviting every one to pass their time in a merry carnival spirit.

The portal of the Palace with its scarlet and gold banners has become a Spanish Market where everything from native herbs to syrupy Mexican punch is sold. Colorful Chimayó blankets fill one stall and quaint carvings, hand-woven carpets and hooked rugs are displayed in the Spanish Colonial Arts Exhibit. Following the customs of earlier days, country people have driven their covered wagons up to the Plaza curb, vending red-cheeked peaches and vegetables, squawking hens and bright-hued flowers. Even the children have a part in the fiesta for the Pet Show is their special affair. They come to the Plaza not only with favorite dogs, cats and ponies but with such pets as caterpillars, turtles, snakes, monkeys and horned toads, equally precious to a child's heart.

Inside the patio, Indian dances are going on, pueblos vying with each other in presenting the best dances and reviving many an old ceremony which might have been forgotten. There, too, is the Indian Fair with the finest examples of baskets, pottery, weaving and turquoise jewelry offered as exhibits and awarded prizes to encourage these original arts. At the Art Museum paintings of Southwestern artists fill the galleries with the Annual Fiesta Show.

The feature which makes the fiesta unique and colorful is the whole-souled participation of the hundreds of native people who come in from tiny mountain hamlets to join with Spanish Santa Feans in making the Pasatiempo truly their own. Under the leadership of a large Spanish-American society they make the most of this opportunity to show their pride of racial heritage, and to enjoy their own type of good time. One year they represent Pancho Villa and his bandits with delightful buffoonery, another year they are the Ciboleros, the buffalo hunters who went forth from Santa Fe to search the plains for herds of buffalo, bringing back dried meat and skins. Their costumes, crude equipment and solid wheeled wagons are authentic, for they are supervised by old men who hunted the buffalo sixty years ago. The buffalo hunt takes place on the College grounds and the supper for the Ciboleros, served by laughing women in old-fashioned dresses, recalls that first dim memory of the cave man being fed by his woman when he came back from the hunt. In the evening they join in old songs and folk dances such as La Cuna, Paso Doble and La Escoba with jokes and laughter, the bright-colored costumes flashing under the lights.

It reminds one of folk dances in Hungary or Russia, yet it is essentially a part of historic Santa Fe as the center of the Spanish Southwest. There is no exhibitionism about it but the spontaneous Latin gayety which is the delight of every native fiesta. As one breathless grandmother exclaimed, when she sank into her seat after the swift steps of the quadrilla, "Qué fun!"

One night is given over to the Conquistadores' Ball when grandees in velvet and lace dance with court ladies in rare shawls and mantillas. Another night offers a highly-colored Western melodrama presented by the Santa Fe Players. Zozobra, Old Father Gloom, is burned on a huge pyre and the Pasatiempo revelry reaches its height. The Conquistadores' Band plays for street dancing, confetti rains in a multicolored shower and the youngsters do a serpentine around the venerable Plaza. Finally the luminarios, those old-time lanterns made of candles set in sand-filled paper bags, gutter out where they have outlined the Palace portal and the fiesta is over for another year.

Other feast days in Santa Fe have their special church significance, though the community fiesta following them has been abandoned. In June there is Corpus Cristi Sunday with the Blessed Sacrament car-

ried beneath a golden canopy for public veneration.
It is preceded by all the priests of the church, while
the archbishop in his rich robes and the deacons of the
Cathedral walk through the dusty roads carrying the
Host. All the bells ring out as the procession leaves
the Cathedral and winds its way between young pine
trees decorating the narrow streets. As the Host
passes, bared heads are bowed and knees touch the
ground like wind leveling summer grain. The morning air is filled with the beat of many feet marching to
slow church chants. Thousands of people make the
pilgrimage, children clinging to their mothers' skirts,
young women with parasols raised against the bright
June sun, and old men with upturned reverent faces.
It is the largest religious procession in the United
States. They stop for benediction before the lacy
altar at the home of Francisco Delgado on Cañon
Road and again at the Sena Altar on Palace Avenue
before the final service in the Cathedral. Watching it,
one is transported with the feeling that this cannot be
the United States—rather some little town in Spain or
Italy where like processions climb the hill. Yet, in the
multitude kneeling on the ground before those altars
when the words of Christ are pronounced, there is
manifest that zealous devotion which founded Santa
Fe so long ago.

The following Sunday afternoon the vow of de Vargas is once more fulfilled, for yesterdays are not buried
in musty tombs in Santa Fe but are relived with the
significance of to-day. De Vargas promised, before

his battle for the reconquest of the City of the Holy Faith, that yearly homage should be paid the Virgin of Victory as a remembrance of her aid. The statue of "La Conquistadora" is the same one that the Conqueror brought with him out of Mexico. She is carried on the shoulders of young girls in white dresses and long white veils and her path is strewn with rose petals. "La Conquistadora" proceeds in exalted state from the Cathedral to the chapel of San Rosario on the site of the camp of de Vargas and his soldiers.

There she reigns before the high altar for a week with benediction in her honor every morning. The special gift of the Mother of Christ is to intercede with Him for the needs of His children, made known to her through prayers. Since the end of June is apt to be a dry season, what is more fitting than that prayers for rain should be included in the benediction? There is a story of long ago when these prayers were so effective that the valley was flooded. The Virgin was taken to the door and shown the melted adobe houses and ruined crops. In consternation many voices implored her aid, crying "See what your Son has done!"

The next Sunday she returns again to her side chapel in the Cathedral, the girls in their white veils as proud of their devotion to "La Conquistadora" as royal maids-in-waiting.

The procession at twilight, October 3, marks the beginning of the feast of Santa Fe's patron saint, Little Brother Francis of Assisi. It is the most beautiful ceremony of all the year. Darkness lends mystery to black-robed figures, and a mystic sense of communion between the sleeping earth and heaven. Gleaming candles on the high altar are seen through the arched doorway of the Cathedral and above it the rose window glows like a jeweled mosaic. Suddenly the boom of cannon shatters the evening silence. It comes from an old anvil filled with gunpowder near the sacristy. A worn playing card—and it must be a playing card, for no other bit of paper will do—has been placed over the gunpowder, another anvil laboriously lifted on top of it, and a red hot poker thrust between the two to ignite the card. The roar that belches forth makes the stranger believe that Santa Fe is once more in a state of siege. But it is only the preliminary for the procession—a combination of the salute of guns and the ancient mode of scaring away evil spirits. Then it is lost in the pealing of Cathedral bells as the procession leaves the doorway.

Pitch-wood fires burn along the road, throwing ruddy lights on the long adobe walls of the Bishop's Garden. Hundreds of humble folk walk between them, men's voices rise in a minor dirge. There are black-shawled women passing, passing, passing like shadows in the dusk, their soft footfalls marking time to the telling of their beads. After them young men and old men passing, with that peace on their quiet faces of which St. Francis sang seven hundred years ago. At the end of the procession, the statue of St. Francis in his rope-girdled gown sways above the heads of those who carry him. Surrounding him are Franciscan monks carrying on the faith, the archbishop in his crimson hat and priests in their lacy surplices.

October and May are known as the months of Mary, with vespers for the children every evening. In May the young first communicants flock to church, their hands filled with fresh spring flowers for the Mother of the Holy Child. There are many wide-eyed little girls in white with wreaths pressed down on their tight black curls, and serious little boys with unnaturally clean faces, a white ribbon and flowers pinned to the arm of their new blue suits and their hands gripping tallow tapers. They cluster around the church doors until the vesper bells ring out. The golden statue of the Virgin on the steeple of Loretto chapel shines out in the twilight, her halo and the crescent at her feet picked out in electric bulbs.

The feast of Our Lady of Guadalupe, December 12, is the gala day in the parish named for this favorite Mexican Patroness. It begins the evening before with a procession, headed by the statue of Our Lady of Guadalupe, twisting in and out the dark narrow streets and back to the church again. A terrifying number of guns are fired into the clear winter night—one way of "shooting the devil."

Later, down on Agua Fría Road, you will hear serenades beneath the windows:

> Lupita, tú eres hermosa
> Como los rayos del sol;
> Eres la flor Nicaragua
> Dueña de todo mi amor.

Recibe pues esta canción,
Recibe pues mi carazón.

(Lupita, to me thy fair beauty
Shines like the rays of the sun.
Sweet flower of far Nicaragua
All of my love you have won.
Accept then, e'er we must part,
Accept this song from my heart.)

All of the many girls named Guadalupe, and Lupita for short, hope to be serenaded that night in honor of their name day. It is a more important anniversary than their own mortal birthday. When the last twanging cord of the guitar dies out, father and mother open the door to see what this noise may be. They bring the serenaders inside and the bashful Lupita serves them homemade wine and sweet cakes. When her long-lashed eyes are lifted, they sparkle with the excitement of this special fiesta for her name day.

Christmas has many sweet old native customs. No one who has ever seen them will forget the little fires that dot the hillsides and burn before the church doors in the early darkness of the Noche Buena. Each adobe home has its ocote bonfire, laid log-cabin fashion of pitch-wood. They flame up like low torches in the night, symbolizing the Christ Child's light coming into the world and entering each lowly door. The flicker of warm firelight and shadows dances over the family group around them, over the seamed adobe walls and the snowy hillsides. Unconsciously the music of "Silent Night, Holy Night" hums itself over in my mind, but the family are singing one of their own songs of the Nacimiento.

Christmas Eve inside the house is gay with happy faces, tender with a velorio for the Santo Niño. The statue of the Infant Jesus is the high light in the simple room. Candles burn around His niche, reflected on the white walls. Good children with big starry eyes are allowed to kiss Him, in memory of that first nacimiento in the manger. Grownups and children join in the games and merrymaking until it is time to go to midnight mass.

After mass and the walk home in the clear frosty night, there is the excitement of breaking the Piñata. It is an olla suspended by cords from the ceiling. The children are blindfolded and strike madly in the direction of the Piñata with a stick to the laughter and cheers of the family. When the lucky one smashes the Indian jar, goodies and toys fall to the floor, and every one joins in a scramble for gifts.

Christmas morning the front doorbell rings frequently with "Mees Christmas" boys—the happiest of Merry Christmas visitors. They are groups of smiling urchins whose voices greet you with "Mees Christmas" and are in turn offered candy, oranges and nuts which they stow away in flour sacks to take home to mother and little sisters. Then they scamper on to another doorbell.

Lent begins with the fast of Ash Wednesday. Many a corner of the small wooden panels painted with saints' pictures, santos de tabla, is burned off that day to make a cross of ashes on the forehead. Maundy Thursday is set aside for visiting the five Catholic churches in Santa Fe. The streets are filled with men and women going from one chapel to the other to do the Stations of the Cross. A fair amount of neighborly chat and passing the day with old friends lighten the gloom of Holy Week mourning as they make the rounds. Young girls murmur special prayers before the shrine of San Antonio, who helps in finding lost trinkets and lost hearts. Perhaps they are rewarded when some dark-eyed youth follows them as they walk demurely from church to church, their eyes half hidden by the folds of black shawls.

Easter Monday was the day for fiestas and the Gran Baile after the six weeks' fasting and penance of Lent. In the days before advertising told how to keep that schoolgirl complexion, girls made the most of Lenten restrictions to bleach their faces behind beauty masks of white or crimson clay. There was no false modesty about appearing hideous and unsmiling for six weeks if they might peel out fair and lovely for the Easter Ball. Besides this bleaching, they used a homemade cosmetic called albayalde de México which calcimined the face with a pale, lavender cast. It consisted of egg shell ground fine in a mortar, mixed with chalk and white of egg and formed into hard balls to be rubbed over the face. The cheeks were reddened by prickling them with a rough mullen leaf, slightly irritating the skin or by rouging them with a homemade cosmetic called "alegría." Their heavy hair, washed with amole root until it shone in blue-black lights, was pinned up with high Spanish combs. A silk dress, an embroidered shawl, a pair of high heeled slippers and they were ready for the Easter baile.

Accompanied by their mothers they went to the town sala reserved for meetings and dances. Even now, it is unheard of for a boy to take a girl to a dance. The dueña-mothers sat on benches around the room, their black shawls making silhouettes against the whitewashed walls. The girls waited impatiently until some youth came to claim them. They did not need to be introduced to dance many times together, but etiquette forbade them to recognize each other on the street to-morrow. While the love of dancing was part of the Spanish heritage, it included a punctilious formality. There was little bantering exchange between partners, though there were many whispered endearments between sweethearts who made the most of this alone-in-a-crowd meeting. Dancing offered the only opportunity for young folks to get acquainted. After each dance there was a stiff promenade around the room and the girl was returned to her dueña.

The musicians, seated on a high platform at the end of the room, were most often a blind fiddler and a one-eyed guitarist, the latter leading his blind partner, for according to the Spanish proverb "In the land of the blind the one-eyed man is King." The airs were those old folk songs which every one knew. There was jiggety music for the schottische and polka and the melody of "Sobre las Olas" for slow Spanish waltzes. Mothers and fathers joined in the square dances, called out in joking couplets, and in the graceful glide of the Varsoviana, with high heels tapping like the click of castanets.

The Easter Monday Baile featured cascarones. These were egg shells saved during Lent, filled with confetti and perfume and a bit of colored paper pasted over the pierced end of the shell. At a signal the girls rushed for the baskets of cascarones, breaking them over the heads of their sweethearts. Then the chase began to snatch a kiss from the girl. Or the order was reversed and the girl with the most perfume and confetti in her dark hair was the belle of the Easter Ball.

IX

Old Plays of Passion, Love and War

DRAMA in New Mexico presents the rare phenomenon of relativity. Three races, three cultures, three periods flow side by side. They are like a great river of Time which does not stand still but runs in currents of differing tempos. There is the swift middle current of the present, the slower tidewater of the Middle Ages and the pools where primitive life scarcely changes in the eddies. During twenty-four hours we may witness the Indian's nature dramas of a thousand years ago, miracle plays of the days preceding Shakespeare and the latest talkie.

This province was settled by Europeans at the time when religion was heightened by drama and drama drew upon religious sources. In Spain it was the golden age of the autos sacramentales of Lope de Vega and Calderón and the fanatic fervor of the Third Order of St. Francis. What was more natural than that Spanish noblemen should transplant the high lights of the mother country to the far-flung colonies?

The extraordinary feature is that these same Spanish plays and beliefs should have survived intact for three more centuries. The reason for their continued existence was, of course, the isolation of a desert-rimmed province. During that time explorations, conquests, contacts changed men as little as they did mountains and valleys. The seed of drama was planted, and its growth nurtured by people hungry for racial tradition. Few new shoots grew up to crowd it and no hand was strong enough to cut it down.

The real American Passion Play continues in the mountain villages north of Santa Fe in all its tragic realism, undiminished by rude curiosity or Roman disapproval. In comparison with it the Passion Play given every ten years at Oberammergau is but a stage performance, in spite of its solemnity and the spiritual interpretation of its actors. "Los Hermanos Penitentes" not only desire no audience but have been known to attack intruders. The "Penitent Brothers" go through their Lenten drama in darkened moradas on lonely wind-swept mesas and drag their crosses down narrow cañon trails. Because it is a personal, mystic exaltation, the Crucifixion is rarely witnessed now by any save the Brotherhood and black-shawled women—grieving Marys who kneel at the foot of the Cross.

This curious molding of fanaticism into intense historic drama is a somber survival of the Middle Ages. At that time the grim practice of self-flagellation spread over Europe like a black epidemic. Kings

beat their own royal backs and gave the support of
the Crown to the Third Order of St. Francis with its
rites of self-torture. Within the next century its fury
died out in Europe, but it was brought to New Mexico
by Don Juan de Oñate in 1598. His journal tells of
the six hundred colonists going through the ritual of
the Penitentes on the eve of their departure from
Mexico in the belief that further Divine Grace would
be given their hazardous northern expedition. After
the colonists settled in the province, this morbid cult
flourished like a thorny-armed cactus. Bleak mountain peaks intensified it with dramatic back drops.
Its zeal grew in isolated settlements where home memories were cherished through twenty generations. In
the daily perils of savage scalping raids, those who
followed in Christ's footsteps were assured of safety
in heaven if not on earth.

The Passion Play of the Penitentes became the
drama of the year, anticipated as an annual outlet for
a melodramatic people. It was more absorbing than
any artificial repertory since the Brotherhood were
actors as well as audience; more intense since the por-
trayal of Christ's agony was of divine origin and its
reënactment the purging of personal sins. In form it
held to the emotional crisis of a four-act drama, yet it
was not so much play-acting as actual participation in
the earliest Christian tragedy.

Its far-reaching membership, like more recent
hooded clans, developed into a powerful organization.
Its officers often dispensed justice in a land where

judges were few. In the last half century it has taken on the color of American political parties. In Abiquiu one chapter house is known as the "Morada Demócrata" and the other as the "Morada Republicana." The Brotherhood is still strong enough to have forced through the State Legislature laws prohibiting criticism of Penitentes in the state press. Antagonism has made it more secret. Membership is never publicly acknowledged although, in the close village life, there are many ways of knowing the personnel of the order.

Only the chosen go through the frenzied initiation, leaving other villagers to scoff at the semi-public services. Families belong to it through fathers and sons and occasionally women are allowed an auxiliary membership. They do penance by binding their arms and ankles with ropes drawn so tightly that circulation stops or by wearing nail-spiked boards under their clothing until their bodies are lacerated. Modern civilization has driven the Penitentes back from the larger towns to isolated mountain hamlets in northern and western New Mexico. There new moradas appear between the old ones as witnesses that this strange cult of the Middles Ages has not died but has become more intensive. When New Mexico filled her quota for the World War, medical examiners were astounded at the number of young native soldiers whose backs bore Penitente scars.

The Friday nights of Lent, most of Holy Week, the first of May, All Souls' Day and the funeral of any Penitente find the Brotherhood assembled at the lonely morada or chapter house of the Order. Of the twelve officers, the Hermano Mayor is the elected head. Another officer is the Reader who chants the story of the Crucifixion from a much-thumbed Bible, peering at it in the dim light of a lantern as he walks beside the flagelantes. The Healer brews soothing herb teas for aching bodies, and other officers have special duties in the initiation. It is the Pitero who plays a reed flute, sending out a high, bloodcurdling minor melody into the night. For five years the Penitentes serve their self-imposed sentence of penance. For another five years they act as officers. After that they are life members, only becoming flagelantes again when some dark sin of the year demands blood expiation.

I saw the Lenten rites of the Penitentes for the first time many years before "Penitente hunting" became a spring sight-seeing feat. Since then, crackerbox picnickers and irreverence have desecrated one of the most profoundly serious dramas to be found in contemporary life. The curiosity seekers have destroyed that which they came to see—not only because they have forced Penitente services to be fiercely private, but because a lack of sympathy made it impossible to perceive the real drama. Modern sophistication makes us soft. While we no longer believe in sadist exhibitions as true religion, I often wonder if any "Penitente hunter" has any conviction for which he would endure five minutes of spiritual or physical agony.

During Holy Week I was visiting a friend who had lived in the Rio Grande Valley since the days before the railroads came in. In a spirit of reverent Spanish graciousness the family coachman took us with him to a remote morada. Plutarco was an ex-officer, bearing the sign of the cross in an indigo tattoo upon his forehead. When we stopped at the morada, he greeted his brothers by kissing the backs of their hands and explained our mission.

The morada was some distance from the village, on the evergreen slope of a mountain. It was a two-room adobe house topping a little hill, and turning blind mud walls toward the road and the village. On the far side there was one black-curtained window and a heavy door. Above it a doleful bell hung in the wooden belfry. Trails from the doorway led down the sandy arroyo and across the mesa to a Calvario with its huge, stark cross. Lying on the ground beside the door there were other crosses waiting to be borne on human shoulders to that Calvario. They were as long and heavy as telephone poles, with the ends worn off on one side where they had been dragged for many painful miles.

One side of the morada was the secret inner room of the Order, the other the chapel where public services were held. The inner room could be seen only by guarded invitation when the Penitentes were not using it. It was a bare, whitewashed room with a few chairs and a pine table. A row of disciplinas hung on the wall—whips made of sharp-edged Spanish bayonet whose fiber cuts the skin. To make penance doubly sure bits of flint and glass were knotted into the fiber. On one side of the room the dirt floor was mudded up into a shallow trough with an opening through the wall. The Penitente crouched there while his wounds were washed with an herb tea. Near it was a pile of the sharp grains of quartz brought in from an ant hill. On Friday nights the Penitentes crawled back and

forth over the sand-strewn path, forgetting their bleeding knees.

Through the partition a door led into the chapel, its simple altar set with candles and saints' statues. Artificial flowers decorated it in that cold month before the Easter anemones dared to peep forth. To the right there was a gruesome crucifix with the blood from the wound in Christ's side gushing out in a red, realistic jet. In the shadows on the left a skeleton was seated in a low cart with solid wooden wheels. A black robe hung on his bony shoulders and his bleached arms held

221

a taut bow and a poisoned arrow. This was the car-
reta del muerto, the chariot of death, whose grim
driver was dragged over the rocky trails to visit other
moradas.

The first Friday night of Lent the Seal brands the
new members. The Hermano Mayor cuts his back at
the waistline with razor-edged obsidian, three times up
and three times across. As the blood streams from it
the initiate begs for the "Seven times Christ spoke
from the Cross," "the five wounds," "the forty days
in the wilderness." Each petition calls for a like
number of lashes, stinging his torn back. The mind
may have reached that state of exaltation where it
invites such agony, but the body is too weak to endure
it. Fasting, loss of blood, and emotional strain are
too much, and the new Penitente often falls into merciful unconsciousness. But when he revives, he pleads
that the Passion service continue to the end.

Lenten rites are a preparation for the climax of
Holy Week. On Wednesday and Thursday there are
pilgrimages to distant Calvarios. The reader walks
slowly ahead reading the story of the last days of
Christ. Penitentes follow dragging their crosses on
their bare shoulders. A blanket over their backs and
a black bag over their heads give them anonymous
protection. Each Penitente is guarded by an officer
who lifts the cross from crushing the initiate when he
staggers under it, and raises it to his shoulder again
when he is able to go on. A group of black-shawled
women and bareheaded men follow behind them, carry-

ing the statues of the Mater Dolorosa and the faithless disciples to take part in the services at the Cross.

I can never forget the deep, monotonous chant punctuated by the thud of whips on human bodies as a file of Penitentes came down a worn trail in the mysterious darkness. Scurrying clouds, driven from the icy Truchas peaks, dimmed the moonlight. The wind was so cold that it pierced my heavy coat but the exhausted Penitent Brothers were exposed to it through the long night, naked save for the short white trunks. Each slow step brought them nearer. There was no deception about those heavy thuds as the disciplinas were raised now over the left shoulder, now over the right, the strength of fanatic zeal marking every step. We were near enough to see the ends of the whips matted with blood and freezing in the wind. Other Penitentes, exhausted from fasting and pain, crawled up the trail on their hands and knees, their burden of crosses giving forth a torturous, low scraping as they were slowly dragged along. Like a starved wraith another followed, chains cutting into his bare ankles, branches of the thousand-needled cactus bound to his arms and his head pierced with a crown of thorns. Last of all came the Pitero, the shrill dirge of his flute rising above earth like the lingering wail of all human agony.

Thursday night the morada chapel was open for the "Tiniebias," that sudden darkening of the world which terrified the Roman soldiers after they had crucified Christ. Now it came before the Crucifixion, with the dramatic emphasis of piling up crises toward the great

223

climax. The flagelantes stayed in the inner room doing penance. The narrow chapel was packed with men and women kneeling or sitting on the floor. The Oficiales stood between them before the crude altar, responding to the litany as it was read by the Hermano Mayor. One by one the twelve candles on the high triangular candlestick were put out as the Elder Brother read of the Master's desertion by each of His disciples after the watch in the Garden of Gethsemane. When the last disciple failed Him and the last candle was snuffed out, the chapel was a chasm of stifling, crowded blackness. Not even starlight penetrated through the heavy-curtained window. Then the pandemonium of Judgment Day broke loose. Men, worked up to a frantic fury, grabbed people by the hair, forcing them to stand. Anything might happen in that seething darkness. Women fainted, others crouched against the wall in fear of being trampled. It was a mob scene of terrifying realism. From the far room there came the thud, thud, thud of Penitente whips, mingled with clanking chains, tin thundering against tin, and the earthquake roar of the wooden matraca. Nearby were the high-pitched prayers of women for their loved ones in purgatory, cries of frightened children, the deep rumble of men chanting and, above the black chaos, the unearthly note of the reed pito.

It seemed hardly an hour. until dawn blessed the world with light again—hardly an hour's respite for those Penitentes filing out of the morada for the Procession of Blood. We crouched behind stone cemetery walls in the chill of early morning, shivering from cold and prolonged emotion. The two moradas had combined for this final act, with forty-two flagelantes walking down the trail. Each step was marked with the blows of the disciplinas. At a level stretch of the trail overlooking an arroyo they stopped, turned their backs to us and raised their whips in the unison of forty-two torturing thuds. In the cold blue light they made a human pattern of emaciated white bodies, splotched with streaming blood, against the evergreen mountains. We closed our eyes, but the scene was etched in our minds for all time, and the thud, thud, thud of the disciplinas went on.

They had drawn lots the night before for the Crucifixion. The Procession of Blood filed on to the Calvario. A large cross lay beside a hole dug in the frozen earth. A Penitente stretched himself upon it while others bound his wrists and ankles to the arms of the cross. The living crucifix was raised in the hole and propped firmly with stones. Though the Cristo's head was covered with a dark cloth, there were black-shawled women near the cross who knew him for son and husband. With shawls drawn over their quivering lips they watched his head droop over his sagging body. Those below him began their prayers and low chanting. The Cristo hung there during the long, still minutes that ran beyond the half hour. Finally his chest slumped forward and a purple tinge covered his unconscious body. The cross was lowered slowly, the ropes loosened and the body borne gently toward the morada. The men and women around the cross melted away to prepare for the resurrection of Easter.

This was the last Crucifixion which has been publicly witnessed for many years. In some placitas an effigy of the Cristo carries on the drama, at others the Crucifixion takes place within the privacy of the morada or at some far mountain Calvario. If death comes for the Cristo, his shoes are sent home to console his family with promises of eternal happiness in Heaven.

Other folk plays in New Mexico have no touch of this grim realism but tell of the miracles of love. The Christmas play of the shepherds, "Los Pastores," and "The Apparition of Our Lady of Guadalupe" belong to the Golden Age of Spanish drama. During this Siglo de Oro, Lope de Rueda drew upon Bible stories and legends of the saints to found the Spanish theater. The plays were performed on movable stages set up before the churches where a great crowd might watch them. Priests encouraged the performances since they told a bookless people the history of the church.

At the time when Lope de Vega and Shakespeare were writing the great plays of Spain and England, the Spanish colonials were moving into their Casas Reales in Santa Fe. There they set up a Teatro de Corral near the Plaza. Possibly some of the manuscripts of Lope de Vega may have been packed away in the baggage of colonists from Andalusia or revived from memory to be played on the open theater of a horse lot in a distant province of New Spain.

"Los Pastores" and "The Apparition of Our Lady," which have had the longest run of any plays on the American stage, are both shepherd plays. Since New Mexico was a pastoral land, these shepherd dramas were deeply cherished and presented yearly through three centuries. Almost every grassy mountain pasture has a cross set up to bless it. Shepherds know so well the solitude of long sunny days following their sheep, the lilac-misted twilights when any miracle might happen, the starlit nights when a flute may sing to the flock and keep away the prowling coyotes. In such a setting shepherd plays were understood and beloved, reflecting the life and faith of simple people.

No one knows how long "Los Pastores" has been played in Santa Fe. The few dog-eared manuscripts bear no date. They were written in copy books, almost illegible in old Spanish letters and confusing in the rudimentary knowledge of spelling the language of Don Quixote. Manuscripts were little needed for the performance, however, for the same men took the same parts year after year, and handed them down by word o' mouth to their sons. Memory transcribed "Los Pastores" so faithfully that even the twentieth century version has the quaintness and form of the miracle plays of the sixteenth century. It is also a Spanish cousin to the "Second Shepherd" play of the Townley cycle, which was performed for the delight of kings and paupers in pre-Elizabethan England. It is like an old court garment put to rough uses in a far land, stained, torn and patched, yet retaining much of the richness of its original satin.

Imagination was not limited by movie photography in 1600. With no back drops, the audience was able to imagine the scene of the plains around Bethlehem from familiarity with their own winter pastures. Even twenty years ago the play was given with the Elizabethan simplicity which is the goal of stagecraft to-day. The players took their places in the center of the hall, not divided from the audience by a raised stage or footlights. Their long journey was suggested by tramping around and around the cleared space, carrying the thread of the drama in their long singsong verses. Hell's mouth was nothing more than a black curtain pulled aside to show the red glare of burning brimstone, the manger a little statue in a crib surrounded by toy oxen and asses. The star of Bethlehem was a candle set in a lantern and pulled across the stage by a rope. There was equally open machinery for the miraculous appearance of the angel announcing the nacimiento and St. Michael coming to fight the devil. They descended from Heaven in a box lowered from the rafters, and neighbors offered interested comments if the pulley stuck. Even the devil had the character of a hard-working young fellow who always got the worst of it, in keeping with his interpretation in old morality plays.

"Los Pastores" was given in long, bare dance halls with kerosene sconces lighting the whitewashed walls.

A stove made the room hot after the outside chill of
the winter night, but the fire gradually died down when
the firemen forgot to put in more wood in the excitement of the play. The benches along the side walls
were crowded with dark-eyed mothers and chubby children, exclaiming over everything in soft Spanish. The
far end of the room was packed with standing men and
boys. On a raised platform at the other end there
was the cradle of the Santo Niño. Between acts good
children were allowed to shyly kiss the rosy, waxen
Baby when it was passed among the audience for homage and offerings.

The Pastores marched into the cleared space between the rows of neighbors and friends wearing white
cambric suits with ruffled sailor collars and short
trousers. A tiny beribboned pillow slung over each
shoulder suggested the shepherd's bed. Each carried
a tall crook, festooned with pink tarlatan and small
tinkling bells. They were accompanied by their cook,
Gila, a serious little girl in a white dress and veil who
sometimes doubled the part of the Madonna. They
marched up and down singing verses about their sleeping flocks, the wondrous new star in the Heavens and
the story they had heard of Mary and "that carpenter
José." After they had camped for the night, an angel
descended from a wooden box lowered from the ceiling. He woke the shepherds to tell them to hurry to
see the Christ child who had just been born in a manger
in "Belén." They spoke wonderingly of the prophecy
that a Saviour would come into the world and planned

gifts to take to the Babe. They began the journey to Belén, following the star drawn along the vigas by a cord, and singing a lullaby:

> Oh, sleep, sweet Child of Heaven
> Who cometh from above,
> That Thy Mother may caress Thee
> In the tender arms of love.
> Singing á la rú, á la me
> A la rú, á la me, á la rú.

In the second act a red flare burst from the end of the room. With clanging of bells and clashing of swords Lucifer dashed out of Hell's mouth. He overtook the Pastores and, enraged at their mission, urged them to turn back with all his devil's wiles. He appeared in different guises, now as a black man, now as a bewhiskered Englishman, now as a helmeted Conquistador, now as a sheep and finally as the true diablo with the long tail, and horns sprouting from his forehead. Between acts he jumped into the audience with a deal of clowning, holding up a little mirror to get a smile from pretty girls and taking down their names in his hell-bent note book. Children shrank back from him and crossed themselves.

A hoary hermit had joined the pilgrimage, brandishing his cross and large rosary at the Devil in slapstick comedy. In his many guises the Devil had almost persuaded the entire party to turn back. Then a box was lowered again and a small boy dressed as the shining St. Michael with cotton wings and a tinsel crown charged into a fight with the Devil. The Pastores watched the fight, as stupid as their sheep. Now St. Michael was uppermost, now the Devil. Finally the saintly sword pierced the Devil and a small foot was pressed down on his poor head.

In the third act the Pastores started on their way again but found the lazy shepherd, Bartolo, had fallen asleep during the fight. He refused to move from his sheepskin pelt, even to see the Christ child. With his long beard, huge shambling feet and mighty yawns, he was a predecessor of Shakespeare's fools. He and the overpious Hermit made the most of clowning, interspersing the original lines with ribald jokes which brought guffaws from the audience.

Finally the Pastores arrived before the cradle, each bearing his gift and presenting it with a long prayer to the Child. At the end they returned to their flocks, striking their crooks on the floor to the beat of string music so that their songs were accompanied by the tinkling of bells.

> Farewell, Joseph, farewell, Mary,
> Farewell, gentle Child.
> Give to us a benediction
> From Thy Lamb, so mild.
> Grant life and health the coming year
> In our mountains wild.

"Los Pastores" is still played in Santa Fe between the feast of Guadalupe and the Twelfth Night after Christmas. The quaint old props are no longer used in presenting it in the St. Francis Auditorium or in a hall down on Agua Fría Road, but the lines and acting are true to the old version. Before the lure of movies encroached upon it, the play ran continuously for the three holiday weeks. Three or four casts presented it in different parts of town at the same time, vying with each other for the best production. Neighbors made the rounds to see other companies, but usually returned for a nightly attendance at the play in their own placita.

Before Christmas another miracle play of "The Apparition of Our Lady of Guadalupe" is given to celebrate her fiesta, December 12. It is like a sixteenth century "Comedia de Santo" by Lope de Vega, a dramatized legend of a saint. This legend, however, originated in Mexico in the year 1531, a century before the Spanish dramatist presented his plays in Spain.

It tells of a poor shepherd boy named Juan Diego who was out in the hills of Tepeyac tending his sheep. He was driving his flock toward the home corral in the early December twilight. Drifts of sunset clouds filled the sky, like rose leaves in a blue bowl. The ringing of vesper bells in the village mingled with the bleating of lambs and the tinkling call of the bellwethers. One lamb strayed away to nibble the last blades of summer grass and Juan Diego climbed the rocks after it. A light sprang out of the rocks and a radiant apparition of the Virgin, clad in robes of gold and rose and azure, stood before him. A sweet voice spoke to him, saying: "Juan Diego, go to thy Bishop and tell

232

him to build a shrine for me here on this hill where I now stand. Tell him that I have sent thee, and that the shrine must be named for Our Lady of Guadalupe, after Her shrine in Spain."

Juan Diego ran to the village, told the Bishop of his heavenly visitor and gave him her message. But the pompous Bishop scoffed that so great a Lady should deign to speak to a poor shepherd. Juan Diego was reproved harshly and warned to dream no more or his sheep would stray away.

The boy had almost lost faith in his vision when at the next twilight a light shone in his path and the Virgin appeared before him again. She asked him what the Bishop had said. Trembling with fear, Juan Diego stammered that the Bishop would not believe him. The Lady sent him back with a second command. But Juan Diego was thought to be bewitched and a guard set to watch his actions.

The third evening when the light appeared surrounding Our Lady, Juan Diego fell to his knees sobbing, "The Bishop will not believe me, Oh, Mother of God! He requires a sign that I am not visited by evil spirits."

"Go up the hill and gather roses, my son," she told him.

To his astonishment he found that white June roses, the "flores de María," covered the rocks in the bleak December weather. He plucked them until he had filled his tilma, a poor ragged blanket such as peones wear. When he came back to the Apparition, she folded the blanket with care so that none of the roses might fall out.

"Go, Juan Diego, and give thy tilma only to the Bishop," she said to him.

He ran to the palace and placed his tilma before the Bishop, telling him that the Lady of the Apparition had sent her roses as a sign.

When the Bishop opened the tilma, the roses tumbled out, luminously white and fragrant. Then the Bishop fell to his knees, for there upon the inside of the blanket was a painting of Our Lady of Guadalupe just as she had appeared to the shepherd. Her robes were of gold and rose and azure, rays of light surrounded her from her head to her toes, and a cherub rested under the crescent moon at her feet.

The Bishop lost no time in building a shrine for Our Lady of Guadalupe on the rocky hillside, for she had honored his country by visiting it herself. The miraculous painting on the tilma was placed above the altar. To this day love gives it the power to perform miracles for the many pilgrims who climb the hillside to pray before it.

The play of the Apparition of Our Lady of Guadalupe closely follows the legend of four hundred years ago. Simple theatrical lighting makes the most of the vision and a madonna-eyed girl plays the lead. The Bishop is haughty in his purple robes, and the sympathy of the audience is with Juan Diego in the faith of his heavenly visitor.

Folk plays in New Mexico are like old Chimayó

blankets. The patterns and colors of the woof are of the new land, but the warp is made of the beliefs and military triumphs which insured Spanish supremacy. In the sixteenth century, miracle plays were rivaled by war dramas. Racial pride was overflowing with the joy of the Christian victor over the hated Moorish infidel and, as always in Spain, national emotion was transferred to the stage. The Christian-infidel plays were as popular then as the doughboy drama is with us to-day. They had even a longer run, for the feud between the cross and the crescent had lasted for eight hundred years with Spain as the dueling ground.

At last Ferdinand and Isabella had driven the Moorish rulers to their last stronghold, the Palace of the Alhambra in the city of Granada. Defiantly facing Granada across the plain, the Spanish rulers set up a luxurious tent city. Isabella chose to call the place Santa Fe for the holy faith in their cause.

Here silken tents were raised for the King and Queen and Court. The richest brocades and satins were used for awnings, until it had more of the appearance of a silken palace than a stern war camp. The tent of the Queen was an immense velvet canopy, divided into apartments with embroidered curtains and screens. One night as Isabella was kneeling before the altar in her private chapel at her evening devotions, the wind blew the draperies too near the lighted candles, and in a moment the royal tent was ablaze. Almost before the court could rush out of their apartments, the silken city was in flames. Ferdinand, fearing that the Moors might take advantage of this disaster, began at once to build a new and permanent city of Santa Fe on the site of the blackened camp. Here the court resided until in 1492 the Moors, prisoners within the Alhambra and overcome by famine, gave up the keys of Granada to Ferdinand.

Columbus came back to present a new world to Isabella at the court in Santa Fe. It was the year when Granada was celebrating "The Day of the Taking"— "El Día de la Toma," with a play called "Ave María." This was the epic story of the Spaniards finally driving out the Moors. Ever since then, the Día de la Toma has been annually remembered in Granada.

A century later, the first play presented on American soil, of which we have any record, was called "Los Moros," a drama of the defeat of the Moors. It was given by Oñate's colonists at their first camp on the Rio Grande in the year 1598. Like the play of the Day of the Taking, it showed the Spaniards on horseback rushing into battle with the scimitared Moors, killing them and leading off the captives in chains. For three centuries it was one of the traditional dramas of Santa Cruz de la Cañada, only twelve miles from the original camp of Oñate and one of the three Christian settlements in New Mexico during the seventeenth century.

Old men have recalled the parts they played in their youth and even retrieved worn manuscripts to revive "Los Moros" for twentieth century fiestas. When it is presented now on a warm July day, it is a jumble of men on cow ponies, charging at each other with raised

236

lances, dressed according to their ideas of Moorish and Spanish soldiers. The broad, brown mesa is a setting that might have been transplanted from the plains below the Alhambra. The lines of the play are lost in the skirmish, and probably the reasons of the historic feud are lost on the actors, but actors and audience continue to delight in the dust-raising bout the occasion offers.

The romance of the Middle Ages, when crusaders battled with infidels for the sacred shrines of the Holy Land, is woven into a play called "The Return of the Crusaders," "La Vuelta de la Cruzada." Although it was probably written during the romantic period of the early nineteenth century in Spain, it is worthy of the genius of Lope de Vega or Calderón. It has the same plot as "Il Trovatore," the story of a crusader who returned from his pilgrimage to find that his betrothed was the faithful wife of a stay-at-home.

"Los Comanches" is a folk play with another war theme, but it is essentially of the far western locale. The Spaniards and the Comanches are antagonists in this seventeenth century colonial drama, and since Cuerno Verde was the war cacique of the Comanches, his name is sometimes given to the many versions of the play. Two Spanish children, a boy and a girl, have been stolen by the Indian raiders. The Spaniards attack the Comanches and rescue the children, ending with the solemn moment when the great Cuerno Verde submits to the defeat of his tribe. For it is an axiom of playwriting, from the siege of Troy to "What Price

Glory?", that the home boy must always be victorious.

"Los Matachines" is unique for many reasons, but especially so because it is the only drama which is given by both the Pueblo Indians and the Spanish-speaking people. The Indians had perfected their own impressive nature dramas long before the colonists first gave "Los Moros." Being religious ceremonies, strict adherence to ritual has left them almost unchanged. But the Indians were quick to burlesque the plays and manners of the bearded Europeans who came into their country. These redmen were not stoical statues, but often laughing children who loved to mimic and joke. "Los Matachines" provided a diversion for them, combining a morality play probably colored with their own interpretation. In Mexico, it is a version of the legend of Montezuma. In New Mexico, there are certain figures, costumes and movements in the weird Yeibitchai chant of the Navajos which are strangely like the masque of the Matachines. Whether this resemblance is accidental, or whether one might have influenced the other, is a question to be ferreted out by ethnologists, but the effect of both primitive dramas is curiously alike.

Christmas morning at San Juan Pueblo or at Cochití finds the Indians giving their version of "Los Matachines," while at many fiestas it is presented in the Spanish manner. It is a morality play of the struggle between Good and Evil combined with a hopping dance that goes on and on like an endless Virginia reel. Virtue, in her white dress and veil, dances up and down between two rows of men whose costumes combine flapping white cotton drawers, fringed and flowered shawls, and high peaked caps with veils and ribbons floating behind. The bridal Virtue trips back and forth, dividing her smiles between two gay Evil Spirits who finally kill each other. Then Virtue, gaining only an old maid's reward, is seated on a throne to impart wisdom to her subjects.

A fiddle and a guitar keep a jiggety tune going, which plays itself over and over in your head for days afterwards. The veils and mitered caps give it an exotic Moorish note, while the white-robed Virgin is of the Christian symbolism. It is a dim combining of paganism and Catholicism: a morality masque grafted with the influence of Moors and Indians; Indian actors, not in their fine athletic nudity, but swathed in makeshift European costumes; a victory of puritan Virtue, but not the Indian's happy, fruitful Earth Mother.

Besides these traditional plays, there were numbers of simple dramas given during the holidays or at fiestas. In the old days, each placita had its own Little Theater group to provide amusement for the long winter evenings. Some were faintly remembered versions of such old dramas as "El Auto de los Reyes Magos," for this allegory of the Three Kings from the East was the first play written in the Spanish language. During the long centuries since then, parts of it have been forgotten and only 168 verses are found in the New Mexico version.

Another play, the Lost Child, "El Niño Perdido.'

shows the life of Christ from the time when the boy of twelve was lost in the temple through the unrecorded years until He was a man of thirty. Mexican influence is apparent here in the added incidents of the Noche Triste tree.

Other plays bear witness to the transplanted love of drama that flowered in New Mexico from purely native roots. They are naïve interpretations of Bible stories and saints' legends. There is the first crime and murder in "Cain and Abel" and the age-old struggle between Good and Evil in "Lucifer and San Miguel."

"Adam and Eve" is still presented in a quiet, golden-walled placita not far from Albuquerque to the delight of the numerous family of Candelarias who make up the entire citizenry of the village. Children are chosen from birth for the rôles of Adam and Eve and play them until they marry. The Garden of Eden is a simple stage with the apple and fig trees resembling small, tapering piñones. The serpent tempts Eve, and she munches the apple con tanto gusto that Adam snatches the forbidden fruit away from her after the first juicy bite. Then God appears and scolds them in a terrible booming voice. He shames them for their nakedness, though Adam and Eve appear to be fully clothed in overalls and a cotton dress. A little boy hangs two aprons on the piñon branches and the first Man and Woman shamefacedly pick the aprons off the "fig tree" and tie them around their waists.

About 1790 the old Spanish custom of Christmas

players going from house to house seeking lodging took the dramatized form of "Las Posadas" in this province of New Spain. On Christmas Eve, Joseph and Mary, riding a burro, stopped before nine blue doorways before they found shelter at an inn. "Las Posadas" is part of the celebration of the starlit Noche Buena in placitas tucked away in the folds of high mountains, distant enough to depend upon their own customs and the pleasure of acting out the story of the weary couple who were quartered at last in a stable.

As the years brought freckled strangers into the Land of Poco Tiempo history became homemade drama. There is a sly, humorous slant to such plays as "La Lluvia delos Ingleses," "The Showers of Englishmen" and the burlesque of the coming of the Americans. Since that time, there have been quaint renderings of Anglo plays seen by some paisano who had journeyed to the "big towns." Later a home talent show was based upon a vividly retold scenario by some one who had gazed at a movie.

The Spanish colonials and their children's children have an inherent love of play acting and a racial ability for dramatic interpretation. But now, except in the back country, the marvel of movies has made them unfortunately self-conscious about producing their original folk plays. The younger generation hardly remembers them. It will take another period of encouragement to restore the native Little Theater pride—if it has not faded out by that time in the blare of radios and talkies.

If you want to see the modern Spanish-Americans really enjoying themselves, go to one of the plays given by a Mexican troupe who have come up the Chihuahua Trail to El Paso del Norte and then on to that most Spanish-loving place, Santa Fe. The one-week engagement stretches into six, and still the house is packed with olive-skinned people who come there as naturally as bees come to honey. Their joy in a play all in their own idiom, their loud laughter at their own kinds of jokes, their Latin "vivas" and eager applause is a homesick symptom.

The plays in the repertory are a combination of *East Lynn* melodrama, French bedroom farce, Spanish stock characters, buffoonery, songs and dances, and the laughter which is always ready to sparkle in any dark eye. The actors are a family group, charming in their flowery phrases and graceful manners.

Or go to hear the Orquesta Típica Fronteriza, here on tour from Mexico City. Half a hundred singers wear peaked Mexican sombreros and silver-braided velvet suits. The soft wail of a marimba or a stringed orchestra accompanies such beloved songs as "Cielito Lindo" or "Viejo Amor." The first familiar bars of the march "Queja Pampera" is greeted with shouts and stamping pleasure. Then, to live up to its advertisement, the Típica Band plays modern "jazz con acento Español!" Later the house resounds to "La Paloma" and "La Golondrina." Girls come out in China Poblana costumes to dance the fandango, and the audience breathes a long Latin sigh when the last encore is over.

I always remember that we Anglos have taken over another's land and substituted our ways for ancient customs when I watch that audience. No doubt we have brought necessary progress, but there is always a question and blush for the intruder. Mexican plays, orchestras and circuses make me glad that exiles have this yearly treat in their own ways and language.

N.V.S

X

The Crafts of the Spanish Colonials

IT is a rare experience to be seated at dinner in New Mexico and discover that the service plates, goblets and candlesticks are the solid Spanish silver of past centuries. It reminds us that the Spanish colonial has given America quite as precious a heritage as the English colonial. In many respects this heritage is of a richer flavor than that of the abstemious Puritans, for Spain reveled in the fleshpots which the world paid in tribute to a commanding nation. Her colonials brought these treasures and traditions to the western wilderness. There they created a new culture by adapting their training to native materials.

The Conquistadores were captained by noblemen who left Mexico City in the arrogant splendor befitting knights of Spain. Like the Englishmen who spread British sovereignty to-day by carrying their bathtubs and dinner coats into African jungles, the Conquistadores were a de luxe foreign legion, subduing the wilderness by culture and faith as well as military force.

Though their long treks lasted many months they had no intention of "traveling light." Crude carretas del rey were piled high with the luxuries of the day. These "king's carts" had crate-like wagon beds and heavy wooden wheels, rounded out from the solid trunks of cottonwood trees. The wheels bulged toward the center where the wooden, greaseless axle groaned and creaked with every labored turn. But eventually the rich cargoes were unloaded in Santa Fe and the Casas Reales gleamed with silver services, which caught the warm hues of brocades hung on simple, whitewashed walls.

When Don Juan de Oñate started for the "conquest and pacification of the provinces of New Mexico, May 19, 1597," his Captain, Luis de Velasco, made an inventory of the Governor's personal equipment. The list included one suit of blue Italian velvet; two suits of lustrous Castilian satin, one of rose with a short gray cape, and the other straw-color slashed with scarlet taffeta; two cloth suits, one of purple Castilian and the other chestnut London cloth; and one suit of flowered Chinese silk. Each of these was elaborately embroidered with wide gold and silver passementerie, and had doublets, cloaks and long, silk hose to match. Garters must have been an important accessory, for they are minutely described with "points of gold lace" and colors to correspond with each costume. He had doublets of kid and royal lion skin, two Rouen linen shirts, six Rouen linen handkerchiefs, six pairs of

Rouen linen breeches with their socks, eight pairs of Cordovan leather boots, sixteen pairs of shoes, and six pairs of spurs, besides Moorish ones with tassels and silk cord. His large hats were of black, gray, or purple taffeta, trimmed with silver cord and plumes. For any real fighting he could protect himself and his two bodyguards with complete suits of armor.

Like a sheik of the desert he carried fifty yards of Michoacán bindweed for a tent with all the appurtenances for setting it up; one bed with two mattresses, a coverlet, sheets, pillows and pillow cases, and a canvas bedding roll bound with sole leather. His personal retinue included thirty war horses and two saddle mules. There were four saddles of Cordovan leather with housings of blue flowered Spanish cloth, three sets of horse armor of buckskin, two shields and one gilded dagger.

Since Velasco left this itemized list of what the well dressed man wore in those days, we wonder how the satin and velvet and gold lace garters stood the dust of long, desert marches? And where was his bathtub? Oxcarts probably carried a large solid silver tub and dinner service as well as the resplendent wardrobe.

The taffeta and plumes disappeared long ago but silver wash basins, pitchers and plate have been unearthed in forgotten villages and form priceless collections of Spanish colonial days. One of these silver basins is as large as a modern washtub, fluted like a shell from brim to bottom. The same pattern is carried out on smaller scales for hand basins and pitchers.

There are many solid silver trays with hinged handles, mugs of all sizes for the vino del país and bowls as varied as rich, Spanish food. The silver plates are of the same dimension but each is an individual pattern in the slight variation of the scalloped pie plate edges. Heavy spoons and forks show that they were different generations of the same family, for the tines of the forks still retain the curving lines of the spoon bowl. The few knives were used for butchering in the kitchen, since it was considered vulgar to cut meat at table.

The texture of this old silver sends a connoisseur into raptures. It was sturdy stuff, meant for long use, but executed with the beauty of design and finish of master silversmiths who learned their art from the Florentines. Most of the plate bears the quinta hallmark of Spanish silver, the one-fifth per cent charged by the Crown for labeling it as of the proper weight. After centuries of buffeting pack trips and garrison banquets, of being thrown out on ash heaps to be replaced by thick, white china, it retains a luster and craftsmanship that have seldom been excelled.

After the Spanish colonials were settled permanently in the river valleys, they began to fashion their own silverware from the plentiful ore in the Mexican mines. This is known as Rio Grande silver and is recognized by simpler lines and a peasant quality. Some of it has been hammered out within the memory of living grandmothers. Doña Mercedes showed me the cup, spoon and fork which her father had made for her before she started away to school. Five decades ago the

child traveled six weeks in a stagecoach to reach Missouri and another week to the convent in Philadelphia. After such a journey she stayed at school for three years before returning to her parents. Her cup, spoon and fork must have been extra precious as mementos of her distant home.

The houses of the ricos gleamed, not only with dinner services and candlesticks, but with solid silver picture frames, household ornaments and chandeliers. They filled the eyes of the pobres with envy. And the pobres were never ones to do without those things which gave significance to life. To do without riches, time-and-space-eating machines, artificial amusements, yes—for what did they really matter? But to do without those arts colored by tradition—never! If they could not afford the originals, their ingenuity fashioned something equally as decorative to take their place. Tin became the silver of the pobres.

Tin chandeliers, sconces and frames copied the patterns of solid silver. The color was as satisfying as the more expensive metal, and tin was even easier to bend and cut into the traditional shapes. That heavy tin, darkened with a patina of time and rust, is easily distinguished from the lighter metal of to-day, containing only a fraction of tin.

Native craftsmen delighted in punching star-pointed sconces, fluting the surface and adding enough bright touches of paint to make the whole look like a silver-framed bouquet around a mirror. Candeleros had a fluted drip pan around the candle holder and a tall tin

back, rounded like a narrow church window, to keep the flame from blackening white walls. Candils hung from the vigas with holders for fifty home-dipped tallow candles, a more thrilling sight than a 100-watt bulb to-day. Old lanterns used the Spanish crown at the top, and the curving side panels suggested Moorish arches. These were glazed originally with mica and later with the much coveted glass. Elaborate motifs, patterned after the silver frames of the ricos, bordered mirrors, colored prints and saints' pictures.

Small tin shrines held the bulto of San Antonio or the Virgin of Guadalupe, sometimes gay with paint, sometimes tooled with the punching and fluting of the metal. Glass doors and sides protected the saints' dresses and the delicate dyed feather flowers surround-ing them.

Tinsmithing goes on here to-day in the little shops of Eduardos and Franciscos. These craftsmen have lost none of their sense of design and proportion nor the joy of the creator. One may order sconces, frames, chandeliers with insets of mirror to reflect the lights, or pick up frames made a century ago. I have one whose three-inch frame is made of waved strips of tin, a bit rusty now. In the center there is a pen and ink sketch of a diminutive Santo Niño de Atocha with shining flakes of gold in his high hat, cape and basket of flowers. Around the picture there is a wide border of what I suspect to be blue wall paper with shaded pink roses.

Before wall paper was used for borders, flowers

249

and zigzag stripes of color were painted on the inside of the glass, perhaps in imitation of tortoise shell.

In keeping with the silver services and picture frames, the gente fina decked themselves with sumptuous jewels imported from Europe and Mexico. For the great balls in the Palace of the Governors, they wore black pearls set in enameled bracelets, square diamonds in stomachers, cabochon emeralds, pearl and coral chokers, jeweled combs and fans. Their rosaries and crucifixes were of jet, onyx and amethyst.

But most of the New Mexicans had only their native gold and silver jewelry as treasured ornaments. Even the most ragged pobres had a few heirlooms locked away in a battered jewel chest. These might be "memoria" rings, given when some daughter had departed from Spain, or puzzle rings with four or five strands of gold wire twisted together and the secret of untwisting them part of the lasting remembrance. Betrothal rings were wide bands with a relief of hearts, grapes and leaves. The leaves were delicately veined in green gold and, by adding enough copper alloy, the locked hearts and grapes stood out in red gold. Lockets of this favorite design concealed miniatures and strands of hair. Clasps for braided gold bracelets, watch chains and necklaces were ornamented with birds and flowers finely cut in the shaded gold.

Added to these were gold and silver filigree, representing savings accounts as well as jewels. Since the gold and silver had only enough alloy to hold it together, filigree could be exchanged for the weight of the metal in times of need. Its price is still measured by the pennyweight, not reckoning the goldsmith's long labor in fashioning it.

Santa Fe became, and has remained, the fountain head for all filigree made north of Mexico. It is a guild of the Middle Ages, where the art descends from father to son, succeeding generations inheriting a patience and sensitiveness for the intricate work. At first, ingots of gold for the jewelers were packed up the Chihuahua Trail on burros. Later filigree received an added impetus from the pure gold found in the placer mines almost at Santa Fe's front door.

Like that street in Lisbon which is given over entirely to filigree makers, you will find goldsmiths at work to-day in shops on San Francisco Street. If you are interested, you will be courteously invited to see Antonio "make hearts"—those romantic lockets of a romantic people. You may be astonished at the simplicity of Antonio's tools, for on his high bench there are only pliers, a bottle of borax and a small blowpipe. There is no mathematically spaced diagram for the delicate pattern before him. He plans the design in his mind and depends upon exactness of eyes and the deft play of pliers to produce the golden fretwork. Gold is melted into small bars and drawn through gauges. The last gauge is set with sapphires and the gold is turned out as fine as horsehair. Two of these gold hairs are twisted together and flattened between steel rollers to give them the serrated edges. Then a narrow gold rim is made as a foundation, and the wires bent and soldered until the fancy of the goldsmith completes the gold lace.

Besides making hearts, Antonio may be working upon a brooch of the old gautchapourri design with tiny rosettes surmounted by a wee gold ball; or "coquetas," earrings with fringes of flat, twisted, gold dangles which suggest coquettes and generals' epaulettes; or "arracadas," the crescent earrings to gleam beneath black hair; or a bracelet of leaves to circle a slender wrist; or the minute hinged scales of the golden fish of San Rafael, fashioned so cleverly that the fish's body twists as though it were living.

Weaving was one of the earliest American arts. It had been evolved by the Indians from indigenous cotton plants long before white men came here. Our first record of primitive weaving goes back to 1540 and the entrada of Coronado. Pedro de Castañeda, who kept the diary for the explorer, wrote of the Zuñis and Hopis "clothed in fine robes woven from cotton" and of blankets of loosely woven strips of rabbit skin.

While the craft of weaving was the Indian's own invention, the innovation of weaving with wool was the Spaniard's contribution. When Oñate and his colonists drove herds of sheep up the trail in 1598, they started the sheep and wool industry in New Mexico. They soon taught Indian slaves to pluck wool from the sheep by hand, spin and weave it.

History was woven into the blankets which then developed in the Southwest. They were records of

Europe and America contending against each other for the ownership of tawny deserts and blue mountains. The web told of scalping raids, and the woof of hostage slaves. The unaggressive Pueblos gave in to the Conquerors, and woolen weaving was incorporated into their art. But the roving Navajos resented this passive acceptance, while they coveted the new, warm blankets. They swooped down on Pueblos and Spaniards and pillaged every blanket they could find. Indian word-o'-mouth history has it that the Navajos finally agreed to stop the raids if the Hopis and Zuñis would teach them to weave. So the now famous Navajo blanket began as a treaty of peace, and afterwards was discarded as wantonly as a "scrap of paper."

From that time, weaving took on the typical divergence of the two races. Where such tribes as the Navajo were only nominally conquered, they continued to use their crude upright looms, weaving heavy yarn into their own primitive designs. Where the Spaniards dominated and intermingled with the Pueblos the horizontal hand looms of Europe were used with finer yarn and a combination of Spanish and Indian designs. These blankets might be called mestizos—half breeds. They are a mixture of Indian technique altered by European looms and weaving. In some cases where a blanket has been woven by an Indian woman using a Spanish loom the combination of technique is so complete that it is hard to classify the blanket.

The fine woolen uniforms of the Caballeros were

fabrics equally as amazing to the Indians as the native cotton mantas were to the explorers. The bright red cochineal dye of this flannel, called bayeta, especially attracted the Indians. When they could find a discarded bit of bayeta they raveled the yarn, retwisted the threads and wove it into their own designs. These blankets of fine, tightly-woven yarn and rich colors are now known as the rare and priceless "Bayetas." They send collectors into ecstasies and have led to labeling many other blankets as "Bayetas." For as soon as the Spaniards saw that woolen cloth was in demand, they imported heavy Turkish flannel for the trade. Then cheaper baize was brought in from Germany and Austria, serge from England and cloth from Mexico and later flannel by Yankee traders of the Santa Fe Trail. Stormy discussion arises to-day over whether a blanket is or is not a "Bayeta." Each collector has his own cunning for proving that the yarn is of the original red cochineal dye and rewoven strands of Spanish uniforms.

In those early days there was no dividing line between the boundaries of Old and New Mexico. Spanish conquest intermingled everywhere with Indian culture in the Mexican provinces of the Spanish Indies. The crafts of the southern provinces crept up the trail to the north and the meager products of New Mexico went south in return. Such provinces as Chihuahua, Oaxaca, Yaqui, Saltillo and San Luis Potosí developed individual types of weaving. They were a characteristic trade mark of the Indian weavers of each locality, a custom which continues to-day throughout Mexico and Central America. Tradition has it that the captives in the prisons at Saltillo and San Luis Potosí vied with each other in weaving the best sarapes for the great blanket markets in those two places. The Saltillo sarape won lasting renown for its "star" design in the center, radiating in jagged edges of other rich colors, and woven as closely as cotton.

In Europe the Saltillos were recognized as being so valuable that imitations were made by printing the many colors on thin, white, woolen cloth. These printed sarapes crossed the seas and are to be found in New Mexico to-day where their transparent effect makes them look like stained-glass windows.

The craft of weaving developed as one of the highest arts of the eighteenth century in Mexico. Blankets for the Hidalgos, or for special occasions, were woven with threads of gold and silver filings. A flag of Maximilian shows the national colors in three wide bands. The green has an olive cast now, and the red is a deep wine color, while the Mexican eagle in the center band of white is crowned with a diadem of gold thread.

During the eighteenth century, herds of sheep had increased in New Mexico, but weaving was done almost entirely by Indians. The government decided to encourage the colonists to return to weaving in order to give the province a profitable industry and sent skilled weavers here from Spain and Mexico. Soon blankets formed a substantial part of the revenue of the great conductas which gathered all the products of the Rio Arriba and Rio Abajo to take them to the exciting annual fairs in Chihuahua and Durango.

The master weaver who arrived in Santa Fe in 1807 was a Spaniard named Don Ignacio Ricardo Bazán. He was a thorough instructor, from preparing the wool to weaving it. Though he insisted upon his Spanish technique, he compromised with the soap and dye of the country. The wool was shaken thoroughly to free it from sand and dirt, washed in foamy suds made from pounded amole root and spread upon the sage brush to dry and bleach. Then it was carded with wooden combs, rolled into balls and spun with a distaff until the yarn was fine and closely twisted. This left the wool in the natural shades of white, black, brown and gray. The black sheep was no longer the spurned outcast of the flock for his fleece gave the necessary emphasis of dark lines in the design.

But the delight of using color was as old as the Moorish influence in Spain. There were only two dyes which the Spanish imported—balls of añil, made from indigo, and Brazil wood which dyed the wool a rich mahogany. For other colors, the weavers adopted native dyes which the Indians brewed from shrubs, leaves and clay. Red was made from the bark of the tag alder, mountain mahogany and red ocher; black from the twigs of sumac and charcoal; yellow from golden blossoms of chamisa (rabbit brush) and yellow ocher; another blue was steeped from Hopi beans. Combinations of these dyes gave green, orange, violet and rose. The dye was tested by burning strands of wool. If the color was of a richness quite satisfactory, the dye was set with a mordant urine.

The first weaving frames were only two feet wide, making two narrow strips of blanket about eight feet long which were sewed together. Often a slit was left open in the center so that the sarape might be slipped over the head as a poncho. Men wore these gay striped blankets folded over their shoulder, ready to serve as jaunty scarfs, overcoats or bed rolls. When the wide looms came into use in later years the warp in the middle was often doubled for added strength and to give the old appearance of being joined together. When the blanket was finished, the woolen warp was cut into a fringe and knotted at either end.

Designs in the old blankets were always simple. They were often only horizontal bands varying in color, width and stitch. Yet each had as much individuality as the uniform pattern of our faces, and two were seldom alike. Even "twins" were rare, where the designs were alike but the color combinations reversed. There were wide bands of the favorite soft indigo contrasted with narrow bands of black, brown and white. There were bands of golden Brazil bordered with blue running into green and set off with brown basket weave stitch against a band of cream. Then there were the heart warming splashes of chile red in a diamond design with ripples of green, black and white. Sometimes the designs were influenced by the blankets of southern Mexico with bands running in diagonal, rainbow stripes meeting in the center and vibrating against each other in saw-toothed outlines. In others, the soiid white body of the blanket was broken with darts of black and insets of arrowheads joined at the point like Indian patterns.

This plastic craft gave the weavers a release into color and design which was part of their racial strain. Each sarape had the handmade quality of a weaver who delighted in creating new patterns. Standardization had not yet nullified them into duplicating an infinite number of the most popular blanket. The story of their lives went into the loom, with the smooth weaving of a good day and the bungling stitch of family quarrels. The blankets that came off the loom were as gay, somber, garish or harmonious as their weavers.

Though it is more than a century since Master Bazán instructed his pupils in this northern province, the native people still retain their hereditary craft sense. In Santa Fe, there are some fifty weavers plying their shuttles in adobe houses, while in Chimayó the guild of weavers follow their old and honorable occupation. At least one weaver may be found in almost any placita, bringing his blankets in trade to Santa Fe.

The name "Chimayó" for all blankets of this region probably came about from the fact that the weavers of Chimayó produced more blankets than those of any other locality. However, the trade mark "Chimayó" is said to have come into use only fifty years ago, sponsored by the forerunner of all curio dealers, Jake Gold. He first used the term in the same joking way the natives used it—"Chimayoso" meaning a country hick to the citified Santa Feans. In half a century the value and art of the country sarape lifted the name out of hickdom and into fame.

For many generations the craft has descended from father to son in Chimayó. Wives used to help with the spinning and dyeing, and daughters were errand girls, but the craft was the masculine trade for providing a livelihood. To-day one room in the adobe house is given over to the weavers and their looms. Sunshine floods in through the open door, catching the bright color in the shuttle as it dances to and fro. Since the weavers use no penciled diagram, they like to be amused through the long, quiet afternoons. The family runs in and out repeating neighborhood news and a few old cronies sit around cracking piñones and gossiping.

In Santa Fe, I was watching a young weaver from Mexico who sang a folk melody as he bent over his frame, deftly adjusting his shuttles to bring out the design. Suddenly his black eyes left the weaving as he turned to me and asked:

"Did you hear me sing last night? I won the prize in the audition. Now I go to Las Cruces to the state contest—maybe I win again—then I go to Chicago!" Nicolás turned back to the loom and began to hum the song again, one of those enraptured love songs he had heard since childhood.

Singing and weaving . . . didn't they always go together until the whirr of machinery drowned out the song? Happily, in New Mexico the song and the weaving accompany each other in the strong racial strain of a native people.

But while weaving continues, spinning and dyeing are lost arts. Time was the unlimited bounty of the Poco Tiempo people in the old days. Now it is gauged by union hours and trebled by buying Germantown yarn. Why should one spend long days spinning and dyeing when skeins of bright yarn may be delivered at the door? To be sure the yarn is not as soft nor the colors as fast as the old vegetable dyes but—a shrug of the shoulders suggests that times have changed.

The future problem in reviving the art of old blankets lies in finding commercial yarns of the quality and colors of handmade ones. Where this has been possible, modern weavers show that their craft sense is as fine as it ever was. Fortunately cotton warp, which began to be used as a cheaper base thirty years ago, is being replaced by the original and longer-lasting woolen warp to-day. Popular taste has been educated in that time to recognize new Chimayós by the solid body of bright red, blue, tan or green with a bold center design of white shadowed by black. To those who love old Chimayós, the revival of using simple horizontal bands of a few harmonious colors for the entire blanket is an indication that the best of the craft will continue with sufficient encouragement.

Woven on narrow looms the jerga designs varied from a red and black plaid to long, vertical lines of brown and white. Layers of paper padded the mud

260

floor, and the long strips of jerga were laid over it, entirely carpeting the room. When the woolen jergas wore out, rag rugs replaced them, woven in narrow heavy runners or braided into ovals and circles. Gay hooked rugs had a special place of honor on the floor before the household shrine, casting a faint prism of colors on the whitewashed walls. They were worked on burlap in quaint, ingenious designs, sometimes representing Santa Inéz with a garland of flowers and an orange lamb at her feet, sometimes clipped into a thick, soft blend of shades.

Years ago the Mexican needlecraft of drawn work was the pastime of gentlewomen, as well as those criadas whose entire days were given over to sewing for the family of the Patrón. You will still see snowy curtains with a drawn work border behind the red geraniums on a window sill up Cañon Road. Inside the house there are drawn work table covers, sheets and pillow cases with cobweb designs wound into the drawn threads. There are also crochet edgings, tidies and door panels with a quaint shepherdess or a snorting horse made to fit the glass door panel. This was a dignified way to tell the world that the housewife was an able needle-woman and that her husband was a Caballero—that title which grew out of the qualification that a gentleman was, cómo no, an expert horseman. The best examples of drawn work and deep crocheted borders are to be found now on lace-trimmed altar cloths and priests' surplices, since churches are always the last protectors of art and tradition.

Heavy bedspreads crocheted with cotton or creamy wool in a design of raised figures were heirlooms packed away in marriage chests. Other colchas were embroidered with wool on cotton twill. The designs were conventionalized flowers, birds and beasts, suggested perhaps by Spanish shawls. They were worked in the rich colors of vegetable dyes with an outline stitch of dark wool accenting them. Patchwork quilts with a multitude of patient piecing from old calico provided warm winter comforts. Silk coverlets and pillow tops were made with overlapping ear-shaped bits from heavy taffeta and brocades of better days, suggesting the early Moorish influence of silken covers and floor cushions.

Savanillas were homespun tapestries embroidered in wool and presented as altar hangings for some special anniversary. They represented years of work of the Patrona who, like some medieval lady, sat before her frame placing fine stitches in her embroidery through the sunny days. One savanilla, or little sheet, probably made two hundred years ago, is entirely covered with stitches of soft tan, blue and green. Its harmony and design are as beautiful as an East Indian tapestry.

Another collection has a priceless tápalo de matrimonio, made for a bride of the Hidalgos. Aurora, riding in her chariot, is cunningly embroidered in the center of this nuptial altar cloth of henna homespun. There are smaller figures of a man and woman and the symbolical lamb and cock on either side. The chariot is of silver thread and the wheels of silver braid, untarnished by the centuries. Heavy silver fringe is tacked to one end. When this tápalo was discovered in a tumble-down adobe inquiries were made about the fringe for the other end. The native housewife smiled, shrugged her shoulders and said, "Quien sabe, señora—years ago the children tore it off to play with." She would probably marvel at the strange ways of the Americana who framed this tápalo de matrimonio under glass and regards it as the rarest decoration of a luxurious living room.

The feminine arts of needlework have all but vanished with the perishability of their fabric and the introduction of machine-made imitations. But the masculine arts, such as carving, weaving, working in tin, iron, gold and silver have lasted through the sleepy centuries. Their materials were not only more enduring, but these crafts offered a means of earning the family living.

Wood carving is as old as Hispanic tradition. It was one of the first arts of those colonials who settled in the New Mexico wilderness and were forced to make everything for their homes out of the native materials of the country. The rare, foreign pieces of furniture brought for the ricos up the Chihuahua Trail vanished with them and their easily spent wealth. But, like the pobres who have lived on to a happier existence, the home-carved peasant furniture has withstood time and change.

Early wood carving was a simply expressed desire to beautify a lonely life; to give to native pine, found so abundantly in the new mountains, the touches of grace and warmth remembered from the homeland. Carvers were limited by their few, crude tools—knives, chisels, planes and Tacuba axes. The elements of their designs were simple but were used in a variation that produced a spontaneous, naïve effect, always well-proportioned to plain lines and surfaces.

The most ambitious carving was naturally used to adorn bare mission churches. We find examples of this early art in the carved panels of doors, spiral columns supporting altars and chalice-shaped pulpits, lintels and corbels. They set off the colored altar backs, depicting a saint in each panel, painted with the same primitive feeling as the carving.

Then carvers turned to beautifying their own homes, whittling on sturdy pine benches and tables through the long winter days when the fields were blanketed under snow. Nails were rare and costly, and the furniture was ingeniously put together with wooden pegs. The pine was rubbed to a satiny texture with sand and left to gray with age. It was strong enough for family use, yet there was grace and balance in the utilitarian lines.

Tables, benches and the many low stools were built close to the puncheon floors suggesting the Moorish influence where every one sat on floor cushions. The carving ran along the chair and bench backs and the supports of tables and stools. Dish cupboards or trasteros had spindle insets and rounded to the top in a half rosette. Long shelves, hung from the whitewashed walls as a resting place where wooden saints might look down at the famliy, were carved with fluted edges, repeating the design of the trasteros. Sometimes the

gouge design was filled in with vegetable paints, but never to the extent of making the decoration ornate or gaudy. The effect of this early carving and furniture was unsophisticated, and perhaps unfinished, but never crude.

The pride of every home was its Spanish chests. They served all purposes from banks to linen closets. Their size varied from huge grain chests, not unlike those found in Normandy for storing winter wheat, to small square boxes for holy oil. The elaborate wardrobe of Oñate was probably carried in such a wooden trunk, carved with his coat of arms. Dower chests were six feet long and half as high, to hold linens, bright silks, shawls and blankets which every groom had to provide for his bride. Heraldic devices with rampant lions and unicorns were worked into their panels. As one publicity pamphlet puts it, "The unicorn was a symbol of virginity. It has never been known in New Mexico." The carving varied with the time and whim of the craftsman, though the favorite design was a central motif of large rosettes, perhaps suggested by the bossing found on Spanish furniture. Traces of blue and vermilion paint, still clinging to the petals of this rosette pattern, carry on the feeling of colored velvets placed under the wrought iron bossing.

Treasure chests protected their golden doubloons with robber-proof bands of iron. Later, leather chests, less heavy than wooden ones, were packed up the trail and became safety-deposit vaults. Some were of solid leather, tooled and carved, others were elaborately decorated with leather thongs woven around insets of red and blue velvet. One of these braided leather boxes was used by La Tules, the gambling woman, when she played monte at neighboring fiestas. Wooden chests with curved tops were covered with deer and horsehide, the marking of the hide cleverly used as the design.

Painted wooden chests have that boudoir air of storing away taffeta dresses and embroidered shawls. Their fanciful painting not only decorated the top and sides but also the inside of the lid. With a background of dark blue or faded Spanish red, the birds and flowers stand out in quaint array. They varied from the six-foot lengths for wardrobes to a six-inch size for jewel caskets.

All chests had handmade locks, hasps and huge keys. On the smaller chests, the lock was almost as large as the front of the box. Handles and hinges were turned and chased after the fashion of Spanish ironsmiths.

With the present interest in Spanish fittings there has been a revival of native wrought iron. Stirrups, bits and bridles, once the pride of Caballeros, are not in much demand to-day. The trade of the village blacksmith dwindled from horseshoeing to repairing broken automobile springs. But iron has returned to its early ornamental uses. Now the forge turns out torchères, sidelight brackets, round basket grates and spear-headed curtain poles. The blacksmith duplicates Spanish grilles and doors, gates and windows. If he is given the freedom of working out his own designs the purchaser will be amazed with the delicate and expert workmanship that comes out of a dingy shop.

The interest in collecting Spanish colonial antiques has had a wide effect. No village is so remote but that some grandam will offer a carved chest or a faded blanket with the tantalizing whisper that it is "muy antigua." It is the echo of Aladdin's call "Old lamps for new! Old lamps for new!" Prices have risen with the collector's zeal, for now one may sell a trastero for enough to buy a shining new golden oak sideboard —verdad? The spindle bed, thrown out in the shed, has been traded for the first instalment on a radio whose programs are the wonder of the placita.

This is partly due to the mail order catalogues, the most potent propaganda of Americanization. They weigh down the mail stage to the farthermost places. With the family Bible and prayer book they often comprise the entire library. And what a temptation the pictures and prices offer—the temptation of buying many new things for an old one.

Originally, Americanization suppressed native customs and crafts with the force of blatant, new standards. It was the law and order code of subduing a hostile territory, a time when personal safety was more important than art. During the sixty years of making an American state of New Mexico, the native arts dwindled but did not die.

The present renaissance of Spanish colonial crafts is a far ripple of the World War. After 1918, many European people were forced to turn to their own handicrafts to earn a living. There was a consequent revival of interest in peasant embroideries, pottery, carving. This extended to "early American furniture" and the earlier American arts of the Indians and Spanish colonials. Its best result has been a reawakened pride in the natives for their own crafts.

The discovery of Spanish colonial crafts still flourishing in our standardized twentieth century is one of the amazing surprises of New Mexico. They belong to the simple folk art brought here long ago by Andalusian peasants. In the isolation of this province the folk art remained unchanged, for the sophistication and ornateness that later swept over Spain never penetrated to this mountain-bound frontier. Time was cheated in New Mexico, and three hundred years passed as but a day, leaving art, language, customs fixed in the early colonial patterns.

XI

Customs of the Country

THERE are many quaint customs of the country clinging to Santa Fe to mark it with the peculiar grace of Latin peoples. If you question any of the ways which may seem strange in America, the explanation will be a lifting of shoulders and eyebrows and the sufficient reply, "Es costumbre del país—it is a custom of the country."

The Anglo is still designated in Spanish as the "extrangero"—the stranger who must be excused because he does not understand these customs. If the strangers' questions have a too insistent curiosity, it is easy enough to turn him off with a Socratic answer, "Quién Sabe?" This has the unequaled value of a polite response but no information for one hundred questions. Used when one does not want to tell, "Who knows?" is as baffling as the Sphinx. Or it may mean quite truthfully, "I don't know," or "I'm sorry that I can't help you," or "I wonder who might know."

It sums up that Latin characteristic of shading the truth so that a refusal will never hurt your feelings.

A washerwoman agrees to come to-morrow morning and your arrangements seem complete. She knows that, for her own reasons, she will not come but to refuse pointblank would be so discourteous! It is easier to allow a non-appearance at eight o'clock to-morrow to offer its own explanations.

This structure of courtesy underlies life to make it pleasant and comfortable. It has made northern New Mexico a land where salutations are expected from friend and stranger alike. As your motor whizzes around a covered wagon or a wood hauler creeping on at a burro's pace, you will be greeted with a smiling "Buenos Días." The woodman may not tip his battered hat, but there is an upward lift of his chin accompanying his "Good Day." You have never seen him before, may never see him again, but he has fulfilled his innate courtesy with one of the delightful customs of the country.

Many a time I have hurried down town arrayed in my Sunday best to be hailed from the middle of the road with a "Hallo Ruth-é." The greeting would come from a delivery truck driver who had once been the family gardener. "Hallo Ruth-é" took away all my grown-up dressiness and reduced me to the child who waited until Manuel saddled my horse. Though many years have elapsed since that day of child and gardener, Manuel preserves the interest in the family, which comes out in his hearty "Hallo Ruth-é."

Riding over the mountains since childhood, fear of

solitary place or of meeting any one was unknown; instead there was always a sense of human protection in meeting another wayfarer. I avoided highways for the lure of climbing to the hilltops or discovering new cañons. Every mountain had its dim woodroads and goat trails. To encounter a woodcutter or a sheepherder was to meet with unfailing kindness and courtesy. Perhaps the woodcutter would tighten my saddle cinch or take out his ax to cut a bunch of pink-berried mistletoe that hung beyond my reach. There would be a few comments on the weather and the fineness of the day, and with an "Adiós" we parted as the best of friends.

This quiet courtesy has led to the New Mexico habit of picking up natives or Indians for a lift in the car, knowing that they would never betray kindness by the hijacking methods of tramp hitch-hikers.

If I meet friends wearing black shawls or driving a string of burros there follows a long exchange of customary questions—"How is your mother? Your father? Your husband? Your sister? The little ones?" One old friend is noted for his pious ways. He has not missed the six o'clock mass for years, and he takes off his hat and crosses himself whenever he passes a church. "How is your family, Don Francisco?" I ask him. "They are well, thank you, señora— Praise be to God." "And how are you, Don Francisco?" "Ah, for myself, the rheumatism troubles me, thanks be to God." Among ourselves we have come to call this friend "Gracias à Dios" for no comment is ever made without the humble refrain of "Thanks be to God."

Though there is no name for our word home in Spanish, there are no people to whom "home" means more than to the native New Mexicans. "Mi casa" is home, house, castle, the focus where life still centers around the family unit.

Stopping before an adobe home one always hears the bark of a lean dog and the cackle of hens announcing the visitor. Little faces peer through the windows, and the father or mother opens the door. For friends, the hearty greeting is "Llegue! Llegue!" a hospitality that insists upon "come in and visit." A gesture toward the open door and a low toned "Pase" is an invitation to pass within the house. Then politeness includes the indispensable salutation of assuring you that everything in the house is yours—"Esta casa está siempre a la disposición de Vd." It is equally a mark of good breeding on your part not to accept it. But if your training has not included this refusal, the acceptance of gift or hospitality is met with the spirit which shows that the proffering was founded on real generosity and not wordy politeness. The Chaves family, for instance, have given away enough priceless treasures to stock a museum. When I spoke of this regretfully, the gracious daughter of the family said, "But it was our pleasure to give them to our friends."

True hospitality is to be found here—the hospitality of putting another plate on the table and opening a can of corn or peaches so that the Anglo guest may have his tinned food as well as the family frijoles.

One night we lost our way in the high mountains between Taos and Questa. In the moonlight we finally discovered an adobe house, dark and quiet as though the family had been asleep for hours. The cold night persuaded us to knock at the door. When the door opened, the candlelight revealed a man with a dark face, black eyes, black brows, and black mustache. As soon as he heard our plight his house was truly "at our disposition." It was "nothing" that they should be routed out of their beds at midnight by strangers, for the little mother insisted upon giving us the family bedroom. A baby was taken up from one corner, two sleepy children carried out from another corner, a little boy stumbled unprotestingly from his pallet in another corner. When there were no other corners left to empty, fresh sheets were put on the bed. We never knew where all the family slept, but at the early breakfast they had the gracious dignity of making us feel that strangers were welcomed every midnight. It is an unfailing custom of the country that no native, no matter how poor, will ever allow himself to be outdone in courtesy.

Family names in Santa Fe are the same as those on the church register in any mountain town in Andalusia. Ortiz and García are as numerous as Jones and Smith. Then there are the Archuletas, Herreras, Hinojos, Jiménez, Gutierrez, Gonzales, Luceros, Montoyas, Muñiz, Romeros, Salazars and Sánchez. There are even such Moorish names as Medina. De la O is the shortest name found in New Mexican records. There are innumerable Bacas and Cabeza de Baca (or Vaca), the latter tracing their family tree to their illustrious ancestor, Alvar Nuñez Cabeza de Baca, the first western explorer. The name goes back beyond that odyssey of the sixteenth century to the time of King Henry of Navarre, when a peasant was knighted for a memorable service to his country. He placed the bleached head of a cow at a hidden passage through the mountains so that the King's troops were able to surprise and defeat the Moors. The signpost of the Head of a Cow was remembered when he was knighted, and the words "Cabeza de Vaca" were included in his title. To-day the "V" is changed to "B," as so often happens in New Mexican Spanish.

As for Christian names, a baby is baptized with a whole calendar of saints. María is the most popular as the name of the Virgin Mother, but she may be María Encarnación Clodovia, María Dolores Lutgarda, María de los Remedios, or María Concepción Marcelina. The favorite name for boys is José, though they are not to be cheated out of the blessings of Mary and combine her name as José María, Manual María, Estéban María. An urchin is apt to be just as mischievous if he is called John of God—Juan de Dios—as he might have been as Jack. Jesús is a very common name, pronounced "Haysús" but always startling to the Anglo eye.

Infants are baptized when they are only a few days

old. The mother may not have revived sufficiently to be present at the baptism and the party following it, but those two most important people, the madrina and the padrino, must be on hand. These godparents assume no little responsibility when they stand beside the baptismal font, for they must look after the child if anything happens to the parents.

Infant confirmation is one of the unusual customs in Santa Fe. It probably survives from that time when hundred-league parishes made bishops' visits, like angels' visits, few and far between. Then the bishop came to the scattered hamlets once in five or six years. Those who had married without the benefit of clergy were remarried during the bishop's visit and children were baptized and confirmed. To-day mothers with sleepy babies in their arms crowd the Cathedral for infant confirmation, wailing and hushing accompanying that service of becoming a full member of the church at such a tender age.

To me the most lovable characteristic of the native people is their genuine family affection. It gives the twenty-sixth baby the same fond welcome the first received. It extends not only to the near and distant relatives but to all who are homeless. Almost every family has one or more cousins growing up with the family. There is never an aged man or woman who lacks a home beside an already crowded hearth, no matter whether that home belongs to one of the neighbors or to his own parientes. There is never a motherless child who is not taken in by some big-hearted woman to share the simple living with her own numerous brood. I knew one such woman in Chimayó who had adopted eighteen children, raising all of them on the profits of her little country store. She has passed now to her reward, and who doubts that eternal happiness was waiting for her who followed Christ's words to "do unto these, my little ones"?

Even the illegimate child inherits no town censure, and under New Mexico's laws shares equally in the father's estate. The unmarried mother, or the man who has spent some time in the penitentiary, are treated with kindness, leaving social errors to the wisdom of the confessional. The simple-minded child is called an "inocente." His babblings are often regarded as prophetic, since an act of God has made him innocent of the ways of the world.

Parental authority is supreme and accepted by even grown sons and daughters. It brooks no disobedience yet seldom witnesses the punishment of children. Many a Juvenile Judge has turned over an incorrigible orphan to some hospitable neighbor in whose home the unhappy youngster loses his waywardness in a normal family life. This is the human heart functioning, not deadened by statistics or institutions. It is that trusting human equation to which modern experimenting laws are returning when they provide mother's pensions, so that children may stay at home instead of being banished to impersonal institutions.

Infant mortality is high here. Many summer mornings I have seen a little white casket in the tonneau of a car surrounded by bright-faced child pallbearers, while solemn men walk behind it down the dusty road to Rosario. That a diet of green chile, beans and coffee is not the best food for babies is a lesson that Americanization has not yet succeeded in teaching. A physician told me of going to see a tiny patient and being met at the door by a sad-eyed mother whose lips trembled as she said that the baby was well. He was laid out in his clean dress, "well" beyond the ills of this world. "One more little angel," she cried over him, "but it is as God wills."

Almost every home has an abuelita, a "dear little granny" who cares for sick children with her simple knowledge of herbs. If the malady is too severe she calls in the "médica," the medicine woman whose ministrations are known even in distant placitas. The médica is an important figure in the community, acting as midwife and doctor, present at birth and death and called upon to allay suffering in between. She goes to sheltered cañons and the sunny slopes of mesas to gather herbs, leaves and roots which must be picked at just the right season. If she cannot reach the high mountains, she depends upon certain sheepherders to bring other plants to her. Her home is like that of any yarbwoman, strewn with drying leaves and roots and precious herbs hanging in crackling bunches from the vigas.

Besides the medicines for pains and fevers, her pharmacopœia includes many household aids. There is, for instance, mountain mahogany whose fumes are

278

guaranteed to kill bedbugs, and horehound to drop in a bottle of aguardiente to lessen the bad effects of bootleg liquor. Her trastero contains bags of savories for flavoring soups and stews, such as the peppermint leaves of yerba buena, the marigold flowers of clavelón and sweet basil. The dried brown roots of amole are heaped in a copper cauldron in the corner. They are pounded between stones until the fiber is loosened, then soaked in a tub of hot water to make bubbling soap suds. Amole lather has the two-fold benefit of not shrinking woolens and of providing a fluffy, lustrous shampoo. Malva is another hair wash warranted to cure "bran of the hair."

The remedios of the médica contain many of the simples used in modern medicine, discovered long ago in the life-and-death necessities of the wilderness. Their efficacy is increased by drinking them as hot, aromatic teas. The faith of long usage makes them universal remedies—often in secret addition to the physicians' prescriptions for dolor de estómago. Alfonso García found a white-flowered plant in Socorro and gave his name to this decoction for rheumatic joints, while other cures for rheumatism are steeped from yerba del oso, hediondilla or plumajillo. Tea from the Romero weed is given colicky babies, and its healing qualities soothe the Penitente's back. Oshá is the popular tonic for dolor de las tripas, or made into a thick syrup with oshá roots and piloncillo—brown sugar cones from Old Mexico—it stops a tickling cough. Other potions for intestinal distress are yerba inmortal, yerba buena, yerba manza and maravilla. Contra yerba checks diarrhea, sabadilla is a physic, and capulín a blood purifier. Dedalera is the native digitalis, used to stimulate the heart. Caimigoria contains the tannic acid used in gargles. Marnilla is a specific for chills and fever. Powdered cachana is sprinkled on a hot stove and its fumes inhaled for "wind in the head." The juice of juniper berries is used in childbirth. A hot compress of silver sage relieves stomach ache after too much green chile.

If these mild remedies made from herbs and roots are not effective, the médica will resort to drastic drugs. As a purgative she will give asogue, a dose of pure mercury. As a heart stimulant she prescribes oro volador, a bit of powdered coral wrapped in a capsule of gold leaf.

Though she has only "good medicines" she knows of poisons concocted from deadly nightshade and of witch's broths made of rattlesnake's fangs to scare a faithless lover to repentance or into the other world. Witches have been tried in court within the memory of this generation and found guilty on the evidence of strange decoctions, though the intangible evidence of evil spells had caused the greater trouble.

The médica brews her potions in a pot simmering on the fireplace coals, crumbling dried leaves between her fingers as she adds a little of this yerba and that. There are blue labels from a tobacco sack pasted on her wrinkled temples to relieve headache. While she waits for the remedio to simmer, she crouches near it

by the dying coals, adjusting the black manta over her head and cupping a twist of a cigarette in her brown hands. That is the time I have learned of witch's spells and beliefs in omens.

She warned me in her cracked, old voice never to drink water at the moment of midnight, for then water is dead all over the world. She was sure that if any one was reported dead while living, he was sure to get well. She cackled that a bride longed for her mother-in-law, if she wept when she sliced onions. And it was certain that sweethearts were true if the fire blazed up when it was first lit, and the piñon logs stood upright against the chimney until they were charred. A wish was sure to come true, if it was made on the thin crescent moon with money held in the left hand or on the first star prick of evening. Another sure omen was to repeat the wish while spinning on the heel three times and stopping when the toe pointed to the east. She whispered that the aspens trembled with shame because, in their proud, silver slenderness, they were the only trees which refused to bow when Christ passed through the woods. There were many dire curses that followed children who disobeyed their parents.

An awful example was the "Mum-mum man" of my childhood. He was a poor, old, paralytic, dragging his misshapen body along the ground by his one active hand and foot. One of the many léperos begging alms, common then in every Spanish town, he stretched out his palsied hand and turned up his wrinkled, bearded face, mumbling "mum-mum."

Nurses told us that he had been stricken by God for cursing his mother and was doomed always to murmur "ma-má."

But even the best of médicas and doctors have no remedies to rout death when the time comes. They can only close the eyes and wind a rosary through the cold fingers of the difunto, offer the consolation of religion and help with the dignified rites of death. Church bells toll for the passing, an insistent, slow, clanging that echoes in the heart with the certainty that death comes to every man.

There is a velorio del difunto that evening, a night-long wake. The raised coffin is surrounded with burning tapers whose flickering light gives a semblance of the quickness of life to still features. Friends come in quietly to sit in mournful stillness on stiff rows of chairs around the room and murmur words of sympathy to the relatives. Between nine o'clock and midnight a supper is served—coffee, steaming chile, frijoles and rice pudding. Toward morning old men and women sing their death songs, no less grief-laden because they are paid mourners. The closed eyelids of a blind man quiver as he sings his original verses of lament. After he has finished, a woman, huddled in a green-black shawl, raises her voice in a long consolation for the bereaved parientes. Then they join in the clear, Latin cadences of a chant. They take their leave of the difunto and the widow and children as the candles gutter out against the dawn.

Cards with black borders have been printed and

dispatched to inform friends of a death in the family and invite them to the last mass and burial. Women stay at home to grieve, and the casket is followed only by bare-headed men, walking two by two. Before the days of motor hearses or "funeral wagons," the home-made pine box was carried to the campo santo on the shoulders of the pallbearers. It was a last, heavy task, necessitating several stops. The coffin was low-ered to the ground, beyond the breathless steepness of a mountain road, for a descanso—a rest for the compadres whose heads were bowed in prayer during the few moments' respite. A simple cross, propped round with stones, marked this place of the resting. It was of narrow pine boards, perhaps put aside only the week before by the departed, and painted now with the black letters of his name—"Juan María Lopez, Rogad por su alma." These wayside cairns reminded all who passed to lay another stone beside the cross and to pray for the soul of one who would spend a year in a nebulous purgatory. Wills, such as that of "La Tules," specified that a sum of money should be set aside for the tolling of bells, the last mass and three descansos. A year later there is another invita-tion for the anniversary mass, a speeding of the soul now standing at the portal of Heaven.

Between the rituals of birth and death there was the happy celebration of marriage. It is characteristic of Latin peoples that girls bloom early and fade early, following the long drain of childbearing. Years ago little girls no sooner left off playing with dolls than they had their own babies to care for. One abuelita told that she was married at thirteen and her boy husband was only a year older. His first task was to make a swing, where they played most of the day. Schools were rare, and real education consisted of being a good housekeeper or a good farmer.

To-day passing through at least the grammar grades is an accepted standard. Forced into our economic basis, many girls earn their living for three or four years before marriage. Invariably, part of the money is sent home to help the family. Education is a matter of pride with the coming generation. Clorinda, for instance, is teaching a country school to pay college tuition for a younger brother.

But even in 1930 there is little comradeship between boys and girls. They are separated in convents and Brothers' schools and, if love did not always find a way, boys and girls would seldom have a word alone until after they were married. There is no calling at home, unless it is a family affair subdued by watchful parents. But there are trysting places along a shady path where such endearments as alma de mi alma—soul of my soul—or lado del lado de mi corazón—side of the side of my heart—may be whispered. Love letters, full of ecstatic phrases, are secretly sent, and treasured more fondly than the formal marriage letters. Serenades offer an accepted and romantic setting to sing of love. To play the bear— jugar al oso—was to creep beneath her window in the evening darkness, sing original couplets of a lover's fancy, catch the rose tossed out by a trembling hand and escape before an irate father recognized the strumming of the guitar.

It was no wonder that dances were the high lights of life. They were meeting places for young and old, where one might make love to a girl even under the wise eyes of her dueña. To be sure, there was no chance for kisses during intermission or of long farewells on the way home, but many vows could be exchanged under the cover of music and a fateful question asked and answered even during the formal figures of a quadrille. That led to a quick-flaming jealousy between youths, a grappling fight in the darkness outside the door, an ear cut off by a flashing knife or pistol shots exchanged.

However, marriages were arranged by parents. If the future husband was not the choice of her heart, the mother might know it by the tears and pale cheeks of her daughter, but there was seldom spoken rebellion against the father's decision. The marriage went on as it was planned. Fortunately love often led to parents accepting the young promptings of the heart, outwardly assuming that no understanding had been reached between the novios even if they had long guessed the magic of smiling eyes.

Then Ramón might hint to his father that it would be well for old families like the Garcías and Archuletas to join their winter ranges and their flocks, hardly daring to mention that Anita was the lovely daughter of Don Antonio Archuleta. If the family thought well of the union, Ramón, his father and godfather would array themselves in clean shirts and their best Sunday suits and pay a formal call upon Don Antonio to present the marriage letter. The village letter writer used to be called upon to inscribe this in his flowery phrases and the curlicues of his quill pen. Some letter writers advertised themselves as never failing to gain a bride with their eloquent documents.

It might have been that the letter writer told the secret to a few close friends—anyhow when the party reached the casa of the Archuletas, Don Antonio was dressed in his best that afternoon instead of plowing the alfalfa field. He threw open the door with surprised exclamations to see his good friends and invited them to enter. When they were seated on the red plush sofa with its crocheted mats, the older men smoked strong cigarettes, but Ramón could not be so disrespectful as to smoke in the presence of his elders. After long perfunctory chatting about crops and weather, Ramón's father ceremoniously handed Don Antonio the marriage letter. Don Antonio accepted it with bowing eloquence and thrust it in his inner pocket. Then he marched to the kitchen door to demand in a loud tone if his poor house had anything to offer his honorable guests. The visit could not have been so unexpected, for in a minute mother, the godmother, the aunts, the sisters and lastly Anita brought out trays with little glasses, a decanter of homemade wine and plates of sugar-frosted cakes. But Anita and Ramón hardly dared to glance at each other.

If two weeks or two months went by in silence, Don Antonio's letter would be a courteous refusal giving Ramón "the squash"—las calabazas. Sin verguenza he might hint that Piedad and Refugio were also marriageable daughters, though he had other plans for Anita. But if only a week elapsed the letter would be an acceptance, reciting the history of his family and naming the land or sheep Anita would receive as her dowry. The answer was returned with the same formal visit that accompanied the marriage letter.

A century ago, if the families were of the gente fina, the groom had to serve a year's apprenticeship to his future father-in-law. He joined a caravan going to Mexico to fill his marriage chest and bring back an Indian slave as a maid for his bride. He also provided linens and blankets of his own dyeing and weaving. Old songs promised "un vestido de seda," and every bride hoped for a red silk dress. Now the groom often goes to Wyoming or Utah to work for a year and save up at least five hundred dollars. What a difference between the "mercenary" Yankee who rushes into love blind-poor, and the "sentimental" Latin who protects the future with a starting stake! To him marriage is a lifetime tenure, though he may grow poorer with increasing years and family. To the Anglo it has become a one-child shifting experiment, while he piles up capital.

Marriage is an expensive luxury for the native youth, beginning before the wedding day instead of waiting until the first month's bills come in. He purchases the wedding dress, veil, bridal trousseau, and a trunk filled with extra dresses, hats, shoes, linen and china. Besides this, he pays for the wedding feast and dance. Perhaps there is not much left of the five hundred dollars, but there is the assurance of the bride's dowry. At the bottom of her marriage chest there are a few heirlooms handed down from her great-grandmother, such as a filigree brooch, an embroidered shawl, half a dozen hand-hammered silver spoons. On top of them are piled linens with crocheted edges, blankets, clothes and shining, modern trinkets.

If Ramón has enough worldly goods to start the new home, the wedding date is quickly arranged with the priest and the bans read in church for three successive Sundays. Two days before the wedding, Ramón, accompanied by all his relatives and friends, comes "to receive the bride." This is a gay and happy reception given by Anita's parents. The bride carries the customary open purse, and every one drops money into it for good luck. Ramón places the memoria ring on her finger, with its shaded gold hearts, flowers and grapes.

Ramón's family have been busy preparing the wedding feast, killing beeves and sheep, baking dozens of loaves of bread, sending over wagon loads of provisions to Anita's home.

Half a century ago the wedding fiesta lasted through two weeks. If the Rio Grande or the Rio Chama divided the haciendas, a boat, padded with blankets and silken pillows and festooned with garlands of flowers, served to ferry the bride and her relatives across the river. After the nuptial mass the bride and groom returned in state, preceded to the house by fiddlers and guitarists singing the marriage song, little girls holding an arch of flowers and guests showering the blushing couple with "felicidades"—boxes filled with fine-cut colored paper. The bride and groom knelt at the doorstep to receive the blessings of the father and mother.

Now the wedding party rides around the plaza in an open car, all eyes gazing at the white satin and flowing veil. There is usually a stop at the photographer's for a picture of Ramón awkwardly seated and Anita standing beside him, her hand timidly resting on his shoulder.

The bride adds her new name to her father's with an "of," becoming the Doña Anita García de Archuleta. Children keep the two names, tying them together with "and." Anita's son would be called Ramoncito García y Archuleta. Anita will always be known to her friends as la Doña Anita, though to outsiders she may be called the Señora Archuleta.

Though Latin generosity knows no bounds, the host must have the security of issuing his own invitations. Crashing wedding parties or funerals isn't done. The wedding invitations are issued in the name of both the groom's and the bride's parents for the marriage of their children. This has its good points, for you don't altogether forget about the groom when he and his family are also giving the feast.

The wedding dance lasts far into the night. One waltz is called the "Vals Chiquillado," when the bride is seated in the middle of the hall, and the groom sings his song to her. If he is so poor a poet that he has no song, he must pay the orchestra to sing his song for him. The blind fiddler has laudatory couplets and long verses of "Advice to Newlyweds," earning his simple living through these courtesies. There are many toasts to the tired little bride before the final ceremony of "entragamiento," when Anita is handed over by her parents to Ramón. Then they leave for the new home, built on for them in his father's placita.

Folk songs are customary accompaniments for every occasion and every season. Though the voices are often off key, the songs of birth, courtship, marriage, death are as much a part of coursing life as the simmer in a pot of beans. Some of them may have originated in Mexico, Central America, or farther away in Spain but they have taken on so much of the color of colonial life that they are typically native around Santa Fe.

The music is a simple, folk melody with a curious rhythm and stressed notes and runs. The tempo is as sure as heartbeats, while the melody wanders in and around it, more often that not in a minor strain. It is the rare "extrangero" who can sing these songs as the native sings them, with accents on unexpected syllables, runs that tumble words together and a final "ay" that starts in a throaty gargle and ends in a nasal falsetto.

There are songs of the buffalo hunters who left from Pecos to hunt on the wide, eastern plains. The last great hunt was in 1869. The songs of farewell to home and sweethearts, the excitement of the chase, the prowess of the ciboleros are still sung by Lucero Rodríguez, merry and hearty at the age of ninety-three.

There are ballads recounting the exploits of native heroes, and many dichos and coplas, twisting a proverb or an epigram into a two-line wise crack, typical of Spanish wit. Of course there were parting songs of novios starting out on the year's pre-marriage service when they joined the conductas going to the tierra afuera, the outside country, as Mexico was called. "Adios, mi chaparrita" has a rhythm suggesting a galloping horse:

Adios, mi chaparrita,
No llores por tu Pancho,
Que si se va del rancho,
Muy pronto volverá.

Verás que del Bajío
Te traigo cosas güenas
Y un beso que tus penas,
Muy pronto olvidarás.

Los Moñitos pa tus trenzas,
Y pa tu mamacita,

CUSTOMS OF THE COUNTRY

Rebozos de bolita,
Y enaguas de percal! Ay! que caray!

Farewell, my mountain sweetheart,
Oh weep not for your Pancho,
Though now I leave the rancho,
I'll return and never part.

From the lowlands, some bright morrow,
I'll bring you gifts and treasures.
And when once again I kiss you,
You'll soon forget your sorrow.

There'll be ribbons for your tresses
And for your little mother,
A scarf of lace and drawn-work,
And muslin for your dresses   Ay! que caray!

Like songs in any tongue love songs outnumber all the others. Unrequited love pulls the heart cords most, lovers enjoying its sorrows in extravagant, plaintive measures. It is the love of olden days and beautiful ladies—chivalrous, languishing, throbbing; the love of Romeo and Juliet; the gesture of a knight to his imprisoned fair lady. Serenades proclaim lovelorn plights which can be told in no other way. They weave the rich imagery of the Spanish language into endless, eloquent verses. Starlight and sunshine, birds and flowers are lover's messengers, as in the quaint little verse of "La Paloma Blanca":

Tú eres mi paloma blanca
Yo soy tu pichón azul!
Arrima me tu piquito
Para hacer cu-ru, cu-cu.

CABALLEROS

Thou art my little white dove,
And I am your pigeon so blue!
Nestle your little bill close to mine,
Softly cooing, coo-roo, coo-coo.

Another has a couplet ready for any type of girl,
to be enlarged upon as suits the occasion:

Ojos trigueños, color de café,
Dame un beso de buena fé.
Ojos azules, color de ciel
Dame un beso, un beso de miel.

Deep brown eyes of coffee hue,
Give me a kiss, loving and true,
Fair blue eyes, clear as the sky,
One honey kiss, for that I sigh.

You wonder if marriage blossoms into happiness
after such raptures? There are a few songs that sing
of it, but "La Firolera" says:

Ya mi marido se murió,
Ya el diablo se lo llevó.
Ora si estará pagando
Las patadas que me dió.

Now my dear husband is dead,
The devil has hauled him away.
I pray he is paying full well
For the beatings he gave me each day.

There is sly humor as well as love's woes in the
songs, like the increasing verses of "Con otro reale que
tengo" which goes on and on like the House that Jack

Built. Or the stanzas of a gay Don Juan who sings that he loves all the ladies, fat or thin, dark or fair, old or young, married or solteras, but the middle ones please him most.

Wandering minstrels had their repertory of songs for an evening's entertainment, singling out the prettiest of the "Señoras y Señoritas" for their graceful couplets. With a guitar swung over the shoulder, black eyes flashing, and gestures of impassioned devotion, these troubadours sang that they were "shameless, for see what love has done to me." They expected a golden coin to be tossed them as an appreciation of the compliment, so that it was an expensive privilege to escort a beautiful Doña to the play.

The bond of race and common language still flows along the Chihuahua Trail, like the underground rivers which so often sink below the sand in this desert country. Outwardly there is sometimes antagonism between New Mexicans and Old Mexicans, but inwardly they like the same things. Songs like the "Virgencita," which gain a season's popularity in Mexico City, are soon played over and over on squeaky phonographs in Santa Fe. Later they are twanged on a guitar and sung wherever a group of boys gather around a doorstep in the summer twilight.

"La Cucaracha," the cockroach, is the song about Pancho Villa, though there were probably other more numerous animalitos with his bandit army. It has that contagious syncopation which never fails to make the body sway to its beat. Up and down the length of the Chihuahua Trail you will hear the tune, but seldom the same words. Each singer makes up his own verses about La Cucaracha, sometimes with the turn of a livery stable joke. Another recent song is "La Rielera," warning that a bootlegger should never have a wife, for his life is too much like that of a tramp stealing rides under a train!

While these modern hits spread among a song-loving people as quickly as jazzy "Blues" among Anglos, the songs that are never forgotten are the old ones composed by shepherds. The greatest number of New Mexican folk songs are the gifts of those who follow their flocks, filling the lonely days by improvising simple melodies and verses.

When they are fortunate enough to meet other shepherds, the night is spent in entertaining each other with their entire repertory. Seated around a camp fire, with the sheep safely bedded for the night, one pulls out a mouth organ, another a música—a worn harmonica. There is sure to be at least one guitar and sometimes a crude violin made with a syrup can set on a whittled neck and four, proud, store-bought strings. The wonder is that the horsehair bow can produce true, rounded tones. All of them join in singing the old songs of the ghosts of a shepherd and his sheep who froze to death in a blizzard, or the happy return to the placita after months in the high mountains. They teach each other their new songs, though each shepherd has his understood right to his own song.

There are tender lullabys, singing children to sleep with the tale of the little owl who was hungry, or the baby coyote. Christmas Eve songs of adoration of the Christ child are sung before His shrine, where He sits in His wooden chair, already dressed in His cape and high, plumed hat. At the velorios de santos there are touching songs of praise for the good offices of the saints, who have brought success in some family undertaking or healed the sick. For this party for the saints, the statues of the neighborhood are brought into the clean-swept sala and assembled on the snowy, drawn work covered table. Rows of candles burn around them. Friends join in the songs and the "Ave María." Afterwards there is merry making and refrescos. But at the velorios de difuntos there are those sad requiems sung by the mourners. These verses of the blind singers have a peculiar pathos, their wavering voices carrying a sympathy which comes out of their own despairing darkness.

Many of the songs are copied in tattered notebooks, often the most prized possession of their owners. There was one tall, bald-headed old fellow at Chamita who was a song collector. He showed me verses copied by his great-grandfather in a foreign shaded hand, and thick scrap books he himself had collected from clippings in Spanish papers from Panama to Madrid. Then he invited me to sit in an inner sala and seated himself in the glory of a barber's chair, bought secondhand because it was so comfortable. He tuned his guitar and sang song after song through the long, lazy afternoon.

I know another family of seven sons who snatch a bowl of frijoles during the noon hour and spend the rest of the sixty minutes playing the guitar and fiddle and improvising songs for their own amusement. The mother goes back and forth from table to stove in her simple duties, humming the tunes as she smiles at her sons seated on the floor in the sunlight of the open door. Fiddles, for they can hardly be called violins, are a luxurious accompaniment for songsters, but the strummed cords of a guitar are as necessary as garlic in chile.

We understand people best through their music, since it needs no translation. Those Sunday night concerts in the half-lighted Plaza are most typical when the Conquistadores' Band plays "Lupita" or "Adelita," and every one joins in the chorus.

In Europe I rose with patriotic fervor when the "Star-Spangled Banner" was played, but when some chance orchestra in Paris began "La Paloma," there were tears in my eyes. It meant home. For New Mexico is a country within a country. And the music of a country expresses the land of the heart, depending upon wheather you were brought up to "Yankee Doodle," "Dixie" or "La Paloma."

XII

The Gifts of God

New Mexico used to be divided in two classes—the rich and the poor. Like all comparisons, the inequality was based on the standards of the day. The division still holds in the language of the native people, though those who are classed as "ricos" would bring a twinkle into the cold, glass eye of a multimillionaire. To-day New Mexico is a land of modest incomes, homes, pleasures, with a one hundred per cent dividend on the investment. It is a product of a more equal if lower distribution of wealth.

A century ago, the difference was between those who had all and those who had none. Los ricos were the small number of lordly Patrones of the haciendas. Los pobres were the large class of peones who depended upon the Patrones for the little cash that passed into their brown hands. Los ricos rode horses bridled with silver, los pobres were lucky to have a burro. Los ricos gambled with gold, los pobres sidled up to the gaming tables in their cotton pantalones and torn, straw sombreros and placed their one copper centavo on the turn of a card. Los ricos owned vast flocks of sheep, los pobres managed to forage two scraggly goats.

The day of los ricos has vanished. There are only a few Spanish-Americans left who own thousands of acres of land grants, where they run thousands of sheep. But los pobres are still with us, bettered in condition, education and independence, since the lordly class has faded out. Los pobres of New Mexico are the luckiest poor people in America, if not in the world.

Take the comparison of a tenement block swarming with eight hundred people and a country where I have passed only one hay wagon in fifty miles. In a tenement there must be rent to pay the landlord for one dark room, crowded with family, cooking, washing, beds. In New Mexico nearly every native owns his land. He digs up the mud in his backyard to build his house with warm, thick walls. There is a well for water and an acequia for irrigation. He leaves the door open on bright winter days so that the sunshine may come in. Toward evening he puts two piñon sticks in the corner fireplace and warmth, seemingly out of proportion to the little fuel, fills the room. The piñon is gathered from the mountains with only the expense of hauling it in. There is no greedy gas meter to swallow precious quarters.

Instead of scuttling out of the way of trucks and people on crowded city streets, children have all outdoors where they play in the sunshine. Instead of an eleventh-story iron fire escape hung with washing, there are red geraniums blooming on a low blue window sill. There is no nerve-jangling roar of Elevateds —only the distant "yip-yip" of coyotes rising through the still night or the nearer braying of burros. Mattresses and pillows are stuffed with native wool, never too thoroughly scoured and sometimes harboring chinches. Furnishings are frugal, but the houses are spotlessly clean from the glistening white walls to the floor swept with a short wheat-straw broom. This neatness extends to the front doorway, swept so thoroughly that the road is almost brushed away. There are fiestas, bailes, masses to weave a happy, simple pattern of life.

I know that there are city dwellers who prefer an electric lamp post to a forest and cannot sleep in Santa Fe for the stillness. But los pobres have been conditioned through countless generations to appreciate the dones de Dios—the beneficent gifts of God.

Cash is always scarce but so are necessities. Poverty often rips the family pocket book to find enough silver half dollars to buy shoes for school children. But it is poverty clothed in dignity.

There is an example of this in the people living in the north and south ends of Santa Fe county. Neither have a yachtsman's surplus. To the north, in the Spanish placitas, los pobres live on meager incomes and the free dones de Dios, sustaining their racial pride with quiet grace. To the south, there are the homesteads of those who drove in last year to plant a beanfield on government land in the Estancia Valley. Their frame shacks and families are down-at-the-heel. There is no beauty or pride about their poverty. They endure a bad year with bad grace, hoping for a better crop next year to take them to distant movies, or pile beds and family in a wagon to drive on to another Promised Land in another state. The northern communities are like silver cedars, forced by arid conditions to live close to the ground and conserving their sustenance by roots as deep under the mountain soil as the evergreen branches above it. The south produces a tumbleweed crop, uprooted by the first cold wind and driven on and on over the prairies. . . .

For the poorest of los pobres are aristocrats. They have the aristocrats' standard of work. If work is enjoyable, it is fine—if it is drudgery, why do it? Economists should study a people who succeed in living without too much work. The five-day week is no novelty here. But to work at one's own business is the aristocratic way of bending all energy to the task, whether it is making filigree or plowing from dawn to dark.

Economic independence has been the salvation of los pobres. There is always enough land to plant beans, chile, corn and melons—the staples of New Mexico since our first records.

With the simplest tools the colonial farmers har-

vested enough from their land to insure a year's provisions. Plows used to be no more than tree branch
with a crooked end, tied to the horses with a homemade harness. Sheep and goats tramped out the
wheat on round, mud threshing floors. Hay was cut
by hand and heaped in fragrant stacks without the
bother of baling it. To me the wonder is that the
country could have gone on without the now indispensable bailing wire, used for everything from automobile parts to hinges.

Mamacita does not miss her luncheon bridge clubs,
for there are husking bees when all the neighbors
gather to strip the corn and save the dry husks to use
for cigarettes or tamale wrappers. The white corn is
thrown into heaps to feed the horses, the colored cobs
are saved for the family. Purple, pink, orange, black
and red in a checkerboard design, the colored kernels
are as gay as jewels and prized for their sweet flavor.
Blue corn is preferred for such delicacies as atole and
enchiladas. Mamacita prepares it with the same primitive machinery her Indian neighbors use. She sits on
her heels behind the metate and grinds the kernels
with the mano. The metate is a smooth, oblong
block of pumice stone hollowed out on the upper surface by long grinding with the pumice rolling-pin, called
the mano since it is held in the hand. She rubs the
mano up and down over the metate as though it were a
wash board. With a deft twist of her hand she throws
the blue corn between the stones, grinding the meal
over and over until it is of a fineness to please a good

housewife. Some one, with an eye for statistics, has figured that each man eats ten metates during his lifetime, for the stone that is inevitably worn away is the same color as the blue corn meal.

In the country, wheat is still ground between huge pumice stone grinders run by water wheels. Up on the high llano at Truchas there are many square log mills beside the swift mountain stream. The first sound of early morning is the splash of water spilling over the mill wheels. Santa Fe used to pride herself on many water mills, but the last one on the Acequia Madre was bought a few years ago and converted into a studio-home. Fortunately the water trough and grinders have been preserved below the old mill to remind us of days of cuanto ha—how long ago?

Fall is the busy season for Mamacita; even busier than the summer work of helping with the hoeing and irrigating, or of following the spring plow with a basket of seeds. During the Indian summer days the harvest must be gathered to provide for winter and the coming year. The pantry shelf with rows of tinned food is still a distant luxury for Mamacita. But she has put away in the low storeroom bags of seeded apricots, peaches and plums, apple rounds and melon rinds dried to a sweetness in her native evaporator—the sun and air. There are also piles of goose-necked squash, fat pumpkins and watermelons.

There is an unwritten law that on the fifteenth of October the bestias may be turned out of the corrals to forage for themselves. Mamacita and the children hurry out to strip the fields before the cows, horses and burros get to them. It is also a game to beat Jack Frost's early paint brush. Beans are gathered in great piles of trailing vines and dried yellow pods. When there is a leisure day the pods are shaken over a cloth until the beans fall out. They are winnowed by tossing them up and down in a blanket or basket, letting the wind blow away the chaff. Unlucky is the family who has not enough beans for every day of the year. They are meaty, brown frijoles, as large as kidney beans and with more flavor. Commercially they are known as "pintos," from the tiny brown specks on their creamy surface.

The autumn colors of northern New Mexico are quite properly the old Spanish colors of gold and scarlet. Mountainsides are vast panoramas of quivering, flaming golden aspen leaves. Even where the pine and spruce are thickest, the flame of aspens shoots up between the evergreen, and gorges glitter as though gold had trickled down the cañons. Below them, pungent, yellow-blossomed clumps of chamisa spread over tawny mesas and arroyos. Sheer cliffs are streaked like a giant layer cake with striations of carnelian, ocher and mauve. Sandhills, dyed crimson with purple shadows, take on richer tones in the mellow, heady sunshine.

Tucked away in the folds of the great mountains earth-hued homes are picked out with surprising scarlet borders. Are these silken banners draped from the flat roofs for some fiesta? Or are they long, vermilion garlands of flowers wreathed on the warm, brown walls? A closer view proves them to be ristras of chile hung from the rooftops to dry in the sunshine. Wherever you go along the river valleys, the landscape is vivid with pure color—blue sky, yellow cottonwoods, red chile festooned over earth houses bubbling out of the earth. Every house flaunts its gay ristras; sometimes hung as thickly as wide red blankets and spilling over onto frames behind the house; sometimes only half a dozen strings, the dwindling harvest of a viejito.

No native crop is more prized or more essential than these strings of red peppers. Early in September every member of the family goes to the fields to pick the shining green pods from the rows of chile. They are heaped in a dark storeroom until the green shows splotches of orange. Then Mamacita and the children leave the fields and sit on the floor all day and into the night to tie the pods, three at a twist, on to a ten-foot cord. The work goes swiftly. Soon the cords are full and tied together at the ends. Then they are hung over the roof to dry, high above straying bestias. Three days in the sunshine, and the ristras are as scarlet as live coals; three weeks and they have deepened to crimson and are beginning to rattle with a dryness when the first cold wind from the Sangre de Cristo shakes them. After six weeks, they are carefully taken down from the housetop, enough hung from the storeroom vigas to provide the family with chile, and the rest heaped high in covered wagons to be driven to market.

Chimayó, that fabled hamlet north of Santa Fe, is

the red heart of chile-land. Chile, blankets and the miracles of the Sanctuario have given it fame. New Mexicans prefer its chile because they say it has more fire to the powdered ounce than that of any other locality. Twenty-five thousand ristras are an average crop for Chimayó. For once it is good credit to be "in the red," for every ristra hung from your roof brings one to two round, silver dollars. Spice merchants seek it for paprika and chile powder, pimento, chile con carne, tamales, pickles and sauces. El Paso, San Antonio, New Orleans, Savannah like its flavor, for the southern states are reputed to consume five times as much hot condiments as all the rest of the United States. The first green chile was canned at Las Cruces, New Mexico, many years before the California packing houses featured their red and green peppers.

There is another arresting red line picked out against the drab houses. It is meat, cut in strips, and hung over a clothes cord to dry in the sun. A cow or a goat has been butchered on the rack back of the house. Why waste the meat when it will provide jerked beef or goat stew for winter? Yes, there are flies and dust settling on the red, uncovered line, but the sunshine and air form a hard, dry crust over the meat before it spoils.

The piñon crop is a true gift of God. It is manna succoring the children of the wilderness. Cabeza de Vaca was saved from starvation by living on piñones for three days, and many a sheepherder depends upon these rich, piny nuts to supply fat in his diet. The piñon shrubs, seldom more than twice as high as your head, dot the red foothills like a thick sprinkling of black pepper. They are generous volunteers. Nature does the planting and watering, natives pick the nuts, merchants market them, but no man can foretell, increase or control this indigenous harvest. It is, of all crops, a free gift to mankind.

Every fall there is a small crop of these tiny brown nuts, but the bumper crop is as unaccountable as southwestern weather. There is a tradition that it comes every seventh year; merchants claim that it is every third or fifth year. Only one fact is sure—it requires two years for the nut to mature from flower to sticky, purple cone. If there is a drouth, the nuts shrivel, the cones turn brown and the bumper crop dies a-borning. But if there are good summer rains, los pobres smile with the promise of a bumper crop for this year or the next.

As soon as the frost turns the aspens to gold and opens the resin-coated cones whole families go to the hills to camp and pick piñones before the first snow turns them rancid. In Santa Fe, where the dwarf pines only give way grudgingly to the city limits, native families spend the long, fall days in the hills picking nuts. A swift blue flame leaps from the trees as the family invades the low forest and a cry of "pi-ñon-e, pi-ñon-e" fills the crystal-clear air. It is a flock of piñoneros, the piñon bluejays feasting on nuts and doing good service by gobbling the worms that bore into the cones.

From grandfather to the tiniest toddler, they take

their flour sacks and creep under the bronze-green branches, making a game of seeing who can gather the first one hundred nuts. Greedy Alfonso grabs the cones for the dozen nuts, like fat apple seeds, that have not yet been shaken down by the wind. But his fingers are so coated with pungent resin that the nuts stick to them, and he loses time. Finally he gnaws off the resin and has chewing gum for the rest of the day. What a gleeful shout there is when little Pedro discovers a pile of cactus thorns and sticks piled up near the roots of a tree! He brushes them away and eagerly burrows into a squirrel's cache, finding twenty-five pounds of nuts. Mamacita smilingly chides him for robbing the squirrel, but Pedro's childish faith insists that Mr. Squirrel will find many other nuts to carry in his cheeks and hide away for the winter.

At evening they trudge home, happy over their harvest. Full flour sacks are tied on the burro's wood saddle, or grandfather and the smallest children take the sacks with them in a rickety buggy. They sing and joke with Mamacita and the others following them, as the lean horse plods along.

At home the piñones are roasted like the coffee berries they resemble. A bumper crop not only means nuts for eating and cooking but ready cash when they are sold to the merchants—more cash than the toil of wheat and corn crops yield. Piñones bring an average of sixteen cents a pound. To any save timeless people even sixteen cents a pound would be little recompense for gathering a thousand tiny nuts. But piñones are free, and picking them is a picnic as well as profit. A bumper crop from New Mexico has filled as many as three hundred freight cars with nuts. More than two million dollars is not a small gift of God.

Navajo and Zuñi Indians get a large share of this for their patient labor. Good piñon years, weavers and woodcutters leave their work and take to the hills, and Navajo blankets and firewood are scarce. Often the piñon crop is a salvation to an arid land, for the little trees continue to bear when all other crops fail. Most of them find their way from the wholesale houses to the pushcart vendors in New York's Ghetto. There the foreign population buys them to take the place of their Russian pine nuts or the Italian pistachio.

While many sackfuls are sold to merchants, there are always enough stored away for winter days when old men sit with their backs against a sunbaked adobe wall. Cracking piñones occupies their minds while they gossip over the affairs of the placita. By long practice they achieve a mechanical efficiency—the piñon goes in one corner of the mouth, is cracked and munched, and the shells flow out the other corner like an automatic feeder. Political campaigners are astounded at a sound, like the deep rumble of waves, that flows over a meeting. It is the continuous cracking of piñones, each person in the audience munching as he listens.

Petrolino, the vendor of piñones, was a famous character on the streets of Santa Fe. He was tall, with broad shoulders and narrow hips and must have been a handsome personage before total blindness overtook him. After that, he lost none of his innate, solitary dignity but his closed eyes gave his face a groping sensitiveness. One shoulder was hunched up carrying a woven brown basket of piñones over his arm, and the other hand held a cane, so that he might tap his way up and down roads. He knew instinctively if a fence had been moved or a gutter had been dug and his cane searched carefully around it. He knew, too, the secrets of the neighborhood, far better than men who could see, for people told secrets before him, falling into that human failing of thinking that because he was blind he was also deaf and dumb. Instead his other senses were more acute and he had the rare intelligence of a blind philosopher. Artists painted him, trying to catch that elusive quality of second sight. As an orator he was famous, carrying the house with his fervent arguments at political juntas. When he died a few years ago, every one mourned for Petrolino, a real town character.

But any sunny day you may see little old Don Marcelo carrying his red willow basket of piñones around the Plaza or stopping to rest on a warm bench if business is not brisk. There is kindly humor in his brown face and a twinkle in the old eyes under the half-moon shadow of his battered hat. You get more than just a jelly glass full of piñones for your dime if you stop to buy from him, for he measures them out with an old-world courtesy and a comment on your good health and the fair weather.

Piñones add a high nutritive value to the simple native diet. All of the oil and sweetness of the pine are concentrated in the small white kernel. Fortunately, cracking them is too tedious a process for most Anglos to get indigestion. Old Spanish recipes called for piñones for stuffing wild turkey and chicken, for fried pies and that favorite brown sugar dulce, piñonate. When many criadas belonged to the hacienda it was nothing for one slave girl to spend weeks cracking piñones with a stone rolling pin. Now electric machines have come to do the work of slaves and shelled piñones are on the market.

The piñon, cedar and juniper trees grow on the red foothills around Santa Fe like the week's beard on a tramp's chin. Piñones with their short sharp needles, not only provide nuts but the most prized fuel for fogones. It burns with a hot, pitchy blaze and leaves the tang of pine in the air. It is especially desirable for open hearths, since it does not shoot out the showers of burning bark that explode with cedar.

The dry, red wood of cedar, called sabina in New Mexico, is used for cookstoves. Larger slabs with rich, lustrous texture are put aside to be carved and rubbed down for furniture. Cedar grows in a spreading bush, often wider than it is high. Against the thick evergreen branches there are curious parasites that shine in the sun like brass filaments. They are mountain mistletoe. The coral-like stems grow into the shape of a ball, sprinkled through with glistening pink pearls. While this mistletoe has no flat leaves nor milky berries, New Mexican maidens find that the pink berries provoke just as many kisses as the white.

Low scraggly cedars of Lebanon sprawl over the ground near their higher sisters. Besides them are their beautiful cousins, the blue and silver cedars, better known as junipers. Their graceful lacey branches are decked for Christmas with platinum beads or purple berries frosted with a silver sheen.

On clear winter nights in the mountains these huddled shrubs take on the eerie quality of an upside-down world. They belong to the fourth dimension sphere, where the real is unreal and phantoms are facts. For by night it is a magpie land of black voids and white shadows. Patches of snow lie on the ground measured by the sunshine into the shadowed shapes of the shrubs. In the moonlight they are Chinese white trees, and the trees are their shadows. Clouds bulk into strange mountains and steep buildings, and the inverted mesas are seas of dark, silver-tipped ether. Clouds prick through the cloud houses like lights in skyscrapers. . . .

But down in the river valley the long rows of twinkling lights are in Santa Fe. A fragrance fills the frosty air as you brush past a trailing branch of juniper. From the little town there is the odor of burning cedar coming up from flat mud houses. It clings to memory like a subtle, scarce-remembered perfume.

One whiff of it brings back a picture of early morning with the first blue-gray smoke spiraling upwards from the low, adobe chimneys. The tingle of the crisp, cold air, the cloudless blue sky, the sunlit radiance and that resinous odor of burning cedar permeate the memory. It is like incense burned to ancient kitchen gods. It drives away the reminder of decaying vegetation, of near-by cowsheds, of a corral where goats are penned at night, of outside privadas. It mingles with the smell of smoldering, brown leaves, and of Russian thistle being burned off the fields where the oils rise in a dense black smoke until they flame up like torches in the wind. Then there is another whiff in the air, acrid and pungent. It comes from cottonwood backlogs, chuckling together in the fireplace long after the piñon and cedar are white ashes.

It is one of the joys of living in Santa Fe to buy these native woods at your doorstep. You watch the wood-laden burros coming down the winding road, nibbling at weeds and leaves as they pass. They vary in color from mouse to brown, always alike in the dust or ashes powdering their rough, thick coats. A baby burro trots beside its mother, the cunningest of all baby animals. It cavorts about on stiff, slender legs, kicking up its tiny hoofs, pointing its long, furry ears and then sidling close to its mother again. You hail the leñador behind them, his coat faded from many years of weather, his old felt hat drooping over a smiling, brown face. With an upraised stick he guides the burros down the road, chiding them by name if they stray too far. The piñon and sabina have been cut stove length and deftly packed in an arc over the wood saddle until the load is larger than the burro's own body. The burro doesn't mind the load, however,

314

as he flaps his long ears and placidly trots along in front of his master's guiding stick. At least he is free of a bit and bridle, for although he may be driven, he can't be led.

If the leñador is prosperous, he will have a string of a dozen burros, bargaining for each load at "seis reales." When you have agreed to pay the "six bits,"

he hangs his ragged coat over the burro's head to keep him blindly still. Instead of using a hitching post, he lifts one small front hoof and catches it in a loop of rope from the wood saddle. With a jerk at the knot the binding rope is loosened and down clatters the wood around the three feet of the immovable, blinded burro. The wood is quickly carried by armloads into your woodshed. Then the other browsing burros are herded together, the leñador jumps into the empty saddle, rolls and lights a brown paper cigarette, whacks the

315

burro's flanks and off they trot to find another buyer. He is a contented Sancho Panza on his donkey, not worrying over windmills or the whims of Don Quixote.

Belonging to the mule family, burros are stubborn little beasts. The wise leñador knows his burros and bends his way to theirs. If they decide to go, they go —if not, they take an emphatic stand, and that's all there is to it. "Stick 'em in the cruz" is the cruel punishment of an equally stubborn leñador. His stick digs into that sensitive spot where the stripes of the backbone and the forelegs cross. He will tell you that this cruz is the divine stigmata, stamping all burros since the Palm Sunday when Christ rode a donkey into Jerusalem.

If the leñador is más rico and less energetic he hitches his burros to a high, iron-wheeled wagon, whose spindle sides form a cradle for the load of wood. Moseying along in the sunshine, humming a tune to the creaking wheels, his indolent voice calls out "Leña! Leña!" to whoever notices him, without stopping the burro's slow meander. The wood loads coming up from Agua Fría have shrunk these last years, sometimes concealing a hollow in the middle of the load. Even a leñador now finds that a small two-dollar bill is not unlucky, since it is needed to buy a dollar's worth of flour and lard and coffee.

What sustains these burden bearers of the West is a mystery. No fodder is provided for them. They are turned loose to forage on dry grass and weeds and lick old tomato cans. In spite of this they have the strength of mules and more endurance than horses. They are to the Western deserts what camels are to the East. Their little black hoofs have hauled ore for prospectors, water-kegs for desert rats, furniture for the first families, wood, Bibles and textbooks.

In 1867 "Uncle Charley" Ilfeld, one of the pioneer merchants of the territory, moved his store from Taos to Las Vegas. The merchandise was packed over the Mora Trail on one hundred burros. The determined young man and his muleros mushed the half-mile string of loaded burros over mountains, blanketed with December snow, to found a great wholesale house and one of the largest fortunes in New Mexico. When he reached Las Vegas, he unpacked the burros, set up store and became the postmaster. The federal equipment consisted of two cigar boxes, one for English letters and one for Spanish.

Burros bear their burdens with stoical success, if they have to, but they are most content to do nothing for days at a time. Moving imperceptibly they keep within the shade on a summer day, yet burros and men are the only animals that have succeeded in surviving in the torrid desert sun. While the animals seem to go without food, they never go without water, for their sure instinct knows the shortest trail to water holes. They are shaggy, ageless philosophers, living on nothing but not worrying about it. The only time they express themselves is at night—the long, loud braying which has given them the sarcastic name of "desert nightingales."

317

It is this night life of burros that sleepy Santa Fe resents. Irate households wake up to find these hungry, braying beasts in their gardens. After the third offense the man of the house turns the burros over to the City Pound. Then the City Fathers worry, for their keep is worth more than their cost. Keeping a burro in luxury may be humanitarian but it runs up a hay bill. None are redeemed, and yet no one has the heart to kill the innocent intruders. The City Pound offers them for sale for twenty-five cents a piece but small boys are the only purchasers. Santa Fe's "burro problem" has led to the suggestion of ferrying them across the Rio Grande at Vallecitos. Future generations will doubtless go there for the sport of hunting wild asses.

In spite of their picturesqueness, burros and leñadores are being pushed out of this land of Poco Tiempo by speedier transportation. Sundays you may notice trucks lurching home in the late afternoon loaded with long branches of piñon cut in the mountains, for a truck will carry as much as seven burros and seven times as fast. Delivery men make the most of a rest day to use store trucks for family wood hauling. There is never a mountainside so remote that it is not veined with wood roads which eventually lead down to the highways or to a sunny placita.

And any late afternoon you may hear the tinkle of a bell from the rounded breast of Atalaya Hill and a childish treble rising with it in an old shepherd song. Then, in the saffron glow of sunset spreading from the

far prairie to the clear green sky in ether waves of
gold, a blue-overalled urchin comes around the bend
in the trail driving his dozen goats before him. They
have found good pasture that day in the potreros, green
grass to enrich goat milk and round, white cheese and
to fatten the little white kids before they are butchered.
But the boy is hurrying the goats toward the home corral, for he is thinking of Mamacita and a good, warm
supper.

Who wouldn't remember, after a long day in the
mountains with only a folded tortilla in your pocket
for lunch, a bowl of chile con carne with its tender
morsels of meat floating in a rich red sauce? Or frijoles cooked in an Indian olla, simmering for days in
the fireplace coals until their brown skins burst of a
tenderness? Or golden apricots, dried in the sunshine
and stewed down to remind you of June in January?

For those who like Spanish cooking, the native menu
offers a savory variety. Of course you may be Nor-
dically inhibited from digesting high seasoning. If so,
you had better fortify yourself with tea and toast before you attend a Spanish supper. For Spanish cooking is no simple matter of broiling a beefsteak and
sprinkling on a pinch of salt. It is an art which tempts
the imagination of a chef, and requires the patience of
a saint in its long, slow cooking. There is a suggestion
of dried mint leaves, a glass of Sherry, a hint of sa-
brosa española, a nuance of orégano, a bit of olives
and olive oil, two or three chile pods, a stain of tomato,

a reminder of minced onion, and the certainty of garlic—one or all in every Spanish dish.

Spanish suppers begin with albondigas, force meat balls rolled in blue corn meal and boiled until the soup is thick and the tender balls are still as round as marbles. For entrées there are enchiladas, the blue corn meal pancakes spread between with chopped raw onions and melted cheese, the stack swamped with chile sauce, and two fried eggs on top staring out like drowning yellow eyes. Chiles Rellenos have good reason to be called Angel's Dreams. They are green peppers stuffed with chicken and cheese, dipped in batter and crisped golden brown in sizzling fat.

Then comes posole, the Spanish for hog and hominy. The corn kernels have been soaked in lye water until the tough, outer skin peels off. The hominy simmers all day with rounds of fresh ham hock until the meat falls to pieces and the bracelets of rind and fat form that delectable tidbit, "cueritos." In the beginning add enough of the chile and onions and garlic, and you have posole heaped in an earthen bowl. Chile con carne is so universally known, even in its canned variety, that it needs no genealogy. Tamales too have found their way into tins, but they are much better made at home, their corn meal stuffing sandwiched with chile and chicken, wrapped in a new corn husk, and boiled in tempting chile gravy. Chicken smothered with sherry and herbs is cooked for hours until the seasoning gives it only a delicate flavor. Carne adobada is pickled for days in brine, chile and spices and fried until the juices stream out of the pork. Mutton stew is disguised with every herb the store room holds.

With any and every dish there are frijoles. These brown beans are to Bernardo what potatoes are to Paddy. They are more of a staple than daily bread and quite as nourishing. They may be cooked with or without meat or seasoning, and the longer they cook the better they are. But there must be frijoles.

And there must be chile. The native housewife turns up her nose at the ground chile on the market. She insinuates that corn meal has been added to its selling bulk and is sure that it is mixed with the tough outer skins, seeds and veins. She prepares her own chile pulp by breaking off the stem ends by which they are tied into the ristra, roasting the pods and steaming them until they are tender. Then comes the process of peeling the meat away from the skin. It makes the finger tips smart for a week when the pods are properly kneaded by hand. But there is a soft red pulp ready for chile con carne. She will show you the discarded skins, seeds and veins that would have been ground up with chile powder if you had not prepared it the right way. It's hot—yes, but that is what gives sauce to life. Chile verde is blistered and sweated until the transparent skin peels off, and the green meat is mixed with salt to add condiment to an already seasoned meal.

For vegetables, there are tender spring greens, called quelites, and known to us as sheep sorrel and pigweed. You will see children picking baskets of them in the cienagas in the spring and summer. They are cooked like spinach, drained and fried with minced onion, and sometimes with the addition of piñones, raisins, and hard-boiled eggs. During the winter the provident Mamacita cooks rounds of dried yellow squash and pumpkin. Chicos is a favorite dish with the summertime flavor of fresh corn. The cobs are boiled when the corn first ripens and dried to be cooked during the long winter. Sliced dried cucumbers, called rueditas since they resemble little wheels, are a Lenten delicacy, along with other dried vegetables and eggs prepared in numberless ways. Beets and carrots, cabbage and celery make ensaladas with a piquant vinegar and oil salad dressing.

After these numerous meat dishes, fruit and a pat of goat's milk cheese are sufficient desserts. But for fiestas there will be sopa, a bread pudding with layers of apples, butter and sugar, cheese browned on top, dusted with cinnamon and served with a hot wine sauce. Or empanadas, those fried pies shaped in a triangle and stuffed with tongue, currants, piñones, spices and wine. Or sopapillas, sweet hollow pin cushions of puff paste, fried like doughnuts and eaten with hot, homemade syrup. Or a glorified rice pudding, called arroz con leche. Or biscochitos, shortbread cut in fancy shapes, flavored with anise seeds and glazed with sugar.

Hot thick chocolate is often served in the afternoon with sopapillas. A dash of cinnamon has been added to it and the whole beaten to a froth with a wooden chocolate pestle. Biscochitos are best with a little glass of wine, for New Mexicans were adepts at making many kinds of wine with native grapes or elderberries. Strong, black coffee simmers on the stove day in and day out. Mamacita has her cup of coffee between meals as well as with every meal. When Americans first came over the trail, they found that water was never tasted until the meal was over. If a guest reached for his glass of water his host assured him that there were other courses yet to come.

For bread there are round, crisp loaves baked in an estufa. A hot wood fire is made within the hive-shaped oven and burns until the thick mud walls are too hot to touch. Then the coals and ashes are carefully swept out and the mud floor covered with loaves in all the shapes of the baker's artistic expression. The door is closed tightly, the venthole stopped with a rag, and in three or four hours, without watching a thermometer, the loaves and rolls are brown. Their fragrance reminds me of warm bread and butter begged from the cook after school. Tortillas are indispensable for numerous hungry mouths. They are large thin pancakes, made without baking powder, and browned on a hot griddle.

I always remember the old camp cook, Pedro, when I think of buñuelos. I was at a sheep camp in the high mountains of Rio Arriba. In the early morning I raised my sleepy head above the quilt beds spread on the ground to see him bending over his iron kettle in the pit of coals. By the time I had dashed cold river water over my face he had a stack of buñuelos ready, great puffy pancakes dropped in deep fat. He smiled when we praised his cooking until the three wrinkles on his nose made one long seam. His buñuelos were crisp and delicate for breakfast, cold and leathery by noon and a sodden nightmare for supper. I found that after they were cooked for breakfast Pedro pressed the whole pack down with all his strength and piled them away in a cupboard box for the rest of the day.

But there was never anything so delicious as ribs of new-born lamb roasted on a spit over the fire, salt rubbed in when they were half done; or morsels of lamb browned in hot mutton fat in the iron kettle; or frijoles simmering all day while the sheep herders were away; or dried prunes cooked until they needed no sugar.

It was late in May when the flocks had been brought from the winter pastures to the lambing grounds. The sheep were run on the partido plan, where the sheep herder was given fifty per cent of the lambs as his share of the year's profit and agreed to return the original number of ewes to the Patrón at the end of three years. Going partido had the advantage of partnership responsibility, for if the sheep herder was careless, his profit was cut down and he had to replace the ewes at the end of his contract.

The lambs bobbed up and down in the flocks like popcorn popping in a pan. Their new, unsteady legs had springs in them that raised all four feet off the ground in a frolicsome bounce. Sunset was filled with bleating when lost lambs and ewes called to each other until that fine sense of smell brought them together. Motherless lambs had the skin of a dead baby lamb tied to them to fool the ewe into thinking the lamb was her own. The shepherds picked up the lambs that were too weak to walk and carried them in their arms, driving the flocks to the night bedding pastures. They flowed along in a white stream, the backs of the ewes making a pattern like the repeated lines left on the seashore after the tide has receded.

After Pedro had washed the tin supper dishes, the sheep herders gathered around the camp fire and brought out a mouth harp, an accordion and a guitar. Soon, the jolly young Patrón, Don Cristóbal, had all of us dancing old square dances near the blazing fire, stumbling over holes in the grassy turf, breathless as we spun around. It was as pastoral as an Elizabethan gambol on the greens, in the remote, wild mountains of New Mexico. Earth beds again and gratitude for the gifts of God, the lullaby of the river lapping through purple Spanish iris, stars caught in the high, pine branches, and the stillness of night broken only by the hoot of some gray owl.

XIII

Wooden Saints

ROMANCE, mysteries and miracles cling to Santa
Fe. If you are sensitive to them, they will seep into
you here as sunshine warms adobe. For long-tried
faith has been molded into customs and arts. If you
believe that cannon are all-powerful, your country will
be planted with cannon. But if you believe that saints
work larger miracles, your home will have a niche for
santos.

The soldiers who conquered this province three centuries ago brought greed, cruelty and oppression. The
colonists who followed them brought sensitiveness,
faith and adventure. As long as war lasted, its crimes
were uppermost. When the conquest had been more
or less effected, the life of the colonials flowed over
the land.

Their needs were more drastic than anything we
can imagine in the twentieth century. There was a

wilderness within and without them to settle and popu-
late. After the weariness of long, parched marches
across the Jornado del Muerto they had no homes to
rest in. They faced the hardships of a bare land,
jealously guarded by the Indian owners. With an
arquebus in one hand to defend their families from
terrible scalping raids and an ax in the other to clear
away the forest, they set about to wring from the wilderness all that home means to man. They were in
a new world, unfurnished, unclothed and unfed by
trains or the mail-order catalogue.

While the captains-general traveled like kings to
the northern province, the meager equipment of the
colonists was reduced to the few, treasured, personal
possessions the women refused to leave behind—a
rosary, a piece of jewelry, silken shawls and sprigs of
geranium and roses of Castile. The six-months-long
entradas made it impossible to pack heavy furnishings
to the new country. As they settled in small groups in
New Mexico's upper river valleys, they gave the place
the advantageous blessing of a saint's name. Their
first efforts were to build homes of adobe, much like
the Indian's practical dwellings. These were sparsely
furnished with beds, tables, chairs and cupboards laboriously fashioned from the trees of the forest. Soon
farm lands and ingenious acequias produced corn, beans
and melons; sheep and wild animals were the meat supply. The material needs were crudely provided but
the needs of the soul were still unsatisfied.

Mission churches rose with the help of Indian con-

327

verts, but masses in them were rare solaces celebrated by the few, scattered padres. There was a need for everyday spiritual comforts, for the blessed images of saints who would allay fear and suffering and bring buena suerte to isolated homes. Accustomed to depending upon religious ritual, the colonists turned instinctively from the terror of marauding Indians and

the struggle with the giant forces of nature which had tipped up mountains into rock-rimmed mesas, to familiar, handmade images which they could love.

However, there were no artists set apart to copy dearly remembered pictures and statues. They were only lonely shepherds and farmers with a hungry need of heavenly help. In spite of the fact that they were not artists, and little skilled as craftsmen, they turned to and carved and painted saints until each fireside niche had its patron, and a galaxy of holy personages watched over the household from the high, scalloped wall shelves.

Images of the saints painted upon small panels of wood were called santos de retablos, while those that were carved into statues were called bultos or vueltos. Since the wooden panels were easier to make, there were many more of them than bultos. They varied in size from a few inches square to eighteen by twenty inches, though the usual size was eight by ten inches. They were like individual sections of the painted, wooden reredos in the mission churches, open portrait albums of the different saints surrounding the Cristo and the Virgin. These altars were splashes of soft pastel colors against the yeso-white walls, where the concealed windows in the high transept brought them out as glowing high lights in the shadowed chapel.

When the paint was applied directly to the wooden panels, it cracked and peeled off. A more durable finish, as well as a smoother and better surface for painting, was made by covering the panel with the native yeso or gypsum mixed with ox-hoof glue. On some of the retablos the yeso was molded into a bas-relief showing the slightly raised heads and figures and a border around the panel, worked at the top into the old design of a half rosette. These bas-relief santos de retablos were of superior workmanship and were painted over in soft colors.

The paint used was made from indigo, clay, the juice of cactus and the dye of leaves and bark, applied as water colors or mixed with oil. Some of them show the realistic stain of human blood which has led to the probable theory that they were the santos of Penitentes. The few, pure colors were used effectively, the figures of the saints and their symbols standing out against the gray-white background with a black outline. Many santos show two curtains pulled to either side to reveal the saint as though it were placed in an altar, a consistent as well as decorative motif since retablo meant an altarpiece.

Through the long winter days when the fields were asleep under snow blankets, farmers spent their time whittling statues of their favorite saints. Though Spanish carving was a traditional art, the colonists were unskilled in the fine points of sculpture. New Mexican bultos have a spontaneous, crude realism in contrast with the more sophisticated statues which the colonists may have brought with them from Mexico or Spain. The latter are recognized by the finer carving of the head, hands, the folds of the gowns and by the tiny, glass eyes. In the northern province the carving was crudely stark and austere, and saintliness was depicted in a fixed stare. Occasionally the head and waist were carved out of solid wood and the skirt flared out in burlap, coated with yeso and painted, and supported by wooden stays. In spite of the rigidness of the figures and their inquisitional stare there is a lovable, human quality about most bultos, for they were fashioned from a desire for sympathy and tenderness to temper the ills of life.

So an art was born out of the necessity for expression—an art not unlike that of the Italian shepherd, Giotto, in its direct, emotional quality. These native santos belong to the stage of development of the Spanish and Italian Primitives in their forthright intensity and realism. They were created, not by following schools of art, but by an inevitable, naïve impulse to satisfy the human soul. As in all primitive art, normal proportions were disregarded in the subconscious desire to express urgent feeling. Just as the Yeibitchai gods of the Navajo or the idols of African Negroes have thin, elongated torsos, so the bodies of the bultos are strangely attenuated—perhaps to endow the image with that sense of more-than-human dignity. Again the primitive unimportance of proportion is seen in the relation of the saints and their symbols. The figure of the farmer's San Isidro may be several times as large as the oxen he is driving, for the saint was important and his special powers of blessing crops and cattle only needed to be suggested.

These far-away artists followed the footsteps of the Church of Rome which encouraged religious paintings and statues for spreading doctrine and history in the days when most people could not read and books were rare. St. Augustine spoke of sacred pictures as the "books of the simple." When European artists had become more proficient toward the end of the fifteenth century, the church ordained which subjects

331

were to be painted, which forbidden, how the saints were to be clothed and in what colors and the strict hierarchical order of the groups.

However, the province of New Mexico was too remote to know or follow Roman dogma. Santos were painted with the colors nearest at hand. St. Francis sometimes wore a red or green gown instead of the prescribed gray or brown, while the Spanish Franciscans and their order in Mexico followed their founder, Pedro Alcantra, and dressed San Francisco in blue robes. Old Testament characters, the heroes of the Israelites, appeared as santos de retablos or bultos even though they had not been canonized by Rome. For instance we find a bulto of Job, evidently appealed to by some one who suffered from boils. The carver represented him in the uncomfortable posture of a man who is painfully seated and covered his naked body with evenly spaced red boils. Moses, in his long gray beard and oriental robes, was venerated since he protected the house from rats and snakes.

Rare bultos of the Trinidad go back to the tenth century version of the Trinity, for it was only during that century that the Holy Ghost was given human form, afterwards being symbolized as a dove. In distant New Mexico such pronouncements were forgotten, and the Trinidad are sometimes found showing three patriarchal gentlemen seated on the top of a round, red world.

Spanish fashions, however, carried over to dress the saints. They did not wear celestial draperies but were pictured in heaven in earthly raiment carrying the symbols of their special virtues. San Felipe wears the cutaway coat and tights of the Spanish Court, San Miguel's wings protrude through a star-spangled coat of mail above leggings and high boots. The saints who were not monks have the royal investiture of the small, black, pointed beard of King Philip. Many of the saints were of the royal blood and were martyred for the new-fangled Christian faith, like St. Catherine of Alexandria. She is pictured in her royal robes, with the worldly crown at her feet, which she spurned, and the heavenly crown above her as her aspiration.

As the colonists became more securely rooted on the prados and mesas of Nuevo México certain men developed greater proficiency as carvers and painters. They were called santeros, the saint-makers, who signed and dated their work on the backs of the santos de retablos. About 1807 there was a break between New and Old Mexico, due probably to the turmoil in Mexico City at the beginning of the revolt against Spain which, in a few years, brought about Mexican independence. The slight intercourse between Mexico and the far northern province diminished, and New Mexicans were forced, more than ever, to turn to their own resources. This stimulated such arts as saint-making and weaving until they reached their peak about 1830-35. Those were notable years for many reasons, for they also dated the greatest number of covered wagons lumbering over the Santa Fe Trail. The impetus of new commerce in Santa Fe balanced the weight of native arts and culture, a slight balance which teetered and dropped as Americanization grew stronger.

After the sympathy and understanding of the good Bishop Lamy had passed, santos and bultos in the churches were replaced by French prints of the saints framed in tin. Since 1890 there has been a decreasing demand for wooden santos, though there are still a few santeros who follow the ancient art. They have, however, an artificial feeling of reproducing antiques and have lost the spontaneity of creating an art because they had need of santos.

In the days when only the santeros supplied these wants, the crucifix was, of course, the symbol every one must have. Some were simple wooden crosses painted in red and black, others were decorated with painstaking inlays of straw. Santos de retablos pictured the crucified Christ in untutored realism. While there was a quality of sympathy and tenderness about the images of the saints, the paintings and carvings of Jesú-Cristo revealed that sense of awesome fear man had in portraying the divine anguish of the Son of God. They were wrought in agony of spirit which was dramatized in their human experience in Penitente crucifixions. They have the emotional intensity of the Middle Ages when the crucifixion became the symbol of the one divine gift, forgetting the hopefulness of resurrection. The little-skilled santeros caught that white light of exaltation in their bultos of the martyred Christ and produced dynamic interpretations

with their crude tools. There was no subtlety about
them. The spear-pierced side gushed with looped jets
of blood and the five wounds and crown of thorns
had their terrible, gory emphasis. Whether the figure
upon the cross was four inches or four feet long, its
simple carving vividly depicted human suffering.

Victorian prudery was shocked by these stark, naked
figures. Petticoats were added in the last generation,
standing out in incongruous white muslin ruffles from
the racked torso, or perhaps the figure was hidden
under a long, red nightgown. Though they would
have denied it by pointing to the enlightenment of the
age, the Victorians were returning to the ideas of
the fourth century. Then the Nicene conference ordained that in sacred art "the human body must be
entirely covered in order that no question of the flesh
might obscure the spiritual issue." Even the pink
toes of the Christ child had to be covered. After that
edict, saints had been swathed in heavily embroidered
Byzantine gowns for fourteen centuries. Red and
gold lacquer had given splendor to Spanish carving,
but the natives followed Victorian modesty and put
lace-trimmed petticoats and silk dresses on the saints
over the carved habits of their orders.

There were finer dresses for Sundays and homespun
ones for work days. Wouldn't a saint be more apt to
look with favor upon your prayers if you gave her a new
silk dress? And if the prayer had been answered,
wouldn't a grateful heart wish to express its thanks with

335

a pearl bead necklace for the stiff, saintly neck? On the other hand, a neglectful saint might be stripped of her fiesta dress and turned to the wall, and sometimes (whisper it) spanked!

Recently I saw a treasured Lady of Carmel, the chatelaine who keeps the household running smoothly. She stood three feet high in her niche and her painted face was stolid under her crown of tin and artificial flowers. She wore a purple taffeta dress trimmed with rows of lace and sky-blue ribbons, and her sleeves were puffed like Velasquez' ladies. Over her arm, and the chubby wrist of the Babe she carried, there hung the scapularies of the Carmelite order. I raised the taffeta skirt to look for the original carving and discovered two other dresses and three ruffled petticoats. A dozen tiny votive offerings were pinned to the top petticoat—a gold heart, a little foot, a crude crutch and a medal. The story of pain and thankfulness was there beneath the painted, wooden face.

You cannot help feeling that the saints are a kindly human lot in New Mexico—good friends to whom you may whisper your hopes and your fears. They will help you with those higher up. For saints play the part of intermediaries, human beings tempered by divine trials until they are fit ladies and gentlemen-in-waiting at the highest court.

Their images reminded the faithful of the mercies which might be granted them through prayers of intercession. In the hamlets clinging precariously to mountainsides, the illiterate invested their santos with peculiar efficacy. A story is told of an aged rheumatic who "borrowed" a bulto of San Antonio from the village church. There was consternation among the faithful when the loss of their favorite San Antonio was discovered and rumors that he had been sold as a curio. Finally the abuelito confessed that he thought San Antonio was cold and lonely in his church niche and needed a warm hearth and company, but the neighbors said that the old man felt that only that particular bulto of San Antonio could take the pains from his swollen knee.

Each santo and bulto represents, not a cold, abstract concept of ethics, but a special human mercy to help in everyday living. Santa Barbara holds in her hand a tower with the three Gothic windows of the Trinity. She fled to this high tower when her father tried to force her to renounce Christianity and was saved by the angels who spirited her away through the windows. She is the patroness of builders and architects and by saintly projection she has power over storms, floods and earthquakes which wreck buildings. You may imagine how precious she is in those hot Latin countries where temblores terrify men by shaking their one foundation, the good, solid earth. Prayers to Santa Clara and San Gerónimo are said to quiet the lightning serpents and the resounding roar of mountain thunder. There is a little verse that is breathed between chattering teeth by those who are terrified by lightning and thunder:

San Gerónimo bendito!
Santa Bárbara doncella!
Líbranos, Señor, de los rayos
Y de las centellas.

Santa Apollonia aids those with toothache and Santa Eloisa had a ministering sympathy for cripples. According to a second century legend Santa Librada was crucified by her father when she refused to marry the King of Sicily. Her bulto shows the figure of a young woman in a long habit and veil nailed to the cross. Those who pray to her and remember her sufferings for the faith will be liberated from hardships and troubles. Santa Inez is the patroness of shepherds, that meek and pure Agnes who has a woolly, white lamb at her feet. Santa Lucía lights the path of the blind with her lamp and helps those with eye trouble, for does she not carry her two eyes upon a platter since she tore them out when their beauty haunted her pagan lover? There is a pitiful prayer that was said to her over and over by a mother who had cried so long after her son's death that she was blind— "Blessed Santa Lucía, well I remember your blindness. I will never cry again. Forgive, O Lord, my wickedness and restore my sight." And soon her eyes were well.

There are many Marías besides the penitent Magdalena and Martha's unhousewifely sister. In fact, there are 288 manifestations of the Virgin Mother, personifying all her attributes in the different types of-Lady and suggesting the tender understanding of a

mother's heart. There is Our Lady of Sorrows, the
Mater Dolorosa, who is known in New Mexico as
Nuestra Señora de los Dolores, or de la Soledad. A
sword pierces her heart, fulfilling the Bible prophecy,
and her feast day is the saddest of all the year—
Good Friday. Novenas recited for nine days before
Good Friday help those who pray to bear the vicissi-
tudes of life with resignation. Nuestra Señora de
Lourdes and de Remedios have special healing powers.
Our Lady of Light stands upon the crescent moon with
the horns pointing downwards until the rays reach
those in purgatory. She was the woman of the Apoc-
alypse of whom it was promised "and there appeared
a great wonder in the heavens; a woman clothed with
the sun, and a moon under her feet, and upon her head
a crown of twelve stars." The favorite Lady of Old
and New Mexico is Nuestra Señora de Guadalupe
with the rays of eternal love shining about her in a
mandorla and a saucy cherub tucked in below her
feet. No Virgin is ever so human as the "Mother
and Child," the mystic mother found in much older
religions than Christianity.

Bultos of the "Holy Family out for a walk" show
Mary and Joseph holding the Little Son by the hand
between them. One of the most beautiful groups is
of the blue-robed Mary and the gentle Joseph bending over the cradle, the whole framed in a box with
a white background.

The Santo Niño is beloved by every one. He has
the universal adoration given to rosy babyhood with

the added veneration of the Christ child. The Santo Niño de Praga wears a long, baptismal robe and holds up his hand in blessing. The favorite is the Santo Niño de Atocha, seated in a little chair, decked in layers of lovingly-wrought garments, a high plush hat and plume upon his head, a basket of flowers in his hand and square-toed shoes upon his feet. Like the Bambino of the Ara Cœli in Rome, He is carried about to visit the sick. But secret errands of mercy keep him running about in the weak hours before dawn, so that he wears out his shoes, and pairs of tiny, new shoes must be brought to him from time to time.

With San Isidro he often makes a tour of the fields to bless the brown land with green shoots of corn. It was San Isidro who helped the farmer plow so that he could go to mass, the farmer plowing one row and San Isidro and the angels miraculously finishing the others. San Isidro also caused the water to rise to the sprouting of the new wheat so that there was no need to irrigate on Sunday. Nowhere else except in the prados of New Mexico would you see processions of devout people, walking across parched fields, praying that the drought may be broken. The bultos of the Santo Niño and San Isidro are carried in the arms of those who walk ahead and the men, women and children following sing their litanies and stop for prayers. The sky is hard, blue enamel, the sun scorches the panting earth, and fine dust rises behind the procession. They go up and down the dry acequia banks, moving slowly so that the Santo Niño and San Isidro may appreciate their need. Their voices rise with that slow, urgent intonation which speaks of the living relation between men and soil.

San Rafael is the patron of fishermen and dangles his golden fish from his hand. He it was who told the poor man to fish in a stream where fish had never been caught and lo—he pulled out a fish of gold! San Nicolás brings gifts to children and aids the poor and needy. San Pedro has two keys, the one of gold to unlock the portals of heaven and the iron one which opens even the bars of hell. San Mateo is the patron of bankers and money-lenders, carrying a long purse or bag, since he was a tax-collector for the Romans before he became one of the four evangelists. San Cristóbal was given his name as Christ-bearer. According to his legend he was a great Canaanite and mighty ferryman who swore to serve the greatest monarch on earth. One night he was asked to carry a crying Child across the turbulent river, but despite his strength and the palm staff in his hand he was borne down by the weight of the Child. After that he became one of the fourteen holy helpers, and travelers sought his watchfulness against accidents.

No saint is more loved than San Antonio. He helps to find lost things around the house like a thimble or a brooch and even misplaced human hearts. He is the good St. Anthony of Padua who was so pure that he was allowed to bear the Christ-child upon his arm. During the World War mothers brought candles to

burn before his niche, praying that he would help their
boys lost upon the muddy battlefields of France.
Prayers go up to him to bring babies to a barren
woman. Later in childbirth his bulto is placed in bed
with the laboring mother. In fact, any very sick person
entertains most of the heavenly host during illness,
for all the family santos are propped up against pillows and bed clothes to work their merciful miracles.
San Ramón Nannato is also invoked for a happy delivery at birth. He was the "unborn" Cardinal, coming into the world through a Cæsarian operation. In
his hands he holds the cross and the triple crown of
martyrdom for his birth, his life as a captive and his
death.

San José vies with San Antonio and "everybody's
St. Francis" as being "good for any trouble." They
are the Big Brothers in this land where help was so
often needed. The long-standing feud between the
pueblos of Acoma and Laguna over the picture of St.
Joseph is of historic record, for the Indians soon
learned to add the advantages of saintly blessings to
the magic of their gods who brought the he-rain to
the House of Dawn. This was a Spanish painting of
San José with the Child on his arm and the other hand
holding his rod which sprayed into lilies, given to
Acoma by Fray Ramírez in 1629. For centuries San
José protected Acoma from black smallpox, smut in
the corn and pestilence, and they prospered. The
rival pueblo of Laguna was envious of these benefits
and when they were threatened with disaster, they

asked for a month's loan of the wonder-working picture. But the Lagunas kept it by force in their own church so many years that they claimed it had always been theirs. In the end, the Acomas resorted to lawsuits, and in 1857 an American judge gave them back their old Spanish painting. When they came to bring him home from Laguna, they found San José's joy was so great in returning that he had already come halfway to meet them, for there was his picture waiting against a piñon tree.

Santiago is the patron St. James of Spain and her colonies, and is often represented as a gallant Caballero on horseback. Naturally he has a special interest in horses and horsemen, and on his fiesta his bulto is carried out to the corral that the mares may be blessed with fertility. There is a precious Santiago at the lovely shrine of Santuario in Chimayó across the chapel from the low door that leads to the miraculous well of healing mud. His small white horse might be mistaken for a mule, if it were not for the proud horse's neck and flaring nostrils. Two diminutive sombreros, woven of Mexican straw with peaked crowns, rest on St. James' head and his shoulder, for his entrada was long from Mexico and one hat might wear out before he reached here! A silk American flag flies on its standard above his sword and sometimes there appears below it another little banner of red, black and white brought back to Santiago from World War battles with the Germans. Votive offerings such as a red celluloid fish and a heart hang from the bridle. The cluster of faded purple roses in his arms was replaced with gay scarlet ones on that recent gala day when the Archbishop took over the old private chapel and dedicated it for the use of the Roman church.

San Juan Bautista with his camel's hair shirt has the honor of having his birthday celebrated while the other saints' days commemorate the death of the martyrs. There are other Johns, such as the Beloved Disciple and San Juan Nepomuceno, who kept the secrets of the confessional so faithfully that his tongue was found incorrupt four hundred years after his death—a lesson for gossips.

Of the shining archangels, there is San Gabriel with his horn and his head cocked to one side as though he were listening for the opening of graves. He watches over little children. San Miguel is resplendent with golden scales to weigh souls, a crown of pure gold on his head and a golden sword to slay the dragon and drive Lucifer from heaven. He has power to ward off black arts and magic.

Santos and bultos are not impervious to the trials of time. The santos may be half-charred where their corners have been burned off for ashes to make a cross on reverent foreheads for Ash Wednesday. The bultos may lack an arm, or head or leg through long family service and the air, which dries out glue. Very often their symbols are gone, for the small objects signifying the individual attainments of earthly careers are easily knocked out of the arms, and the identification of marred figures becomes an expert's problem.

St. Michael minus one leg still has somewhat of his fierce military gesture, but here is a saint without arms and her tin crown awry. She might be any one of the virtuous ladies, if you did not know which order her habit signified. San Antonio with no Child resting in his arm always seems to me the most pitiful of bultos, for though he had helped to find many lost things, no one thought to restore the Child to him. Sometimes new hands and arms of a different style of carving are fitted incongruously onto old maimed figures, or the Cristo may be fastened to a new, wooden cross.

These santos and bultos have added their friendly offices to many crises or have been called upon for the simple blessings of the day. Sometimes you wonder, as you stumble into a sunny, quiet placita, if anything ever happens there. But under the sleepy stillness there is the deep flow of life, as eventful as life can be anywhere in its personal experiences, and richly colored here by old traditions and faiths.

You may enter the unpretentious adobe houses and be met with courtly courtesy. On the whitewashed walls, cracked like parchment, the santos hang by knotted strings, and a bedecked bulto has his rounded niche. They are but painted boards while you look at them. But if you could see them when darkness fills the room, and there is only the light of a flickering candle stuck onto the mud floor beneath the santos and a kneeling mother beside it, the santos might give you, too, a sense of mystic grace.

Now you would be lucky to see such an array of bultos or santos de retablos, for collectors have combed the placitas for these ancient household saints. Instead you may find a new made-in-Germany white china statue, prized for its spotless modernness by the younger generation. They lack all the heart-hewn significance of worn, wooden panels, but already the new image has been invested with old mercies.

XIV

Lost Treasures

ONE of the charms of Santa Fe is that she offers a different lure to each of her lovers, for each finds in her composite character a reflection of his own interests. One of her many names might be the City of Lost Treasures.

An outstanding characteristic of the country around here is the search for hidden gold. It began long ago with the Conquistadores who hoped to smell out gold from the Indians living in the Seven Golden Cities of Cíbola. Centuries later, lanky American frontiersmen plodded over the Santa Fe Trail, lured on by the promise of wealth in the mountains or in quick-profit merchandise. They followed the golden mirage of the desert, the potent magic waiting for them in an undiscovered, mysterious land.

347

To-day the possibilities of New Mexico's shimmering distances are still the fascinating, unknown quantity in the equation. Gold mingles with sand waiting for water to run over the placers, vast basins cry out for moisture to turn them into billows of purple-blossomed alfalfa. Mountains are echoing walls for Greeley's advice, "Go west, young man, go west." Each man who heeds the slogan comes to New Mexico seeing the undeveloped wealth of a virgin land—a land old to Indian and Spanish civilization and yet new to the age of machinery. They bring a spirit of hazard and pioneering adventure to the twentieth century undertaking of making the land yield them livelihood. They have been rewarded by finding rich veins of gold, silver, copper, iron, lead and zinc, made profitable with the latest processes of separating metals, by discovering hills of rare and precious non-metallic ores necessary in modern inventions, and oil pools far under the dry, tawny soil. New Mexico is the richest of Southwestern states in enormous beds of coking coal. The turquoise mine, near Los Cerrillos, gave the Indians their sacred sky stone, of such beauty that its fame lured the mining Spaniards up from Mexico.

The gold rush to California in '49 and the silver stampede to Colorado in the seventies spilled over into enthusiasm for the neighbor territory, fabled with the gold and turquoise of the Indians and the lost mines of the Spaniards. A few men found these El Dorados in the eighties and nineties. When they struck it rich, their wealth gave credence to all other dreams. Mushroom camps grew up around the conical hills of Los Cerrillos while the boom lasted. Carbonateville and Bonanza are now ghost camps of those days, mounds beside the highway where there is not one adobe left upon another to show where the walls stood. Placers in the Ortiz Mountains, discovered a century ago, gave their name to Golden, a somnolent settlement now guarded by one great, yellow, cottonwood tree. Its leaves gleam in the autumn sunshine like golden coins and drop to the earth as symbols of the vanished dollars. Each spring brings them back in a new green with the hopes of nature and men to find the gold again.

As the boom days passed in the nineties, soiled maps with cryptic symbols and landmarks became part of the mining stock of the country. Such a map of a lost Spanish mine brought more cash than came out of the ground during the boom. It was an unfailing bait for dudes. Romance was always thrown in gratis— the story of how the Conquistadores forced the Indians to lead them to the secret mine, of the Spaniards growing rich and old working it, of a beautiful heiress who was kidnaped and the location of the mine lost until. . . . Then followed a lusty, western yarn of the last confession of a dying man who relieved his conscience by confessing murder and sending his partner the lost map.

Yes, of course the map gave the exact clew as to where the lost Spanish mine was to be found. See the zigzag line here marking Deadman's Gulch, the crosses

349

for a granite butte and a lone pine tree, the circles with the names of Red Rock Mountain and Bloody Hill. Deadman's Gulch was just over there to the northeast, easy enough to find with this map. The prospector had been waiting until the right man came along to make working it worth while. A few thousands spent now would mean hundreds of thousands in a year!

The deal was on, but it required several months to perfect all the plans—at the expense of the dude. Then in the dead of night the prospector started out on his mysterious journey, for no one must see him leave camp or follow him to discover the location before the new claims marked it. The dude cooled his heels at the camp waiting. His enthusiasm cooled also when months passed and no word came from the prospector. Perhaps he had been waylaid and killed and the map stolen once more. The dude's money was gone, the prospector was gone—not to return until the dude had shaken off the disappointing dust of the country. Then the wily prospector came back, another dude arrived at camp, and the soiled map was unfolded again.

One miner had an egg-sized lump of ore, worth perhaps two hundred and fifty dollars, that had kept him in comfort for twenty years. Its yellow free gold was there for every man to see. He had only to show it to mining enthusiasts to have them stake him for months at a time. The miner promised to lead them to the rich vein, going out alone to locate it. But time after

time he came back with empty pack saddles and a be-
fuddled story about how every cañon looked alike,
lightning must have burned down the lone tree land-
mark, and the vein could not be found.

There was a fabulous mine known in the legends
of the Southwest as that of "Peg-leg Pete." Peg-leg
always came back to camp with nuggets of gold, unfailing proofs that he had found a rich vein somewhere
in the distant hills. His aim was too sure to allow any
one to stalk him, but when he died, other prospectors
turned his burros loose and attempted to ferret out
his trail. One by one they came back disappointed,
for Peg-leg's secret had gone with him to the grave.
Years later a man claimed that he had found Peg-leg
Pete's mine. There was great excitement when he
led a party to a deserted cañon not far from the well-
worn ore trail.

"Here is Peg-leg Pete's mine," he said pointing to
a freshly dug hole in the sand. But there were only
stained, human bones in it.

"There's no gold in that hole!" exclaimed the party.

"Peg-leg found his gold ridin' on top of a burro,"
the man explained his theory. "He wasn't the best
aim in this here country for nothin'. See that hill—
he laid there in wait for pack trains. The fellows that
packed their gold were buried here and Peg-leg brought
their nuggets to camp."

High-grading ore was another pastime. There is
a story of a mine in Taos County that we will call the
Toltec, whose gold was in a rich, true vein, cashed

351

into millions of dollars when it was shipped to the mint in Denver. Near it, but beyond the vein, was the claim of the Mystery Mine. Miners at the Toltec hid lumps of high-grade as they worked and salted them in the Mystery. When they sent the high-grade to the mint they swore that it came from their Mystery Mine. But partners will quarrel over profits. One partner disappeared, and his dismembered skull was found on the top of the mountain twenty-five years later. The remaining partner took in others to help him dispose of his unlawful riches. He was killed, and the third member came to a grewsome death last year. The facts of his brutal murder are more astounding than fiction.

Not all prospectors sell salted mines or live on the profits of faked maps. Many of them lose their minds over the lure of hidden gold. They wander off into the mountains with a burro, a little grub and a head-ful of golden dreams. After long, solitary months they return with lumps of fool's gold, shown with that secrecy which sees spies behind every door. And when they remind you that eighty million dollars' worth of gold was taken out of a mine on Taos Baldy within their memory, who are you to dispel their faith in having found the mother lode again?

Sheep herders were apt to go as simple as their sheep until the state passed a law providing that at least two herders must be sent out together. The two provide human contact and often encourage each other's hallucinations. There was a sheep herder's mine that went so far as to be incorporated as "La Luz Misteriosa."

It was called that because the shepherds had seen a mysterious light one night when a wolf frightened their sheep. It was a pale, green will-o'-the-wisp hovering on the mountain across the arroyo. To them it was a sign that some spirit had returned to look for the gold he had hidden. At daylight they clambered over the rocks to examine the spot and there, plain to see, were two large, smooth slabs with a crevice that might have been a grave. They forgot their sheep and dug down until they broke off rocks veined with a metallic sheen. They had found a lost Spanish mine, haunted by the long dead owner. It cost them incorporation papers and an assayer's report, which they did not understand or believe. Their grandchildren will have a tale to tell of "La Luz Misteriosa" and the gold hidden in a maze of cañons.

The legend of gold thrives on such disappointments. There is hardly a cañon near Santa Fe but is riddled with prospector's holes, and there is hardly a native but has some worn map of a lost Spanish mine. Fortune tellers say—and running the cards has a black but potent charm—that the one universal question they are asked here is concerned with finding lost mines or buried treasure. Inevitably this tantalizing treasure-seeking is woven into folk tales.

Like all people living in a wild and lonely country, the natives have a passion for story telling and an insatiable delight in the marvelous. During long win-

ter evenings grandfathers sit by the corner fireplace
and recount strange tales they have heard from their
father's father, the hundredth telling losing nothing in
imagery and drama. Some of these cuentos are so
long that they are continued from evening to evening.
The simmer of a pot of strong, black coffee near the
flaming piñon logs and the munching of piñons and
popcorn dripping with homemade syrup is the constant low accompaniment to the rising and falling in-
flections of the old man's voice, for every one is too
spellbound and respectful to interrupt his art. Each
abuelito has a story-teller's pride in holding the absorbed interest of his audience, adding and inventing
incidents to dress up his old tale.

This folklore is often the New Mexican version of
the Arabian Nights or fairy stories. "El Cotón de
Jerga" tells of the carpet-jacketed country lout who
won the King's doleful daughter by succeeding in
making her laugh when the courtly suitors had failed.
But the cuento doesn't stop with marriage bells. The
king was not too pleased with having to keep his bargain by making Carpet-Jacket his son-in-law. "El
Cotón" was shrewdly aware that the King and the
beautiful Princess looked down upon him, and determined to win their respect. He went with his rival,
the Duke, and other courtiers to cut logs in the woods,
and when the others stopped work at noon "El Cotón"
refused to eat. He insisted that on the following day
the Princess should bring him his lunch. The Duke
swore that the Princess would not demean herself by

acting as a servant and "El Cotón" bet his life on the outcome. The Princess rebelled at being asked to perform such a menial task but the King, in spite of his pride in the matter, agreed that the good, old Spanish custom required a wife to serve her husband. So the Princess carried forth the lunch basket the next day. El Cotón's life was saved and, after this little experiment in husbandly prerogatives, "they lived happily ever after."

Picaresque tales are as popular in New Mexico as they are in Spain or Old Mexico, carried on in the new locale with all the flavor of the old. The hero is a clever rogue who makes his way in life by "borrowing." He seldom steals or commits a crime but he always deceives the honest fellow by sharper wit and a bit of chicanery. The father of all rogue stories is the long cuento of Pedro de Uidemalas.

In the many quaint animal fables the native coyote is substituted for the wily European fox with the dog as a trusting dupe, while the serpent outwitting man is as old as our first story. One of these, "Juan de Oso," is the fable of a boy who was half bear, and "Juan sin miedo" was the Johnny who was fearless until his own shadow terrified him.

Witches' stories have a morbid, superstitious element where Indian magic has added to the firm native belief in brujas. When a wizard has been killed in Bernalillo and his evil practices are vividly described by grandfather himself, who would not believe in these fantastic spells of brujos? Contrasted with witches who weave black magic are the legends of saints whose miraculous appearances help the humble in times of need and danger.

The most popular of all cuentos in New Mexico centers around the perilous adventures of finding lost treasures. These folk tales add to incredible fancy an authentic and historic setting of early days—the mixture of one part fact and nine parts imagination is the recipe every story-teller uses. Flattering his audience by building upon their own definite knowledge, it is an easy jump to soar from there into the dreams of wishes-come-true, the unexpected luxury of finding buried treasure. They never spoil a good story for the sake of too much truth. It is nature's kind way of comforting with fancy those who lack fortune, for the hungry man dreams of food and the poor man of riches.

These riches do not come from hard toil but from visionary sources long forgotten and revealed only at the propitious moment. The coming of the Caballeros colored the imagination of the country and is still the origin of fabulous legends. The Chihuahua Trail is ghost-ridden with traditions of hauling gold in ox wagons or packing it on burro caravans and hiding it before a sudden raid. Parchment scrolls with directions reading "nine paces toward the rising sun; three paces toward the setting sun, three paces to the right" are enough to lead any one to search for the cache in the strange, bare place beneath an old cottonwood tree.

Within the last six months a lost treasure story has been revived by finding an old ox wagon on a mountain ridge near the Chihuahua Trail. It is dated as belonging to the long ago, not only by the solid wheels cut out of tree trunks, but by living trees two feet in diameter growing through the wagon.

The legend has it that the Spaniards were bringing up from Mexico a heavy wagon loaded with three thousand pounds of bullion and a small box of diamonds when they were surrounded by Apaches. Realizing that they were trapped, the Spaniards sank the bullion and diamonds into the soft mud of a cienaga. They left the wagon and tried to escape by running along the top of the ridge. All of them were killed except one boy who returned to tell his mother the story of the flight. In every generation since that time some of the descendants of the family have probed the cienaga for the sunken treasure. Finding the ox wagon led to the latest, unsuccessful hunt.

Every treasure story has this same pattern. There is always one boy, one man or one woman who escapes the massacre and lives to tell the tale. The gold may be hidden in a cavern near Clayton, it may be secreted in a deep crevice in the rocks near Gallina, it may be buried with altar vessels in the walls of an old mission deserted after the rebellion of 1680, it may be concealed in one of the thousand caches along the Santa Fe Trail where a fire was built over the spot to leave no clew for the pursuing Indians. But always there is one person left to spin the thread of romance and ad-

venture for future generations to follow. If the Spaniards left all in gold in New Mexico which is attributed
to them in every county and hamlet, the King's Highway could be paved with golden pesos.

In Santa Fe, gold is not only hidden in caches or in
the depths of mountains but it may be lost in wells,
walls or under mud floors. In the days before there
were banks to fail, you pocketed your money for selling wool or spring lambs and later on, when the family
were expected to be asleep, you dug a hole in the adobe
wall under the Santo's niche or preferably into the
raised hearth of the fogón, slipped the sack of golden
pesos into it and mudded it over so that no one would
ever suspect the hiding place. Sometimes grandfather
himself forgot where he had buried it. Sometimes one
of those sudden acts of God took him off before he had
a chance to tell the eldest son where it was. Then the
family search began, tapping walls and floors, digging
into abandoned wells and around the roots of old trees.

During a dry summer twenty-five years ago workmen were excavating a filled-in well on San Francisco
Street. By accident they came across a treasure trove
which was later valued at eighty thousand dollars. An
old house was torn down on Cañon Road and a hidden
pot of gold was revealed worth twenty-eight thousand
dollars. Is it any wonder that romance and mystery
flourish here?

An ancient native couple owned a rambling manor
house set in an orchard on the sunny slope of the Santa
Fe Cañon. Romance clung to its adobe walls, and a

peaceful seclusion made it attractive to restless Americans. For years the old couple refused to sell their home. Though they toiled not and neither did they spin, they always had enough silver to exchange for groceries.

There was a tale of treasure buried in the house that was worth more than mounting real estate values. It harked back to the days of the great-great-grandfather, a miser who once asked a neighbor to help him count his gold and silver. He sewed up the gold coins in a calfskin and buried the silver in Indian jars in the walls of his room and under the mud floor. Before he died he called his children around his bed and left one ranch to María, one to Tiburcio, one to Antonio, doling out the property to all of his twenty-nine children.

"But the calfskin full of gold—where is it?" the neighbor reminded him.

A crafty smile came over the dying man's face as he whispered. "That I worked for by the sweat of my brow. It came from the earth, and it shall return to the earth."

In spite of diligent searching, the calfskin of gold was never found, but the ollas of silver probably kept the Rodriguez family in comfort in those five generations of living in that same sunny spot. When they finally consented to part with the hacienda, they were allowed to build a little home in the corner of the orchard, for they could not bring themselves to break the traditions of the home place. As excavations went forward for newfangled water pipes and radiators, there was always the exciting expectation of coming on the calfskin of gold. True to the old man's vow, the golden calf must have returned to the earth. The only coin was a silver peso of 1832, found in the wall of the old man's room, and ceremoniously returned to his grandson.

In almost every old town from New Orleans to Quebec money is occasionally discovered buried in the walls. Santa Fe adds to this the romantic treasure chest filled with Spanish "pieces of eight." A confiding abuelita has told me of seeing these strange square coins dating back to three hundred years ago when Spanish pirates roamed the seven seas. Or perhaps her cousin found heavy ingots of gold and silver, packed up the Chihuahua Trail and cached in a sudden raid.

Last year there was great excitement here when four natives found a "stone in the shape of a shoe with certain numbers and strange marks on it." They believed it pointed to a treasure trove buried fifty or one hundred feet deep. No one ever knew whether they carried away the treasure in the secrecy of night or whether their energy gave out in that cansada feeling. Perhaps their love of gold was scared away by the superstition that devils haunt treasure troves, and follow the finder. The men would only reply to questions with a baffling shrug of their shoulders. "Quién sabe" was the anonymous authority. As long as old adobes stand, there will be the lure of hidden treasure to spur the adventurous.

Fifty years ago when my father came to the wild
West where anything might and did happen, the young
bloods took treasure hunting seriously. Spades became
more fascinating for digging into adobe walls than they
were in a poker game. By chance these young men
found a cryptic map of an old house on lower San
Francisco Street and the fatal cross marking the spot
where the chest of gold was buried. With Yankee
shrewdness they rented the house and secretly set to
work to find the treasure chest. They worked at night
with tallow dips shaded against prying eyes and outside guards to give the warning signal. They took up
the floor and found two other floors of wide hand-
hewn boards just as the map showed. They lifted out
spadesful of dirt noiselessly. They whispered and
peered. The spade struck something solid. They
slipped into the hole and dug as silently as prairie dogs.
It was the chest, large, ironbound and locked. The
lock was rusted together. They pried it loose and
flung up the heavy lid. Empty! Some one had known
of the chest before their day.

During the fear of the Santa Fe-Texas raid and
later when the Confederates ran up their flag over
Santa Fe, merchants stored their most valuable stock in
the adobe walls of their stores. Walls four to six feet
thick were hollowed out and bolts of calico, bags of
coffee, silks, shawls and jewels were stacked in the hole,
and mudded over so that the raiders would not guess
the cache. For calico and coffee, that had been hauled
over the perils of the Santa Fe Trail, were worth their

weight in greenbacks. Silks and embroidered shawls represented fortunes in frontier trade. Usually the crafty merchant dug out his stock after the fear of the raid had passed, but occasionally the hiding place was forgotten. Later generations found these spoils when an adobe wall caved in, weakened from the extensive excavations.

Jewelry and Spanish shawls, as well as bags of gold, were tucked away in treasure chests, along with the marriage letter and the baptismal record. Spanish shawls were, of course, not Spanish at all but Chinese. They took their name from the Doñas who made them fashionable in Castile. They are still known in Spain as "Mantas de Manila" since, long ago, these silken squares were smuggled from China to the Spanish port of Manila and then across the seas in full-sailed caravels to Spain. Though they were oriental in origin, it was the sinuous grace of winding them around lithe figures and draping them over bare shoulders which forever substituted that "made-in-China" trade-mark for "used-in-Spain."

Some were brought directly to the western ports of Mexico and started on their way up the trail to be bartered for turquoise and salt. One and two hundred years old, the Spanish shawls of Santa Fe are as fine as any found in Seville. For fiestas they are shaken out of their linen bags and draped around Spanish beauties in all the rare hues of a flower garden. A century ago they may have looked like garlands festooned

362

around the boxes of the bull ring near the Plaza or even, in a moment of adulation, been thrown at the feet of a favorite matador. They are of heavy black crepe de chine with vines and flowers of flame color, tobacco brown with lemon sprays, orchid with large shaded roses, magenta embroidered in the same rich tone, or all ivory with a fringe so long that it swishes about the ankles. The embroidery is so perfect that both sides are alike, the wrong side only distinguishable by the narrow hem.

After the fiesta, if the hard years have lightened the family purse too greatly, these heirlooms pass into other hands. One of these creamy shawls had small, brown, cedar needles caught in the fringe, recalling the long days when it had been laid away in a chest in an adobe store room. Another of pale blue satin, with a circular Chinese design in the center and butterflies and flowers spraying over it in pastel colors, is said to have been the bedspread used by Governor Manuel Armijo. A typical Mexican fringe of blue and red and yellow had been tacked around it. What a story it makes— a satin mantle embroidered for some Mandarin bride resting at last in a far-away mud fortress! Can't you see the portly Manuel in his shiny brass bed, covered with a lustrous satin spread, bloated with success that exceeded even dreams of that ragged sheepherder?

Spanish laces found their way here too—blonde for gala wear and black with shadow patterns of a respectability for grandmothers of thirty years. Mantillas were triangle-shaped with Spanish flouncing along the edge and caught against the ear with a spicy carnation; or they had a wide frill of lace to drape over the high tortoise-shell comb and a straight lace cape to fall over the shoulders. Fine black silk net was embroidered in gay colors for mantas, making the flower garlands look as though they were invisibly suspended in the air. What a picture women must have been a century ago with their taffeta dresses so heavy that the skirts stood out in rich folds, and mantillas, shawls and jeweled fans as alluring adornments!

In time, costly embroidered shawls were imitated with cashmere squares printed in bright colors. They found great favor with both the Spanish and Indian women. These shawls are now made in Czechoslovakia and imported to Old and New Mexico.

Before fashions distracted New Mexican women with changing styles in hats and coats, one could save up for a rebozo which would last a lifetime. These were long, wide scarfs woven in brilliant stripes and used for all occasions. The silk was soaked in olive oil before it was woven to ensure its lasting softness. The broad stripe of Virgin Mary blue gave the name to the rebozo de Santa María. Fringe at the ends was often of pure silver and gold filings.

Then, men were not limited to gray tweeds. Their suede jackets had silver braid and silver buttons down the long, tight trousers. Gay sarapes were folded over one shoulder, the bright stripes woven of silk and wool. With a slit in the center like ponchos these became overcoats, and folded they served as blankets on long horseback journeys. With a saddle for a pillow, a sarape for a bed, and the starry heavens as a canopy, the Caballero considered himself well accommodated.

The black shawls which delight us with their foreign note along the streets of Santa Fe to-day are somber successors of those gay days. All black, they hark back to that only shade of respectability in Spain. Their value is gauged by the fineness of the cashmere and the length of the heavy silk fringe. If you should fail to estimate properly these two items, you should have been present at the Battle of the Shawls.

It began when a church sodality met at the home of one of its members. Shawls were laid off upon the bed. The hostess, knowing how much they looked alike, suggested that each guest lay her shawl on different chairs. But the women laughed at such a suggestion—wouldn't they know their own shawls just as they would know their own newborn babes?

Nevertheless, when the meeting was over, there was one who raced back to claim that she had gotten the wrong shawl.

"See—this fringe is only a foot and a half long and mine was two feet. How could I have mistaken this poor one for mine which Enrique gave me only twelve years ago? This one is green with age and mine is of the blackness of night. Válgame Dios, haven't I put it carefully in the chest and only worn it for mass? It is that Doña Apolonia who has gone away with mine. Que sí—all these years she has coveted it!"

Off she went to get the sheriff and rout the sly Apolonia. But la Apolonia insisted that the shawl was her own. It started a neighborhood feud with voluble innuendos, and "talking more than seven" with hands and eyes and lips. It ended with attorneys appearing before the justice of the peace and the court room as crowded as for a murder trial. Relatives to the nineteenth cousin blocked the doors. The merchant who sold the shawls was subpœnaed to testify as to the value of cashmere and fringe, and the possible date of sales.

Doña Teresa's story won the shawl back for her. Making a cross with her thumb and forefinger she swore that it was hers. How did she know?

"Every morning I go to six o'clock mass," she explained. "Lately my grandson Tonito, who lives with us, has accompanied me. He is but a child, and while I prayed, he played with the fringe of my shawl, knotting it. Here, Señor Juez, are the knots he made."

Doña Apolonia had no alibi ready for such proof. The judge turned over the shawl to Doña Teresa, who put it over her head and marched triumphantly out of the court room at the head of her family. Doña Apolonia stalked off in the other direction with her band, still muttering imprecations against such a trumped up story.

Doña Teresa had a right to be annoyed for nothing is more becoming than one's best, black shawl. There is an intriguing beauty about them which suggests mysterious femininity, half-revealing, half-concealing oval faces and slender figures. Their graceful lines do not change with freakish modes in hats and coats, and they have the added economy of being as useful in the cool summers as when covering a heavy jacket in winter.

There is a special art of wearing them. The deep fringed triangle points down the back to the ankles, the fold is drawn flat over the forehead and turned in on each side like a nun's veil. With one end thrown over the chin and shoulder the brown hands are free to tuck numerous packages under the shawl and to hold the hand of a toddling child. Skirts are all that show—full enough to be comfortable and long enough to be interesting. For everyday they are of black sateen, but for fiestas they may be purple with rows of pink and green and gold braid. If the shawl falls loose, a simple white blouse is revealed, caught at the throat with a gold filigree brooch. Anatomy is not modernized under the shawls.

Unfortunately, black shawls are not worn as universally as they used to be. The older women still cover their heads in these dark folds, and the younger ones respect tradition by wearing them for velorios when they pay visits to the dead, or for the anniversary mass. Otherwise the younger generation follows the herd in shifting American fashions. One must acknowledge that they do it well, too, achieving with a little money and a department store outlay the chicness of Parisian midinettes. The Latin eye sees color and line and leaves the quality of textures and lack of style to their Nordic sisters. Handsome, black eyes, black hair dressed in the latest fashion, olive skins and painted lips, their skirts swinging high above trim ankles, their hands flashing imitation jewels, the modern señorita is the composite of old and new influences.

But it is the black-shawled women who walk in beauty, passing as silently as shadows, their footsteps

noiseless in worn, black shoes. Half revealed under the dark folds, their fine faces are intricate studies in character. Some are thin, brown faces, almost mummified by the dry air. They are etched with a thousand lines around tight-drawn lips and old eyes that remember past glories and question strange new ways. Others have the round apple cheeks of placid age, with a wisp of white hair blowing out under the folds of the shawl.

Sad faces, I have heard people say. The sadness is the street mask of women who were sheltered, dueña-guarded—the turn of flashing, dark eyes was all that decorum permitted in public. At home the faces laugh, are illumined with the devotion of motherhood, sparkle and pout with the repartee of quoted proverbs. But it is the gentle, black-shawled faces that we remember longest on the narrow, twisting streets of Santa Fe —sensitive and proud with Castilian dignity and a trace of Indian stoicism, marked with the struggle of at once accepting and reviling the conditions of modern life.

The story of Santa Fe is behind all the faces that pass in the historic Plaza. Some are old and withered as dry, brown leaves, some are round and laughing with the hopes of youth, some have curving nostrils and fierce, black moustachios that suggest flaming Latin passions. Some have red fillets binding their straight, black hair and an Indian's primitive candor in their childlike, bronze faces. Some have graying heads and thin white noses bent forward in the preoccupation of business competition. Some have the consciousness of flattering bystanders on their smooth, rouged cheeks and in their keen, speculative eyes.

Many trails have brought these faces to Santa Fe. Daring and adventure, hardships and war, customs, arts and faith bit into the plastic flesh inirradicable patterns. They came with their racial strains to this focus of western dominion. Then the country itself took hold of them, transmuting them into deep-rooted, characteristic types.

Beyond the little settlement of the Holy Faith, mesas, valleys, the twilight-flushed Sangre de Cristo, the vagrant rivers give one a sense of a land that God left to sunshine and that has been little changed by man. It is a country of shimmering, tawny distances subtly overcast with green, of shadowed cañons of rose and silver and violet, of massive blue mountains whose snowy peaks only divide them from the sun-filled turquoise sky. Yet the red earth itself and the far, clear spaces have had their effect upon New Mexicans. For the history of a country is the sum of man plus environment.

In other states, not so isolated from the marts of trade and more generous in the gift of water, Indians and Spaniards have all but lost their racial heritage by intermingling with the Americans.

But in New Mexico they remain sharply differentiated into three races. The Indian follows his old ways of working with nature, the Spanish-American is strangely arrested in the traditions and customs of the European renaissance, and the descendants of the sturdy Scotch-Irish pioneers of the Santa Fe Trail days carry over a spirit of adventure in life.

Indians, Spaniards and Americans—they have molded Santa Fe as the centering place of their cultures. The venerable Palace of the Governors and the domed Capitol are their monuments of conquest. Around the two are the low adobe homes of Spanish people whose hopes and fears and loves have colored life for three centuries, of churches erected by their faith whose bells still count the sunny half-hours. For Santa Fe is the Villa Real where old and new trails meet, the ancient capital of history and romance.

INDEX

373

INDEX

INDEX

375

INDEX

377

INDEX

378

INDEX

THE CHICANO HERITAGE

An Arno Press Collection

Adams, Emma H. **To and Fro in Southern California.** 1887

Anderson, Henry P. **The Bracero Program in California.** 1961

Aviña, Rose Hollenbaugh. **Spanish and Mexican Land Grants in California.** 1976

Barker, Ruth Laughlin. **Caballeros.** 1932

Bell, Horace. **On the Old West Coast.** 1930

Biberman, Herbert. **Salt of the Earth.** 1965

Casteñeda, Carlos E., trans. **The Mexican Side of the Texas Revolution (1836).** 1928

Casteñeda, Carlos E. **Our Catholic Heritage in Texas, 1519-1936.** Seven volumes. 1936-1958

Colton, Walter. **Three Years in California.** 1850

Cooke, Philip St. George. **The Conquest of New Mexico and California.** 1878

Cue Canovas, Agustin. **Los Estados Unidos Y El Mexico Olvidado.** 1970

Curtin, L. S. M. **Healing Herbs of the Upper Rio Grande.** 1947

Fergusson, Harvey. **The Blood of the Conquerors.** 1921

Fernandez, Jose. **Cuarenta Años de Legislador:** Biografia del Senador Casimiro Barela. 1911

Francis, Jessie Davies. **An Economic and Social History of Mexican California** (1822-1846). Volume I: Chiefly Economic. Two vols. in one. 1976

Getty, Harry T. **Interethnic Relationships in the Community of Tucson.** 1976

Guzman, Ralph C. **The Political Socialization of the Mexican American People.** 1976

Harding, George L. **Don Agustin V. Zamorano.** 1934

Hayes, Benjamin. **Pioneer Notes from the Diaries of Judge Benjamin Hayes, 1849-1875.** 1929

Herrick, Robert. **Waste.** 1924

Jamieson, Stuart. **Labor Unionism in American Agriculture.** 1945

Landolt, Robert Garland. **The Mexican-American Workers of San Antonio, Texas.** 1976

Lane, Jr., John Hart. **Voluntary Associations Among Mexican Americans in San Antonio, Texas.** 1976

Livermore, Abiel Abbot. **The War with Mexico Reviewed.** 1850

Loyola, Mary. **The American Occupation of New Mexico, 1821-1852.** 1939

Macklin, Barbara June. **Structural Stability and Culture Change in a Mexican-American Community.** 1976

McWilliams, Carey. **Ill Fares the Land:** Migrants and Migratory Labor in the United States. 1942

Murray, Winifred. **A Socio-Cultural Study of 118 Mexican Families Living in a Low-Rent Public Housing Project in San Antonio, Texas.** 1954

Niggli, Josephina. **Mexican Folk Plays.** 1938

Parigi, Sam Frank. **A Case Study of Latin American Unionization in Austin, Texas.** 1976

Poldervaart, Arie W. **Black-Robed Justice.** 1948

Rayburn, John C. and Virginia Kemp Rayburn, eds. **Century of Conflict, 1821-1913.** Incidents in the Lives of William Neale and William A. Neale, Early Settlers in South Texas. 1966

Read, Benjamin. **Illustrated History of New Mexico.** 1912

Rodriguez, Jr., Eugene. **Henry B. Gonzalez.** 1976

Sanchez, Nellie Van de Grift. **Spanish and Indian Place Names of California.** 1930

Sanchez, Nellie Van de Grift. **Spanish Arcadia.** 1929

Shulman, Irving. **The Square Trap.** 1953

Tireman, L. S. **Teaching Spanish-Speaking Children.** 1948

Tireman, L. S. and Mary Watson. **A Community School in a Spanish-Speaking Village.** 1948

Twitchell, Ralph Emerson. **The History of the Military Occupation of the Territory of New Mexico.** 1909

Twitchell, Ralph Emerson. **The Spanish Archives of New Mexico.** Two vols. 1914

U. S. House of Representatives. **California and New Mexico:** Message from the President of the United States, January 21, 1850. 1850

Valdes y Tapia, Daniel. **Hispanos and American Politics.** 1976

West, Stanley A. **The Mexican Aztec Society.** 1976

Woods, Frances Jerome. **Mexican Ethnic Leadership in San Antonio, Texas.** 1949